Thackeray:

THE
SENTIMENTAL
CYNIC

By

LAMBERT ENNIS

NORTHWESTERN UNIVERSITY PRESS
EVANSTON, ILL.
1950

NORTHWESTERN UNIVERSITY STUDIES

Virgil B. Heltzel, *Editor*

Humanities Series Number Twenty-five

Composed and printed at the Waverly Press, Inc.

Baltimore, MD.

TO MY TWO SMALL DAUGHTERS
who taught me that—legend notwithstanding—
books can get written despite frequent and
clamorous interruptions

AND

TO MY WIFE
who proved far stronger than Isabella Thackeray
in resisting the temptation to interrupt.

Preface

THE reader who picks up this book expecting a full-dress biography of Thackeray will be disappointed. A minute proportion of the thousands of known facts about his life are included. This study is, if anything at all, a chronicle of Thackeray's attitudes. To achieve this goal I have attempted to trace his conduct during the major crises of his life in terms of those attitudes. Secondly, I have had my fling at what is now a prevailing activity among Thackeray biographies: the detection of more or less unsuspected, quasi-biographical elements in the major novels. This seems to me part and parcel of the study of an author's attitudes, since those attitudes control to a large extent the insertion of his own experience into his work.

Any author's experience will of course be altered to a greater or less degree as it finds its way into his books. This fact hardly needs repetition were it not that present-day reviewers so often attack biographers for explaining a creative process as conscious, when in fact they never meant to interpret it as other than subconscious.

It is almost supererogation to say that this book could not have been written without the help of Professor Gordon N. Ray's edition of *The Letters and Private Papers of William Makepeace Thackeray*. Whenever I have quoted from this work, I have preserved Thackeray's spelling and punctuation intact, but have regularized such orthographical conventions as the writing of wch for "which." I am further indebted to Professor Ray for his careful reading of this manuscript, his many valuable suggestions, and his permission to use certain items in his vast, unpublished store of Thackerayan lore.

I am also grateful to Mrs. Hester Thackeray Ritchie Fuller for permission to quote from the text of the correspondence in *The Letters and Private Papers* and to The Harvard University Press for allowing me to copy certain editorial matter in that edition. The Oxford University Press has graciously accorded me permission to quote from Professor J. Y. T. Greig's *Thackeray: A Reconsideration* and Charles Scribner's Sons to use material from Professor Lionel Stevenson's *The Showman of Vanity Fair*.

I am deeply grateful to my colleagues: Professor Frederic E. Faverty, Professor John W. Spargo, and Professor Arthur H. Nethercot for reading portions of my manuscript and offering valuable suggestions about it. To Professor Virgil B. Heltzel thanks are due for his careful editorship and to the directors of the Northwestern University Studies for making possible this publication. To Mrs. Phillips Davies and Mrs. Martha Torchiana I am grateful for typing the manuscript, and to Miss Zelma Leonhard for reading proof and preparing the index.

The greatest debt is expressed in the last sentence of the dedication.

L. E.

Evanston, Ill., July, 1950.

Table of Contents

CHAPTER I

Boyhood and Schooldays

WILLIAM MAKEPEACE THACKERAY was a man of contradictions. As a satirist, he waged war on cant and false emotion, yet he could be as sentimental as a schoolgirl. He was famous for waging war against snobs, yet was not free of the imputation of snobbery. He was dreaded by Victorian women for exposing their pretenses and follies, yet he was in the vanguard of the movement for women's rights. Secretly in love with the lax moral code of the eighteenth-century man of fashion, he was also a staunch defender of Victorian morality. He reveled in thinking himself lazy, yet his pen could pour out manuscript almost as fast as that of Sir Walter Scott. He had enormous compassion for the suffering, yet in him was a savage streak. These contradictions epitomize Thackeray.

The most important of all Thackeray's "ambivalences"—to use that currently popular term—is the opposition within him of cynicism and sentimentality. This conflict has been noticed by commentators at least since his obituary notices appeared in December, 1863. Thus the commentator in *The Spectator* observed:

The peculiar power of Thackeray's genius lies in the strange effervescence of those widely different elements,—a profound tenderness of feeling, a pathos of more than feminine delicacy and more than masculine comprehensiveness, with a power of cynical fury which is always impelling him to spring upon the selfishness and duplicities of human nature.[1]

Of the two halves of the ambivalence, the tenderness grows first, usually during the man's early childhood. Then comes a succession of wounds to his spirit which makes him retaliate aggressively. Here the wounded man's aggression takes form in a wish to destroy commonly accepted values. In other words, cynics start as men of unusual sensibility, and a schoolmate of his days at Charterhouse described the boy Thackeray as "sensitive of blame to a degree scarcely ever found in men satisfied of their own powers."[2]

[1] Reprinted in *Littell's Living Age*, XXIV (February 6, 1864), 325.
[2] John Frederick Boyes, "A Memorial of Thackeray's School-Days," *The Cornhill Magazine*, XI (1865), 121.

A neighbor of Thackeray's during the 1850's, Sir Theodore Martin, described the novelist's nature as

one that yearned for sympathy. It was full of tenderness, and showed it, where he was sure that it would be understood. In fact, of all men I have known he was the most tenderhearted ... almost womanly.[3]

Another friend, Herman Merivale, writing his recollections of the great novelist many years after his death, similarly pointed out:

He had all the nervous susceptibilities, as he had all the loving-kindness of a woman ... more than any other man I have known of Goethe's ewigweiblichkeit.[4]

In our generation, a recent biographer has written:

The clue to Thackeray's personality is his acute nervous sensibility, which not all his bluff heartiness, his love of the ridiculous, his full-throated delight in the commonplaces of living could hide.[5]

In his sensibility may lie the basis of another strong Thackerayan trait—the preoccupation with masks. The man of sensibility is obsessed by feelings of inadequacy, and his most trivial act may be traced to the need of covering some one of those inadequacies. Hence his ways of conducting himself are usually masks or shells. A reader of Thackeray soon notices a fondness for imagery that suggests a shell over something which needs concealment. Such is his devotion to the Bluebeard legend and to talk about "skeletons in cupboards." Even the title of his greatest book, *Vanity Fair*, is a sort of shell when one recalls that the true meaning of "vanity" is emptiness. And Thackeray's constant poses, such as that of the jester or buffoon, are masks or shells.

Another of Thackeray's traits was his dislike of hard, abstract thinking; he preferred knowledge that came to him clothed in tangible and familiar symbols. A great Victorian critic, Walter Bagehot, saw—without benefit of Freud—that this trait also grew out of Thackeray's sensibility:

Thackeray ... looked at everything—at nature, at life, at art—from a sensitive aspect. His mind was, to a considerable extent, like a woman's mind. It would

[3] Gordon N. Ray, ed., *The Letters and Private Papers of William Makepeace Thackeray*, 4 vols. (Cambridge, Mass.: Harvard University Press, 1945–1946) IV, 122n. Henceforth all references to this work will be referred to as *Letters*.

[4] Herman Merivale and Frank T. Marzials, *Life of W. M. Thackeray* (London, 1891), p. 12.

[5] John W. Dodds, *Thackeray: A Critical Portrait* (Oxford University Press, 1941), p. 57.

comprehend abstractions when they were unrolled and explained before it, but it never naturally created them.[6]

Thackeray himself was conscious of this limitation, especially with respect to his trouble remembering historical facts and dates. Envying Macaulay his vast memory for such details, the novelist observed ruefully, "whilst everything but impressions I mean facts dates and so forth slip out of my head in which there's some great faculty lacking depend upon it."[7]

Going through life thus, conscious of many inadequacies, Thackeray inevitably shared with his fellow mortals the habit of building up protective devices. These took the form of various poses or masks or shells. Having achieved such protection as these afforded, his particular aggressive counter-attack was aimed at tearing the shells from the inner personalities of other people with whom he came face to face. This counterattack had a threefold purpose: it helped him ward off unexpected treachery; it gave the assurance that he was not uniquely weak since he could find shortcomings in others; and it averted their scorn from his weaknesses by placing them on the defensive.

The unmasker has to visualize his victims in terms of his own picture of himself; hence Thackeray considered other mortals as outward shells frantically striving to cover up inner weaknesses. And he deemed it his duty to unmask this inner self so that the world might know it. As such he was avowedly a satirist. When he created a character like Dobbin in *Vanity Fair* or George Warrington in *Pendennis*, whose inner self was superior to its exterior, he promptly used him as a touchstone. His function was to measure the hollowness of his fellow characters, "snobs" and others, whose fair exteriors cover sham interiors. Persons whose inner worth equaled their outward value and who therefore needed no mask or front were the ones who received Thackeray's highest accolades: if they were men, he called them "frank and manly"; if they were women, they were "artless."

For "arts" are the devices by which women preserve the fronts they maintain to the world. And the fact that women, like the men, have to face that world means that the world's regard is their chief concern. In other words, such people are "worldly." For next to his

[6] "Thackeray and Sterne." Reprinted in *Literary Studies* (London, 1895), II, 315.
[7] *Letters*, III, 38.

view that appearance is a shell which covers reality, Thackeray cherished the view that life is a struggle between worldly and un-worldly people. The latter may be either anti-worldly men like George Warrington, who understand but scorn the world, or un-worldly beings like Helen Pendennis and Colonel Newcome, who are truly ignorant of worldly arts.

Many were the protective shells which Thackeray himself assumed varied at different times in his life. During his earlier career as professional author he sought a reputation as a daring young writer of slashing articles. In his later years, conversely, he loved to think of himself as the kindly old worldling, preaching "lay sermons" as he beamed through his spectacles at the entire English-speaking world. For the whole of his working life Thackeray enjoyed playing the part of an indolent sybarite, too weak to resist temptation. He was also prone to regard himself as a buffoon, or jester or "traveling quack."[8] In fact when he drew the pictures of "the showman of Vanity Fair" to illustrate his most famous novel, he depicted in motley the clown who symbolized himself and, in one case, bestowed on him his own features plus a jester's staff and mask.[9] In his correspondence, he liked to attach an honorific title to his favorite *nom de plume* and call himself the Chevalier de Titmarsh. He even drew a caricature of himself in that role,[10] riding forth to battle with the famous spectacles looming benignly under the raised beaver.

All of this brings to mind the "clothes philosophy" of Thomas Carlyle, especially in the form which was expressed in *Sartor Resartus* (1833–4). One is reminded that Thackeray was, in his formative period during the 1830's, "an enthusiastic convert to Carlyle's crusade against cant and humbug."[11]

Two of Thackeray's most recent biographers, Professor Lionel Stevenson[12] and Mr. J. Y. T. Greig,[13] have both stressed the events of his childhood that made for insecurity. And a contemporary author who knew nothing of twentieth-century psychiatry but who had experienced a childhood even more unhappy than Thackeray's,

[8] See below, pp. 201f.

[9] Lionel Stevenson, *The Showman of Vanity Fair* (New York: Scribner's, 1947), p. 383.

[10] *Letters*, IV, 355.

[11] Gordon N. Ray, "Biographical Memoranda," *Letters* I, cvi.

[12] *The Showman of Vanity Fair* (New York: Scribner's, 1947), chapter 1.

[13] *Thackeray: A Reconsideration* (London: Oxford University Press, 1950), pp. 10–14.

who was to become his close friend, and who was to write the novels most closely similar to his—Anthony Trollope—put his finger on the center of his elder contemporary's character, when he wrote:

He was not a man capable of feeling at any time quite assured in his position. . . He doubted the appreciation of the world; he doubted his fitness for turning his intellect to valuable account. . . Though he was aware of his own power, he always, to the last, was afraid that his own deficiencies should be too strong against him.[14]

The facts of Thackeray's early life are by now so familiar as to require only a few words. He was born in Calcutta on July 18, 1811, the only child of a beautiful, charming, and devoted mother. His father, who had kept a native mistress, was a successful bureaucrat in the Indian Civil Service. He married Thackeray's mother in 1810 and died in 1815. The mother had experienced a girlhood love-affair with Henry Carmichael-Smyth, whom she was to take as a second husband eighteen months after Richmond Thackeray's death. There is more than remote possibility, therefore, that she was not deeply in love with her first husband, a circumstance which may account for her unusually strong attachment to her only child.

There can be no doubt but that the attachment was reciprocated. The tacit evidence of the novels bears witness to the fact that a mother-and-son relationship lay at the center of Thackeray's personal universe.[15] Such relationships are integral to the plots of *Pendennis* and *The Virginians*, and the pivotal relationship of Rachel Castlewood and Harry in *Henry Esmond* is of a quasi-mother-and-son order. Furthermore, these and all the other novels have many more such mothers and sons somewhere on their peripheries. *Vanity Fair* provides Amelia Sedley Osborne and her son Georgy; *Pendennis* shows us Foker and his mother; also Lady Clavering and her little Frank; and *Esmond* brings forth young Frank Castlewood, as well as Henry, to receive Rachel's maternal devotion. One of the subplots of *The Newcomes* anticipates *The Virginians* in drawing a mother of twin boys, Mrs. Sophia Alethea Newcome; another provides a French variation of the basic theme in the picture of Mme. de Florac and Paul; *Lovel the Widower* juxtaposes two such pairs, the name character and Mrs. Bonnington on the one hand, Captain and Lady Baker on the other. Each of these pairs of mother and son has a counterpart in *The Wolves and the Lamb*, an earlier work-

---

[14] *Thackeray*, "English Men of Letters Series" (New York, 1879), p. 15.
[15] Greig likewise stresses this fact in *Thackeray: A Reconsideration*, pp. 7f.

ing of the same matter in a play. Denis Duval is the only son of a widow who is stern to him in early childhood, but is becoming affectionate when the book is interrupted by its author's death. An almost identical basic relationship exists in distorted form in much of the fiction of Thackeray's younger days, where doting mothers beget slightly comic sons, as in *The Great Hoggarty Diamond* (1841), or scoundrels as in *Stubbs's Calendar* (1839) and *Barry Lyndon* (1844), or villainous mothers bear criminal sons as in *Catherine* (1839).

The tendency in all of these situations to reflect Thackeray's own family position is apparent. All but five of these fourteen mothers are widows at the outset or become so during the course of the book. The other five—Mrs. Foker, Lady Clavering, Mme. de Florac, Mrs. Bonnington, and Catherine Hayes—have husbands who are contemptible or insignificant, either personally or in the action of the story. In this insignificance it is possible to read a subconscious protest by Thackeray against the existence of his own stepfather. All the mothers dominate their sons, either by doting fondness like Mrs. Carmichael-Smyth and her antitypes Amelia, Helen Pendennis, and Rachel Castlewood, or by more militant tactics like Sophia Alethea Newcome, Mme. Esmond Warrington, and Mme. Duval. The children are all only sons except the two sets of twin brothers, and nearly all are indolent and pleasure-loving, thus mirroring in fiction one of the greatest sources of contention between Thackeray and his mother—his indolent, pleasure-loving ways.

Moreover, the two novels—*The Newcomes* and *Philip*—which Thackeray built around the similar central relationship of a widower and an only boy, seem to be deliberate efforts to break away if only slightly from the mother-and-son pattern. Yet in both books there are older women, Mme. de Florac and Caroline Brandon, who gradually assume the position of virtual foster-mothers in the lives of young Clive Newcome and Philip Firmin.

Thackeray's love for his mother obviously struck deep roots during those early Calcutta years, and those roots were in no sense killed when they were violently wrenched loose in his fifth year. Then, like seemingly all Anglo-Indian children, he was sent to be educated in England. Entrusted there to relatives with whom he was not unhappy, Thackeray was nevertheless miserable at a sequence of badly selected boarding schools. It was at this time that the sensitiveness born of insecurity and fear was strongly implanted in him.

The first of these institutions, located at the Polygon in Southampton, was to be recalled vividly in *The Roundabout Papers*, after forty years:

We Indian children were consigned to a school of which our deluded parents had heard a favourable report, but which was governed by a horrible little tyrant, who made our young lives so miserable that I remember kneeling by my little bed of a night, and saying, 'Pray God, I may dream of my mother!'[16]

His chief recollection of the place was "cold, chilblains, bad dinners, not enough victuals, and caning awful."[17] On the other hand, he only mildly disliked his next school, Dr. Turner's at Chiswick, which his fiction was to transmute into a girl's academy and immortalize as Miss Pinkerton's in *Vanity Fair*.[18] Thence he progressed in 1822 to the famous Charterhouse School in London, which was to appear in his books under a variety of names ranging from Slaughter House in *The Fitz-Boodle Papers* (1843).[19] and *Men's Wives* (1843)[20] to Whitefriars in *Vanity Fair*, Chartreux in *The Virginians*, and Grey Friars in *Pendennis*, *The Newcomes*, and *Philip*. It is the house of a Charterhouse master, the Reverend Edward Penny, to which Thackeray refers in a passage written in 1854:

We were flogged at school; we were fifty boys in our boarding-house, and had to wash in a leaden trough, under a cistern, with lumps of fat yellow soap floating about in the ice and water.[21]

When he stood on the threshold of celebrity in March, 1847, the mature novelist wrote: "I think the chief good I got out of Charterhouse was to learn to hate bullying and tyranny and to love kind hearted simple children."[22] And in penning his self-portrait as a schoolboy a year-and-a-half later Thackeray took pride in the fact

[16] George Saintsbury, ed., *The Oxford Thackeray*, 17 vol. (Oxford, 1908), XVII, 553f. Henceforth, unless otherwise stated, all quotations from Thackeray's writings except those from *Letters* will be taken from this edition, which will be designated as *Works*.

[17] The same, p. 495. For a briefer recollection of the school, see *Letters*, II, 669.

[18] Chapters 1 and 2.

[19] *Works*, IV, 283.

[20] The same, pp. 317-323.

[21] "Pictures of Life and Character." *Works*, II, 706.

[22] *Letters*, II, 284.

that his hero while at school "never bullied little boys." Another year went by and he confessed to a sympathetic female correspondent: "I was so unhappy myself as a child that I don't think I have said a rough word to one twice in my life."[23]

Fear of the birch became an obsession with Thackeray.[24] Yet granting the rod to be almost symbolic of boys' schools in the nineteenth-century mind, other writers—with the notorious exception of Swinburne—do not hasten to write about it on such slight pretexts as does Thackeray. Even Dickens in *Nicholas Nickleby* drew his famous picture of Dotheboys Hall and had done with it. But the very mention of the word "school" sent Thackeray's mind to running on the subject of flagellation. His schoolmasters are all—with the exception of the Doctor in *Pendennis*[25]—either pampering, sycophantic divines like the Reverend Otto Rose, or tyrants whose names—despite comic implications—are usually lurid plays on the dread topic: Dr. Birch,[26] Dr. Swishtail,[27] Dr. Block of Switchester College,[28] and a whole related group comprising Dr. Tickler,[29] Dr. Tickleus,[30] and their female counterpart, Miss Tickletoby.[31]

A deep impression was made on Thackeray by a rather trivial incident that befell him in January of 1841. He met an old gentleman who had just dreamed at the age of sixty-five that he was "flogged at Charter-House."[32] Four months later the story went into a sketch entitled *A Saint Philip's Day at Paris*,[33] and some time before the end of 1846 it became matter for a digression in *Vanity*

[23] The same, p. 574.

[24] There is some question as to whether Thackeray was actually ever caned at Charterhouse. Arthur Pendennis, whose experiences there were based on his, "never was flogged, but it was a wonder how he escaped the whipping-post" (*Pendennis*, Chapter 2. *Works*, XII, 19). But since Thackeray states explicitly that he was beaten at his first school (see above, p. 7) and since fear of the rod could be as serious a traumatic experience as the rod itself, the point is not too important.

[25] See below, p. 14.

[26] "Dr. Birch and His Young Friends," *Works*, X, 147–212, and *passim* throughout.

[27] *The Professor*, chapter 2; *Works*, I, 118. "Stubbs's Calendar; or the Fatal Boots," February–March; *Works*, I, 423–432. *Vanity Fair*, chapter 5; *Works*, XI, 48–60, and *passim* throughout *Works*.

[28] *The Book of Snobs*, chapter 13. *Works*, IX, 316.

[29] *Barry Lyndon*, chapter I. *Works*, VI, 14.

[30] *Vanity Fair*, chapter 56. *Works*, XI, 711.

[31] *Works*, VII, 251–313.

[32] *Letters*, II, 9.

[33] *Works*, III, 490.

Fair.[34] Foker confided to Pendennis a few weeks after leaving Grey Friars School, " 'by gad, sir, I sometimes dream, now, that the doctor's walking into me,' " to which "Pen smiled as he thought that he himself had likewise fearful dreams of this nature."[35]

Finally near the end of his life, Thackeray dined with three old Etonians who regaled a pleasant hour mimicking, with the greatest veneration, the flogging technique of their famous headmaster, Dr. Keate. The next day the experience was worked into the novel, *Philip:*

the very *hwhish* of the rods was parodied with thrilling fidelity, and ... the subject was brought to a climax by a description of that awful night when the doctor called up squad after squad of boys from their beds ... whipped through the whole night, and castigated ... many hundred rebels.[36]

Thackeray concludes, with a deeper irony than he intended, "their talk greatly amused and diverted me, and I hope, and am quite ready, to hear all their jolly stories over again."

Inevitably men who had thus endured flogging had to retaliate when opportunity presented itself in later life. And since the original oppressor was unavailable, the victim was often someone in authority to whom they could transfer their animosity. Those who, like Thackeray, found themselves before many years in the literary profession discovered symbols of quasi-authority in successful writers like Edward Bulwer-Lytton. If those men were of the opposite party, they made fine targets for reviews of the type called—significantly—"slashing." And even if they were not famous, the fact of their being of the opposite party still made them meat for a "slashing article."

Thackeray makes the relationship abundantly clear during an incident in *Pendennis*. Captain Shandon, editor of *The Pall Mall Gazette*, recognizes the style of George Warrington from a "slashing article" in that magazine and comments succinctly on it:

I know the crack of his whip in a hundred, and the cut which the fellow's thong leaves. There's Jack Bludyer, goes to work like a butcher, and mangles a subject.

---

[34] "I know ... an old gentleman of sixty-eight who said to me one morning at breakfast ... 'I dreamed last night that I was flogged by Dr. Raine' ... Dr. Raine and his rod were just as awful to him in his heart, then, at sixty-eight, as they had been at thirteen" (chapter 2. *Works*, XI, 14).

[35] Written in October, 1848. Chapter 3. *Works*, XII, 37.

[36] Chapter 2. *Works*, XVI, 12. Written in December, 1860.

Mr. Warrington finishes a man, and lays his cuts neat and regular, straight down the back, and drawing blood every line.[37]

Quite naturally Thackeray fell into the habit of regarding any hostile reviews of his books as whippings. He was to tell of a sympathetic fellow-guest in a New York hotel who popped under the table-cloth her copy of *The New York Herald* when he came into the dining-room because an Irish reviewer in that paper had attacked his lecture on Swift. "I told her I had had my whipping already upstairs in my own private room, and begged her to continue her reading."[38] And in "An Essay on Thunder and Small Beer" (1851), Thackeray confessed that "it is all very well for a writer to affect to be indifferent to a critique from the *Times*. You bear it as a boy bears a flogging at school, without crying out; but don't swagger and brag as if you liked it."[39] And just as the schoolboy's air of stoicism during a caning is only a pose, so Thackeray on one occasion confessed that his pose of disregarding hostile criticisms was only a mask over his anguished feelings. Comparing two reviews of *Vanity Fair*, he confessed to Mrs. Proctor:

If we put on our cocked-hats on account of the Examiner article, that of the Spectator caused us to remove a part of our dress and submit to a whipping. I don't care for the praise or for the blame or anything. Yes I do. I care for kind friends who are always good and cordial to me.[40]

Because he cared so much "for kind friends," Thackeray was prone all his life to make confidantes of women; after all it is the traditional role of that sex to confer sympathy. Moreover, the craving for kindness played a large part in developing Thackeray's democratic instincts. The great revelation that buoyed him up during his worst ordeal—the trip to Ireland when his wife's insanity became known to him[41]—was the kindness in the hearts of simple people.[42] And during the days of his greatest glory, when his younger daughter had been spoiled by being the guest of Lord and Lady Ashburton,

[37] Chapter 53. *Works*, XII, 672.
[38] "On Screens in Dining-Rooms." *Works*, XVII, 409. The incident, as it occurred at the time, is told in *Letters*, III, 120f., 123. The sympathetic fellow-guest was originally a man.
[39] *Works*, X, 220.
[40] *Letters*, II, 403. Written on July 25, 1848.
[41] See below, p. 21.
[42] See below, p. 116.

he decided that the cure lay in sending her on a visit to his "simple, kind" friends, Dr. and Mrs. John Brown.[43] Nor did Thackeray fail to see that his extraordinary dependence on "kind friends" had originated during his schooldays. The schoolboy Arthur Pendennis, who was more recognizably a self-portrait than was that hero at any later stage of his growth, "loved with boyish ardour . . . those masters or seniors who were kind to him." Furthermore, he had been "known to take a thrashing for a crony without saying a word; but a blow, ever so slight, from a friend would make him roar."[44]

It was thoroughly in keeping with the high valuation which Thackeray placed on his shell of courage that when he had armed himself for the expected blow, he should quake in mortal terror of a blow from a friend, or in fact from any unexpected quarter. A study-hall episode from the Charterhouse days, when he attempted the age-old feat of hiding a boyhood classic inside his Latin text, sheds light on the roots of the phobia. After forty years he evoked the picture:

As he reads, there comes behind the boy, a man, a dervish, in a black gown, like a woman, and a black square cap, and he has a book in each hand, and he seizes the boy who is reading the picture-book, and lays his head upon one of his books, and smacks it with the other.[45]

Thackeray was always a courageous man, only one of many proofs being the fortitude he was to display during the painful ailments of his later years. A public whipping, humiliating as it might be and deep as were the scars it might leave on his soul, was direct and foreseeable aggression. In the *Roundabout Paper*, "On Screens in Dining-Rooms," he was to admit that:

I may have undergone agonies, you see, but every man who has been bred at an English public school comes away from a private interview with Dr. Birch with a calm, even a smiling face. And this is not impossible, when you are prepared. You screw your courage up—you go through the business.[46]

In keeping with this attitude, Thackeray always had a sneaking fondness for direct aggressors, whether they were Bluebeard, Lady

[43] *Letters*, III, 3.
[44] *Pendennis*, chapter 2. *Works*, XII, 19.
[45] "De Juventute." *Works*, XVII, 422.
[46] The same, 409.

Kew, or the Marquis of Steyne. But his utmost loathing went to underhanded villains like Iago, Tartuffe, Blifil,[47] or Barnes New-come. He is speaking as much for himself as for George Washington when, in *The Virginians*, he causes that hero to say: "An open enemy I can face readily enough. 'Tis the secret foe who causes the doubt and anguish!"[48]

This exaggeration of a normal human fear not only explains much of Thackeray's concern with inner realities under outward shells; it also explains the inconsistency between his usual kindness and the acrimony of some of his quarrels, notably those with Deady Keane in 1843 and with Edmund Yates in the famous Garrick Club affair of 1858.[49] Both controversies resulted from attacks of a personal character on the novelist, but since he himself had indulged in simi-lar personalities with Bulwer and others, he could not with any fair-ness base his counterattack on Keane's or Yates's personal jibes at him. So he took the position that Keane was a fellow-writer for *Fraser's Magazine*, and Yates a brother member of the Garrick Club; hence their lampoons of him were treacheries within a closed circle. And he took a vindictive revenge by hounding the two men out of those circles.[50]

With this attitude in mind, one better understands not only such preoccupations as Thackeray's concern with appearance and reality in friendship, but with minor themes such as the right of servants to pass judgment on their masters when they are below stairs and out of the employer's hearing.[51]

The desire to placate potential enemies, which brought out that insight into the needs and attitudes of others, was, like the fear that created it, born during Thackeray's schooldays. There his first need was, obviously, to win the favor of his schoolmates. Yet in his case it clearly could not be bought by athletic prowess, which he did not possess. The best substitute was amiability and bribes. When Arthur Pendennis—alias Thackeray—"had money he spent it royally in

[47] See *Philip*, chapter 21. *Works*, XVI, 307.

[48] Chapter 92. *Works*, XV, 988.

[49] See *Letters*, II, 103–105; I, cxx–cxxiii.

[50] To accentuate the point that Thackeray regarded Yates as a treacherous villain, see *Letters*, IV, 102, for a reproduction of Thackeray's drawing of the incident, "The Smiler with the Knife." Yates extends the hand of friendship to Thackeray while holding a dagger behind his back.

[51] See below, p. 115.

tarts for himself and his friends; he has been known to disburse nine-and-sixpence out of ten shillings awarded to him in a single day."[52] When there was no money for tarts, he learned to buy the approval of his fellows in a different way. Thackeray had found in himself a talent that afforded escape from the terror and boredom of the schoolroom into a pleasanter world. He could draw. Again *The Roundabout Papers* recapture the vivid moment with a scene in the schoolroom where his cronies are clustered around the youthful Thackeray. " 'I say, old boy, draw us Vivaldi tortured in the Inquisition,' or, 'Draw us Don Quixote and the windmills, you know.' "[53]

All his life Thackeray was to win favor of children by gifts. In time the tarts of childhood were replaced by those "tips" to schoolboys which symbolized to him the happiness of school life, just as the birch rod symbolized its miseries. When the children were too young for tips, Thackeray drew pictures for them as did the heroes of his books, Clive Newcome and Henry Esmond.[54]

The most striking aspect of Thackeray's first series of lectures, *The English Humourists of the Eighteenth Century* (1851), is the lecturer's fondness for recreating his subjects in his own image. Oliver Goldsmith is a case in point, and Thackeray does not fail to mention that the author of *The Vicar of Wakefield*, as a school-usher, "spent his earnings in treats for the boys. . . . When he met his pupils in later life, nothing would satisfy the Doctor but he must treat them still."[55]

Thackeray, like Goldsmith, continued his schoolboy generosity throughout his adult life. His handouts to indigent authors and artists were legion. Furthermore he maintained the expensive practice as editor of *The Cornhill Magazine* of slipping his personal check into rejected manuscripts that he was returning to needy authors. Noble and admirable as such practices were, they can—nevertheless—be traced back psychologically to the schoolboy's need of winning his fellows' regard. And that regard will go far to compensate for the tyranny of schoolmasters—whether it take the form of overtly aggressive flogging, treacherous sneak attacks by ushers, or worst of all, verbal sarcasm.

[52] Chapter II. *Works*, XII, 19.
[53] "De Juventute." *Works*, XVII, 430.
[54] *The Newcomes*, chapter 14; *Works*, XIV, 187. *Henry Esmond*, chapter 5; *Works*, XIII, 376.
[55] "Sterne and Goldsmith." *Works*, XIII, 679.

Thackeray was treated to the sinister weapon of sarcasm in ample measure during his last year at Charterhouse. Dr. John Russell, headmaster of the school at the time, was a master at ridiculing a boy's self-esteem to the point of annihilation. In fact, the novelist's memory of these torments was so strong after forty years that readers of *The Roundabout Paper*, "Thorns in the Cushion," were implored not

to *castigare ridendo*. Do not laugh at him writhing, and cause all the other boys in the school to laugh. Remember your own young days at school, my friend—the tingling cheeks, burning ears, bursting heart, and passion of desperate tears, with which you looked up, after having performed some blunder, whilst the doctor held you to public scorn before the class, and cracked his great clumsy jokes upon you—helpless, and a prisoner! Better the block itself, and the lictors, with their fasces of birch-twigs, than the maddening torture of those jokes![56]

During this last year at Charterhouse or soon afterward, one of Thackeray's schoolfellows wrote a poem called *Horae Carthusianae* which has survived in a manuscript now owned by the John Pierpont Morgan Library. It graphically describes the feelings of a typical young Carthusian as the morning bell awakens him to the prospect of Dr. Russell's class, knowing well that not a flogging, but an imposition will await failure. The boy wishes he could be ill so as to escape the ordeal. Just such a youthful preference for illness to unpleasantness may lie behind Thackeray's later valetudinarianism. His sicknesses then were real enough, but he rather enjoyed them and encouraged their onset by almost deliberate intemperance. Moreover, expert medical opinion has suggested that the headaches he suffered while still at Charterhouse were probably of psychosomatic origin. They "seem to have been directly associated with the persecutions of a rigid headmaster . . . and with examinations."[57]

On the typical unhappy morning, however, which Thackeray chose to describe in *Horae Carthusianae*, no convenient illness saved him from Russell's persecution. The poem sets forth in detail the pedant's sarcasm at the boy's flounderings in the *minutiae* of Greek

[56] *Works*, XVII, 400. Cf. Henry Esmond's first experience at Cambridge, where because of his Jesuit-trained pronunciation of Latin, "Mr. Bridge, the tutor, made him the object of clumsy jokes, in which he was fond of indulging," and at which the "little flock of boys . . . raised a great laugh at him" (Chapter 10. *Works*, XIII, 109).

[57] Dr. Chester M. Jones, "The Medical History of William Makepeace Thackeray," *Letters*, IV, 454.

grammar. With the same remarkable persistence of memory which he attributed to the Etonians' recollections of Dr. Keate's floggings, Thackeray recreated the identical scene twenty years later in *Pendennis*. There young Arthur is more thick-skinned than his creator had been under the diatribe of "the doctor":

"Miserable trifler! A boy who construes δε *and*, instead of δε *but*, at sixteen years of age, is guilty not merely of folly, and ignorance, and dullness ... but of ... deadly crime, of filial ingratitude."[58]

Another of Thackeray's contemporary analyses of that persecution went home to his mother in a letter which shows remarkable insight for a sixteen-year-old boy. He reports:

Dr. Russell is treating me every day with such manifest unkindness and injustice, that I really can scarcely bear it: It is so hard when you endeavour to work hard, to find your attempts nipped in the bud—if I ever get a respectable place in my form, he is sure to bring me down again; to day there was such a flagrant instance of it, that it was the general talk of the school—I wish I could take leave of him tomorrow—He will have this to satisfy himself with, that he has thrown every possible object in my way to prevent my exerting myself.[59]

Here Thackeray displays at least a precocious knack for rationalizing and putting into words his conduct in a difficult personal relationship. Thanks to this expressive power, one sees how Russell's oppressive educational methods could turn a sensitive boy's willingness to learn into withdrawal and sullen rebellion. Then, to justify that rebellion, the boy was building up in his mind the legend of his own indolence. Psychological insight, which Thackeray acquired at an early age, is used in youth generally for self-exculpation; only with maturity does a man see that he himself may have to assume a share of the blame for unhappy situations.

To defend himself against tyranny—whether physical, written or oral—the sensitive person must study himself constantly to perfect his defenses,—in effect, to become highly introverted and a master of self-exculpation. Hence such attacks as Russell's impelled Thackeray to study and know himself by constantly greater introversion. This situation may, in fact, explain why he became the most introverted of any male novelist yet born in Great Britain with the possible exception of Sterne. From this introversion derives the quality

[58] Chapter 2. *Works*, XII, 21.
[59] *Letters*, I, 24. Written on February 19, 1828.

in Thackeray's writing that has been called "the humorous ego," that state of mind which expresses itself in constant personalized digressions. These often amount to mere apologies to his readers for some fancied offense.[60] From this constant self-appraisal comes also Thackeray's well-known dispassionate fairness, which caused his sudden abrupt turnabouts in the middle of some passionate indictment. The introvert is usually the first to see both sides of a question.

His introversion accounts also in large part for Thackeray's habit of building himself into the heroes of his books, whether as George Fitz-Boodle, Arthur Pendennis, Henry Esmond, Clive Newcome, George Warrington in *The Virginians*, Bachelor in *Lovel the Widower*, or Philip Firmin in *The Adventures of Philip*. Of these six men, Fitz-Boodle is the narrator of his own adventures, Arthur Pendennis those of Clive and Philip, and either Henry Esmond or George Warrington gradually slips into the role of narrator in the books of which he is the hero. In other words, Thackeray found it nearly impossible to tell a story except from the point of view of a character who is really himself. Even the notable exception, Barry Lyndon, has points of resemblance to his creator.

Thackeray's temperament was of course compounded, not only of the unpleasant experiences—the floggings and Dr. Russell's sarcasms; into it went also the experiences which compensated for those miseries, chief among them the approval of schoolfellows, the hours of reading, and the vacations with Mrs. Carmichael-Smyth, Thackeray's mother under the new name she had taken with her second marriage. Since her return with Thackeray's stepfather from India in 1819, the contrast between school and home had been even more pronounced for her son than for most schoolboys in that age of educational cruelty. School was the symbol to him of oppression and shattered *amour propre*, while home meant security, restored self-respect, and love, with Mrs. Carmichael-Smyth enthroned as the household spirit. On revisiting boyhood scenes after twenty years, Thackeray wrote in his diary: "all sorts of recollections of my youth came back to me: dark and sad and painful with my dear good mother as a gentle angel interposing between me and misery."[61] The strain of mother-worship expressed here led to a sort of aesthetic

[60] See below, p. 217.
[61] *Letters*, II, 361. Written in March, 1848.

adoration of madonna-like figures in Thackeray's maturity.[62] Its simpler aspect was epitomized by a famous phrase in *Vanity Fair:* "Mother is the name for God in the lips and hearts of little children."[63]

Apparently Mrs. Carmichael-Smyth used to pray over Thackeray's bed before he awakened in the morning, and it was his belief that these prayers imparted sanctity to the moment of awakening. Hence that was the time when he received the greatest ecstasy from her presence. He wrote in *Catherine* (1840):

do not you, as a boy, remember waking of bright summer mornings and finding your mother looking over you? had not the gaze of her tender eyes stolen into your senses long before you woke, and cast over your slumbering spirit a sweet spell of peace, and love, and fresh-springing joy?[64]

When Arthur Pendennis has been jilted by Miss Fotheringay, and his mother sits by his bed holding his sobbing form in her arms, Thackeray decided to draw the incident for one of the illustrations to the book so that he could savor more fully its sweetness. Characteristically he adds:

the gentle creature ... thought with a strange wonderment and tenderness, that it was only yesterday that he was a child in that bed: and how she used to come and say her prayers over it before he woke upon holiday mornings.[65]

Similarly when Henry Esmond comes home from the wars to visit Rachel Castlewood at Walcote, his sleep on the first night of his visit is "deep, sweet, and refreshing . . . He woke as if angels had been watching at his bed all night. I dare say one that was as pure and loving as an angel had blest his sleep with her prayers."[66]

This making of his own bed a shrine of sacred observances reminds one of the way in which Thackeray's friend Alfred Tennyson regarded a man's sickbed as somehow hallowed if it was tended by loving hands. Thackeray's thought is a strand of the same fabric of emotions as that which made him linger in bed and wish he were ill on school mornings when he had to face Dr. Russell. Since the

---

[62] See below, p. 155. Greig also emphasizes this maternal apotheosis (*Thackeray: A Reconsideration*, pp. 14–16).

[63] Chapter 37. *Works*, XI, 478.

[64] Chapter II. *Works*, III, 154.

[65] Chapter 7. *Works*, XII, 88.

[66] Book 2, Chapter 7. *Works*, XIII, 218.

bed was a symbol of security, it naturally became—when associated with these maternal prayers—invested with a veil of sanctity.

Less sacred to Thackeray, however, even in his schoolboy days, was another aspect of his mother's piety—her growing Evangelicalism. When his daughter Anny, at the age of fifteen, was undergoing strong Evangelical pressure from Mrs. Carmichael-Smyth, her father wrote the girl:

When I was of your age I was accustomed to hear and read a great deal of the Evangelical (so called) doctrine and got an extreme distaste for that sort of composition . . . for the preachers I heard and the prayer-meetings I attended.[67]

Thackeray's instinctive rebellion against Evangelicalism, acquired at this time, accounts not only for the pronounced anti-Puritan bias of his fiction; it lies back of most of the stresses and strains which his relationship with his mother was to undergo. These stresses, moreover, provide the literary material for at least three parallel situations in his later novels: the rebellions of Thomas Newcome, Lord Kew, and the Warrington twins against Evangelical stepmothers or mothers.

As bed and mother were symbols of home to Thackeray, so he found in the stagecoach a symbol for the passage from school to home. In *The Roundabout Paper*, "De Juventute," he asks:

Where are the coaches? and where the youth that climbed inside and out of them . . . that rubbed away the bitter tears at night after parting, as the coach sped on the journey to school and London; that looked out with beating heart as the milestones flew by, for the welcome corner where began home and holidays?[68]

The return to school from the holidays was to be the stick by which Thackeray measured painful separations for the rest of his life. Hacking away at *Pendennis* in the boredom of a London July and yearning to be at Ryde with Mrs. Brookfield, Thackeray confided to that lady that he felt "just as I used five and twenty years ago at school the day after coming back from the holydays."[69]

When Thackeray was separated from his daughters after his wife's insanity, he was to weep when he tried writing to the elder child, Anny, because "something always" took place then "similar to what used to happen when" he first wrote to his mother "after

[67] *Letters*, III, 93f. Written in October, 1852.
[68] *Works*, XVII, 434f.
[69] *Letters*, II, 570.

the holidays."[70] Analyzing the experience more fully in a subsequent letter, he concluded:

the paper gets dim before my eyes and it is the scene of parting over again—Don't fancy that I'm unhappy though: it's only the abstract pathos of the thing that moves me. I never could bear to think of children parted from their parents somehow without a tendency to blubbering: and am as weak to this day upon the point, as I used to be at school.[71]

Thackeray followed the traditional course of authors-to-be who are unhappy at school—he escaped into books. Since adventurous books are normally preferred by boys and since Thackeray attended Charterhouse in the 1820's, his favorite reading can easily be guessed. His joy over *Thaddeus of Warsaw* and *The Scottish Chiefs*, the Gothic romances of Ann Radcliffe, the Waverley novels, *Don Quixote*, and *The Arabian Nights*, is testified to directly in *The Roundabout Papers*,[72] indirectly by countless references to those books throughout his writings.

Because Thackeray felt unusually weak and inadequate during the hours when he stole away to these boyhood literary refuges, the experience of relief which they provided was extraordinarily intense and they etched themselves on his memory with unusual strength. It is a truism that knowledge of the books which men read as boys stays with them longer than does any recollection of the scanty reading possible in the interstices of time afforded by adult life. But Thackeray had what psychologists call a reactive mentality. It kept reverting nostalgically to early life. It preoccupied itself with children. Quite naturally then, his literary frame of reference was made up to an unusual degree of the books he had read as a boy.

In *The Roundabout Paper*, "On a Peal of Bells," Thackeray listed his favorite heroes from Scott. They were: The Baron of Bradwardine, Fergus, Ivanhoe, Locksley, the Templar, Quentin Durward, Quentin's uncle, Saladin, the Scotch knight in *The Talisman*, Claverhouse, and Major Dalgetty.[73] The boy's natural identification of himself with the courageous hero is here obvious. This admiration may also account for the persistence and generally sympathetic

[70] *Letters*, II, 172. Written on June 1, 1844.
[71] The same, p. 197.
[72] "Tunbridge Toys," "De Juventute," "On a Peal of Bells." *Works*, XVII, 413-435, 599-608.
[73] The same, p. 602.

treatment of military types in Thackeray's books, although his attachment to his stepfather, his interest in military history, and the prestige of the uniforms in the fashionable world each played its part. Yet immediately after writing the passage in "On a Peal of Bells," the middle-aged Thackeray apologized for his not-yet-dead liking for these favorites of his youth:

> about all those heroes of Scott, what a manly bloom there is, and honourable modesty! They are not at all heroic. They seem to blush somehow in their position of hero, and as it were to say, 'Since it must be done, here goes!' They are handsome, modest, upright, simple, courageous, not too clever. If I were a mother (which is absurd), I should like to be mother-in-law to several young men of the Walter-Scott-hero sort.[74]

Discounting from this statement the paternal feeling toward young men which marks the novelist's later years, the ideal Thackerayan man is here. Distrustful of too great an intellect because it might conceal some deceit which he in his inadequacy could not plumb or match, Thackeray's need for frank artlessness at all costs found vent thus early. Later he was to embody this craving in a row of male characters somewhat like this engaging, if not too stimulating ideal. Most striking are Frank Castlewood the Younger, Clive Newcome before he knows unhappiness, Lord Kew, Jack Belsize, Harry Warrington, and—in embryo—Denis Duval. They are not to be confused with the more introspective autobiographical heroes like Arthur Pendennis, Henry Esmond, the second George Warrington, or Philip Firmin.[75]

A second archetype for this sort of hero was the "head boy" at school. By Thackeray's standards he should be "frank and manly" (whatever those beloved words mean), handsome, athletic, a champion of weaker boys, and not too intellectual. George Champion in *Dr. Birch and His Young Friends* (1849)[76] fills the part almost perfectly. Significantly, he has one most devoted younger adherent, "Jack Hall, whom he saved when drowning out of the Miller's Pool. The attachment of the two is curious to witness. The smaller lad

---

[74] The same, p. 602.

[75] Greig also notes this parallelism between the two basic types of hero. To him Harry Warrington "resembles the improvident and gullible Thackeray of the thirties; George, the Thackeray of the forties, when misfortunes have sobered and aged him" (*Thackeray: A Reconsideration*, p. 127).

[76] *Works*, X, 158f.

gambolling, playing tricks round the bigger one . . . They are never far apart."[77]

George Osborne in *Vanity Fair*, before his degeneration into a coxcomb, had many of the traits of a "head boy." And William Dobbin, who is in part modeled on Thackeray himself, "flung himself down at little Osborne's feet, and loved him . . . he was his valet, his dog, his man Friday. He believed Osborne to be the possessor of every perfection."[78]

In *The English Humourists* Thackeray is prone to make certain eighteenth-century authors into scapegoats for certain shortcomings which formed part of his own self-portrait. Such is the case with Richard Steele, who became, in Thackeray's eyes, most striking for his inability to resist the festive bowl. During his own career as a Charterhouse gownboy, Steele felt toward Addison, by Thackeray's account, just as Dobbin felt about Osborne and—by implication— Thackeray himself about some unnamed schoolmate:

Dick Steele . . . contracted . . . an admiration in the years of his childhood, and retained it faithfully through his life. . . . Joseph Addison was always his head boy. Addison wrote his exercises. Addison did his best themes. He ran on Addison's messages: fagged for him and blacked his shoes: to be in Joe's company was Dick's greatest pleasure, and he took a sermon or a caning from his monitor with the most boundless reverence, acquiescence, and affection.[79]

It should not be assumed, however, that Thackeray always looked on "head boys" from the point of view of their admirers. With characteristic ambivalence, he likewise enjoyed putting himself in the place of one who was—if not a head boy—at least an admired senior. That feeling partly explains Thackeray's statement that at Charterhouse he learned "to love kind hearted simple children."[80] It also explains the protective relationship in which Arthur Pendennis stood toward both Clive Newcome and Philip Firmin when they were his juniors at Grey Friars.[81] Arthur is the ostensible narrator of both *The Newcomes* and *Philip* and, during the description of his schooling at Grey Friars, is very much a spokesman for Thackeray himself.

[77] The same, p. 161.
[78] Chapter 5. *Works*, XI, 56.
[79] *Works*, XIII, 551.
[80] See above, p. 7.
[81] *The Newcomes*, chapter 4; *Works*, XIV, 44f. *The Adventures of Philip*, chapters 1 and 2; *Works*, XVI, 9 and 15.

The apparent contradiction between Thackeray's many sentimental passages about Charterhouse and his equally violent diatribes against the place is not really a contradiction at all. He disliked the institution, but he loved the boys who attended it. Nor was the dislike a constant emotion; it diminished with time and was greatest during the novelist's early years of struggle and poverty. Consider, for example, the summer of 1840, a few weeks before Isabella Thackeray went insane. At that time his resentments arose from a multitude of minor tensions, but these in turn stemmed from a major unhappiness. Thackeray felt rejected from the privileged station which his so-called "gentleman's education" had led him to regard as a birthright. Casting about for a scapegoat to bear the onus of that misery, he lashed out at the education which had so unfitted him to fight the breadwinner's battle. With deepest irony he advised the young aspirant to education to "go for ten years to a public school" that he may lose "the ties and natural affections of home," become selfish in the urge to compete with wealthier boys, go "many hundreds of times to chapel" without improving his morals, "get a competent knowledge of boxing, swimming, rowing, and cricket, with a pretty knack of Latin hexameters, and a decent smattering of Greek plays," and end up a first-class snob valuing above all things "the honour of dining and consorting with" his betters.[82]

An agricultural school at Templemoyle which Thackeray visited on his tour of Ireland in 1842 won his unstinted praise. Its students were trained for the actual vocation they were to follow rather than "being fagged and flogged into Latin and Greek at the cost of two hundred pounds a year."[83] Moreover the author had now recognized that "of the race of Etonians, and Harrovians, and Carthusians . . . very few *can* read the Greek." Even the great Sir Robert Peel's quotations in the House of Commons are tags of Horace wadded into a pocket-pistol "to astonish the country gentlemen who don't understand him." Yet the five hundred boys at Eton are proud of being "kicked, and licked, and bullied by another hundred," not to mention "putting their posteriors on a block for Dr. Hawtrey to lash at."

On another tour in 1844, when Thackeray visited the Eastern Mediterranean, he flared up at the suggestion that he should go into

[82] *Works*, III, 299.
[83] The same, V, 344.

neo-classical ecstasy at the sight of Athens: "I was made so miserable in youth by a classical education that all connected with it is disagreeable in my eyes; and I have the same recollection of Greek in youth that I have of castor oil."[84] He was even able to toss Dr. Russell's enthusiasm for Greek poetry into the limbo of humbuggery which received all emotions that he himself did not share:

I had my doubts about the genuineness of the article. A man may well thump you or call you names because you won't learn—but I never could take to the proffered delicacy; the fingers that offered it were so dirty. Fancy the brutality of a man who began a Greek grammar with 'τύπτω, I thrash'![85]

Here Thackeray's sensitive soul outweighed his sense of fair play. He was appalled by the dirt, fleas, and general tawdriness of Athens in 1844, and he felt a want in himself because he could not go into the desired raptures, so he saved face by deciding that those raptures were—like most emotions he did not feel—humbug. The old wound to his self-esteem inflicted by Dr. Russell reopened, and he decided that the schoolmaster's love of Greek antiquity also was humbug because the man seemed to him a tyrant.

A breach was made in Thackeray's hostility toward his old school when, in March, 1847, he found himself listed as one of its illustrious alumni in Peter Cunningham's "Chronicles of Charter House."[86] Secretly pleased at the honor, he disclaimed it on the ground that "Titmarsh . . . was a very bad scholar, who bitterly regrets his place of education." A year later more official overtures came from the school when the success of *Vanity Fair* had turned Thackeray into a celebrity. The librarian urged him to "come and dine and look up old friends and young, and see how 'Georgy Osborne' is getting on."[87]

Gradually thereafter he allowed himself to slide into the comfortable role of distinguished alumnus. He attended formal functions; he tipped the boys liberally; and he bestowed priceless publicity on

[84] *Notes of a Journey from Cornhill to Grand Cairo* (1846). *Works*, IX, 122.

[85] *The Fat Contributor Papers*, " 'Punch' in the East." *Works*, VIII, 36. The brutal schoolmaster who began the study of Greek verbs with the conjugation of "τύπτω, I thrash" seems to have been a legendary Victorian figure. Naturally the legend strongly impressed Thackeray because of his obsession with the subject of whipping. In a denunciation of two French classical painters for lacking a true classical education, he wagers "that neither of them ever conjugated τύπτω" ("On the French School of Painting," *The Paris Sketch Book*, 1839. *Works*, II, 50).

[86] *Fraser's Magazine* (March, 1847), pp. 345–346. Quoted from *Letters*, II, 283n.

[87] *Letters*, II, 368n.

the school in the famous closing chapters ot *The Newcomes*. Yet in all these dealings with the school, it is clear that the charm of the boys themselves rather than any approval of the institution as such was responsible for Thackeray's predominant feeling.

The fascination that the boys exerted on Thackeray was of course enhanced by the boost which their admiration gave his ego. It made him feel like a sort of superannuated "head boy," no longer near-sightedly helpless at games or lacking in manly beauty because his schoolmate George Venables had broken the bridge of his nose and disfigured him for life. Though he always pretended to make light of this misfortune, there is no doubt that it seriously undermined his self-confidence. Its most curious effect was the recurrence in Thackeray's writings of his wish to retaliate by disfiguring the noses of men more blessed than he with physical beauty.

In at least three incidents Thackeray causes a male character with whom he identifies himself to injure a rival in that manner. In *The Fitz-Boodle Papers* a duel takes place between Lieutenant Klingenspohr and George Fitz-Boodle, one of Thackeray's semi-autobiographical heroes. The German has wrested from his English rival the love of Dorothea von Speck, reigning beauty of the Duchy of Kalbsbraten-Pumpernickel. Before the wedding, however, Fitz-Boodle boasts that he "placed a sabre-cut across the young scoundrel's nose, which destroyed *his* beauty forever."[88]

The redoubtable Redmond Barry, while still an adolescent, flings a glass of claret into the face of Captain John Quin, a successful rival in love. As a result, the captain's nose "was cut across the bridge and his beauty was spoiled for ever."[89]

In *Vanity Fair*, the turning point of the epic battle between Dobbin and Cuff at Dr. Swishtail's school occurs when Dobbin "hit out a couple of times with all his might—once at Mr. Cuff's left eye, and once on his beautiful Roman nose." The *coup de grace* is delivered when the same champion "put in his left as usual on his adversary's nose, and sent him down for the last time."[90]

Dr. Swishtail's school is another thinly disguised Charterhouse, where Swishtail is Dr. Russell, and Cuff is the head boy. The latter is, however, a renegade to the Thackerayan tradition of the "head

[88] *Works*, IV, 296.
[89] *The Memoirs of Barry Lyndon, Esq.*, chapter 2. *Works*, VI, 37.
[90] Chapter 5. *Works*, XI, 54.

boy" in that he maintains his power by bullying. His loss during the fight to Dobbin of the allegiance of little George Osborne represents a much-desired, vicarious winning by Thackeray of a pretty younger boy's affection. Significantly it is won from a precocious young man of fashion:

Cuff . . . smuggled wine in. He fought the town-boys. Ponies used to come for him to ride home on Saturdays. He had his top-boots in his room, in which he used to hunt in the holidays. He had a gold repeater: and took snuff like the Doctor. He had been to the Opera, and knew the merits of the principal actors, preferring Mr. Kean to Mr. Kemble.[91]

Pendennis makes it clear that the heroes of Charterhouse were boys in the upper form who

assumed all the privileges of man long before they quitted that seminary. Many of them, for example, smoked cigars—and some had already begun the practice of inebriation. One had fought a duel with an ensign in a marching regiment in consequence of a row at the theatre—another actually kept a buggy and horse at a livery stable in Covent Garden, and might be seen driving any Sunday in Hyde Park with a groom with squared arms and armorial buttons by his side.[92]

Had Thackeray been a little younger and had he been sent to Rugby, the heroes of his books would no doubt have reflected his suppressed boyhood desire to be an athlete. But since outdoor sports were badly organized at Charterhouse and since that school was set down in the heart of George IV's London, its heroes in the 1820's were regency bucks, its favorite book, Pierce Egan's *Life in London* (1821). Although the Thackeray of later years laughed at Egan's naïve portrayal of fashionable vice, he took it quite seriously during his schooldays. Most probably the Charterhouse boys really felt that Egan's trio of heroes, Jerry Hawthorn, Corinthian Tom, and Bob Logic were "types of the most elegant, fashionable young fellows the town afforded." We have Thackeray's testimony that, to the schoolboys, the occupations of those "bucks"—seeing "life" in ginshops, knocking down watchmen, boxing with Jackson, attending cockfights, dancing with courtesans at Almack's—"were those of all high-bred English gentlemen."[93]

But absurd as were the occupations of the regency buck to the

91 The same, p. 49.
92 Chapter 2. *Works*, XII, 20.
93 *Works*, II, 423.

middle-aged Victorian moralist, Thackeray, and sincere as was the moral feeling that led him here to ridicule, often to castigate youthful license, there lurked in him—bowed down as he was with terrific responsibilities—an attraction toward the irresponsibility enjoyed by the bucks of his boyhood and the dandies of his maturity. So although Thackeray ostensibly depicts the manners of bucks and dandies as a form of satire, neither he nor his readers ever accepted these portrayals primarily as such. Rather they found in them a form of escape. Both he and they lived vicariously the sins and adventures of Barry Lyndon, Rawdon Crawley, Jack Belsize, and the rest.

Moreover, I doubt whether Thackeray ever got over his envy of the Charterhouse schoolmates who were more precocious than he in becoming men of the world. Only such an envy could explain the persistence of his hostility toward such boys. He of course would have defended it as an effort to correct a social abuse. But the constancy of his iterations is altogether disproportionate to the seriousness of the offence. The description of Cuff's early swaggering and the passage from *Pendennis* about the upper formers are but two of many.

Thackeray's fiction is studded with other boy characters who are like Cuff but more fully developed. The younger George Osborne when he goes to live with his grandfather is just such a youth. So is the younger Frank Clavering in *Pendennis*. A counterpart of these, although slightly older, is the military type represented by Captain Grigg in *The Book of Snobs*. "This last-named little creature . . . was flogged only last week because he could not spell." Now, however, he will "command great whiskered warriors . . . because he has money to lodge at the agent's."[94] Similarly Arthur Pendennis is shocked to find Tom Ricketts, "a little wretch whom he had cut over the back with a hockey-stick last quarter," now standing "surrounded by bayonets, crossbelts, and scarlet, the band blowing trumpets and banging cymbals—talking familiarly to immense warriors with tufts to their chin and Waterloo medals."[95]

The same paradox served Thackeray's need as late as 1859 while he was writing about the American Revolution in *The Virginians*.

[94] Chapter 9. *Works*, IX, 300.
[95] Chapter 3. *Works*, XII, 28.

There Harry Warrington, an officer on the staff of George Washington, voices his resentment and that of his comrades over the rapid promotion of the young Lafayette. Washington accuses Harry of jealousy and the latter exclaims: "Jealous! sir, . . . an aide de camp of Mr. Wolfe is not jealous of a Jack-a-dandy who, five years ago, was being whipped at school!"[96]

Thackeray makes this too-rapid promotion of schoolboys appear a matter of justice, as he makes the too-rapid advance of others seem a matter of morals. Yet one feels sure that jealousy lay behind both attitudes. He wanted to see younger boys suffer the humiliating status of being under the schoolmaster's rod as long as he had.

The same feeling accounts for another strange obsession which occurs again and again in Thackeray's fiction. He had a violent objection to the new type of boy's school where a clergyman took a small number of pupils into his home. Normally these establishments provided a more humane discipline and greater physical comfort than did the large public schools. Thackeray, as a champion of suffering childhood, should have applauded this kinder treatment. Instead, however, he took the stoic attitude of an old soldier trained under more Spartan conditions. To him the gentler methods of a newer age were effeminate and corrupt. Bantering as were his jests on this topic, the constancy of their repetition suggests a genuine underlying animus:

Are our sons ever flogged? Have they not dressing-rooms, hair-oil, hip-baths, and Baden towels? And what picture books the young villains have! What have these children done that they should be so much happier than we were?[97]

The masters of these schools, Thackeray felt, catered to the parents by toadying to their sons—encouraging them in luxury, relaxing educational methods, and winking at precocious vice. These pedagogues, if they looked forward in their methods to the Twentieth Century, went back nevertheless in literary tradition to that stock symbol of sycophancy, the nobleman's private tutor or chaplain. The Reverend Clement Coddler, who maintained such a school in *Cox's Diary* (1840), had been tutor to the Duke of Buckminster.[98]

[96] Chapter 92. *Works*, XV, 985.
[97] "Pictures of Life and Character." *Works*, II, 706.
[98] *Works*, III, 240. Coddler required each of his pupils to bring to school a personal table service of silver, dressing-gown and slippers, pomatum and curling-irons. With parental

In *The Book of Snobs*, the Reverend Otto Rose's Preparatory Academy at Richmond is built around the patronage of the Marquis of Bagwig, whose son, Lord Buckram, is its star boarder.[99] And young Georgy Osborne in *Vanity Fair* attends a school in Bloomsbury owned by the Reverend Lawrence Veal, domestic chaplain to the Earl of Bareacres.[100]

The reader of Thackeray must always remember the existence of two separate factors in such writings of his maturity as concerned the experience of his youth. One is the quality of the experience itself; the other is his literary handling of it. The former is primarily a personal matter, whose deepest effect on the author was made long before the book was written; the latter is an artistic problem, which most concerns the author at the moment of writing. Sometimes Thackeray's problem as an artist was to convert the experience into nostalgic reminiscence; more often it was to convert it into satire, particularly the satire against snobbery which had become his special stock-in-trade.

So Thackeray, as a middle-aged satirist, faced the task in books like *Vanity Fair* and *Pendennis* of making precocious vice or the coddling of schoolboys appear as forms of snobbery. In the first case, the schoolboy was made out to be a snob because he imitated the vices of grown men; the clergyman became a snob because the coddling of his pupils was a form of toadyism to their parents. Yet Thackeray, the human being who observed these practices—whether during boyhood or manhood—did not feel them personally as forms of snobbery, but as blows to his ego. To him the precociously worldly schoolboy was exempted from an inferior and insecure role in life sooner than he himself had been exempted. The coddled pupils of the Reverend Lawrence Veal were liberated from such a position at

---

permission, a boy could have unlimited spending money. Wine was consumed but charged extra for, as were warm, vapour, and shower-baths. Cigar-smoking was discouraged but not forbidden.

[99] Chapter 5. *Works*, IX, 282f. By the time young Frank Clavering in *Pendennis* is sent to the Otto Rose establishment, it has moved to Twickenham. The boys dress for dinner, have "shawl dressing-gowns, fires in their bedrooms, horse and carriage exercise . . . and oil for their hair." Whipping was abolished, for Rose thought "moral discipline was sufficient to lead youth." The boys drank spirits and smoked cigars "before they were old enough to enter a public school" (Chapter 44. *Works*, XII, 560).

[100] Chapter 56. *Works*, XI, 715.

the outset. And Thackeray could never forgive the fates for that injustice.

Yet since snobbery became a ruling prepossession with our novelist, his thoughts about snobbery in educational institutions are worth consideration. In his generalized diatribes at the "English gentleman's education," as we have seen, the turning of the boy into a snob is a stock complaint. A more specific type of snobbery is practiced by the Doctor Russell in *Pendennis* when he pumps Major Pendennis on the prospects of young Arthur's inheriting "a good . . . property."[101] Hence the big public schools were tarred with the same brush as the small private institutions. Furthermore, as we shall see, Thackeray was to indict the universities for the same offense.

Thackeray's most telling story of snobbery among schoolboys themselves was the crucifixion of young Dobbin at Dr. Swishtail's. The boy was called "Figs" because his father was a grocer.[102] On the other hand, the author tried to make out in *The Newcomes* a case for the boys. At least their social distinctions were not, like those of their seniors, based on wealth or rank, but on good-breeding. So Clive Newcome, while still a student at Grey Friars, says to his father:

It isn't rank and that; only somehow there are some men gentlemen and some not, and some women ladies and some not. There's Jones now, the fifth-form master, every man sees *he's* a gentleman, though he wears ever so old clothes; and there's Mr. Brown, who oils his hair, and wears rings, and white chokers—my eyes! such white chokers! and yet we call him the handsome snob.[103]

But Clive's speech sounds suspiciously mature, like a concealed digression by the author on his beloved theory of gentility as an inward and not an outward quality. Thackeray devised this doctrine

---

[101] Chapter 3. *Works*, XII, 23.

[102] *Vanity Fair*, Chapter 5.

[103] *The Newcomes*, chapter 7. *Works*, XIV, 88. Clive is using the word "snob" in its older sense of one who was not a gentleman, the same sense in which Thackeray and his friends commonly used it in the 1820's and 1830's. In the parts of this study which are not quoted matter, the word will be usually written in quotation marks—"snobs" when it is used in this older sense. When it appears without quotation marks, it can be taken to have the current meaning, which to all intents and purposes coincides with the one Thackeray himself was largely responsible for giving it and of which he supplied a classic definition in *The Book of Snobs* (*Works*, IX, 269): "he who meanly admires mean things."

many years later to convince himself that his lionization by the aristocracy was due to his innate gentility and not to his literary reputation.[104]

His natural timidity and his mother's strong hold over him retarded Thackeray's progress in mastering the fashionable vices. Yet holidays with friends who had homes in London gave opportunity to visit the theater.[105] This in turn naturally whetted the romantic side of the boy's nature and supplemented his debauches of novel-reading. Many of his classmates were more precocious than he, if we are to believe *Pendennis*, in the predominant cult of chaste romantic love, which had received fresh impetus from the recent extravagances of romantic literature, although it has always of course been the style among senior boys in public schools. At Charterhouse many of these youths "were in love, and showed each other in confidence poems addressed to, or letters and locks of hair received from, young ladies—but Pen, a modest and timid youth, rather envied these than imitated them as yet."[106] So did Thackeray too, no doubt, but he certainly was not at this time as naïf as a Joseph Andrews.

Before he was twelve years old little Pen had heard talk enough to make him quite awfully wise upon certain points—and so, madam, has your pretty little rosy-cheeked son, who is coming home from school for the ensuing holidays. I don't say that the boy is lost, or that the innocence has left him . . . but that we are helping as much as possible to corrupt him.[107]

The truth is that, apart from the inevitable sex talk of boys, a fairly broad sexual education from their reading was available to pre-Victorian schoolboys. It was general practice to emulate Colonel Newcome, who as a boy had happened to fall in with *Tom Jones* and *Joseph Andrews* in his father's library, an experience he later recalled as "low and disgraceful."[108] Sterne and Smollett usually stood beside Fielding on the paternal book shelves, and when one

[104] See below, p. 150.

[105] Cf. Boyes, *Memorial*, p. 119: "he had a passion for theatricals, of course kept under restraint at school, but now and then gratified when he visited friends in London on the half-holidays."

[106] *Pendennis*, chapter 2. *Works*, XII, 20.

[107] The same, p. 20.

[108] *The Newcomes*, chapter 4. *Works*, XIV, 49. Cf. "Pictures of Life and Character" (1854, *Works*, II, 709f): "there were some prints among them [eighteenth-century portfolios] very odd indeed; some that girls could not understand; some that boys, indeed, had best not see. We swiftly turn over those prohibited pages."

considers that Thackeray and his fellows topped off this substantial fare with *Life in London*—largely a book about courtesans—it is no wonder that they possessed the theoretical worldly wisdom attributed to *Pendennis*.

The problem of Thackeray's attitudes toward sex at this stage of his development is crucial to understanding his war with his readers later over the issue of Grundyism in his writings. The general trend of European social manners has permitted a young man to seek sexual experience soon after puberty with tacit understanding that all talk or knowledge of such activity will be excluded from the home. Such of course were the family manners of Thackeray's more precocious schoolmates. But the period was a difficult one for all of them, inasmuch as the growing strength of both the Evangelical and the feminist movements was already working to impose the single sexual standard. Mrs. Carmichael-Smyth was of course an ardent advocate of the reform.

Under these circumstances, young men were confronted by a dilemma: they could continue under the old system or they could sublimate their sexual instincts into chaste romantic passions for ' pure" girls. If they continued in the old ways, they lacked the comforting assurance enjoyed by their fathers, who had known that their own mothers were shutting their eyes to their sons' "wild oats."

Faced by this predicament, Arthur Pendennis was so much his mother's son that he unhesitatingly chose to sublimate his first passion into pure and romantic adoration, just as he was to maintain— rather unnaturally—his later interest in Fanny Bolton on the level of a pleasant flirtation. It was clear to everyone but the boy himself that a marriage to the object of his first *amour* was ridiculous, but Pen's mother Helen was unable to extricate him. The "purity" of his passion and the technical chastity of the lady herself—a bovine actress with an eye to the main chance—gave Helen no effective means of breaking off the affair. She saw clearly the practical unsuitability of the match, but was weakened in combating it by her own emotional involvement, for she was at the same time jealous of her son's new love and so dotingly fond of him that she could refuse him nothing. The living symbol of the old morality, Major Pendennis, had to unravel the mess, which, he announced most explicitly, would never have existed but for the new standards.

'If it were but a temporary liaison,' the excellent man said, 'one could bear it. A young fellow must sow his wild oats, and that sort of thing. But a virtuous attachment is the deuce. It comes of the d——d romantic notions boys get from being brought up by women.'[109]

So realistic is the description of the Fotheringay affair that efforts have been made to find a counterpart for it in the corresponding period of Thackeray's life—his stay at Larkbeare from the spring of 1828 until February, 1829.[110] Yet to oppose such conjectures, one need only look at Thackeray's statement that at this time he "had not learnt to love a woman."[111] The remark, of course, does not rule out actresses for whom he felt romantic infatuations across the footlights. In fact, the Fotheringay affair was inspired partly by an anecdote which a friend told to Thackeray[112] and partly by the actresses he had specially admired during his late adolescence. In February, 1828, while in his last phase at Charterhouse, he wrote his mother: "I went to the Adelphi on Saturday night, and fell in love with . . . Mrs. Yates. Mrs. Yates. Mrs. Yates. She is so pretty, and so fascinating and so ladylike and so—I need not go on with her good qualities."[113]

The Roundabout Paper, "De Juventute" (1860), speaks ironically of the "decay of stage beauty since the days of George IV" and recalls nostalgically the same "Adelphi, and the actresses there."

When I think of Miss Chester, and Miss Love, and Mrs. Serle at Sadler's Wells, and her forty glorious pupils—of the Opera and Noblet, and the exquisite young Taglioni, and Pauline Leroux and a host more![114]

The real infatuation that Thackeray dwells upon in this essay was the one he felt for Henriette Sontag, later Countess de Rossi, a German soprano who was the Jenny Lind of her day. She scored sensational London successes in a repertory of operas by Mozart and Rossini during the summer months of 1828 and 1829. Quite conceivably Thackeray's enthusiasm for the works of these two

---

[109] Chapter 9. *Works*, XII, 113.

[110] See Lewis Melville (pseud. for Lewis Benjamin), *William Makepeace Thackeray* (Garden City, N. Y., 1928), p. 46.

[111] *Letters*, II, 453.

[112] Greig, *Thackeray: A Reconsideration*, p. 121.

[113] *Letters*, I, 23. Ironically, this Mrs. Yates was the mother of Thackeray's enemy-to-be, Edmund Yates (see below, p. 199).

[114] *Works*, XVII, 428.

composers, attested to by numerous literary references, is associable with his devotion to Mme. Sontag:

Think of Sontag. I remember her in *Otello* and the *Donna del Lago* in '28. I remember being behind the scenes at the Opera (where numbers of us young fellows of fashion used to go), and seeing Sontag let her hair fall down over her shoulders previous to her murder by Donzelli. Young fellows have never seen beauty like *that*, heard such a voice, seen such hair, such eyes.[115]

When Sontag returned to the stage many years later, Thackeray heard her sing in Paris in March, 1850. He met her at a dinner soon afterward and was so delighted that he cadged an invitation to a reception where he might see her again.[116] When she died on July 18, 1854, he began a poem for the occasion "but stopped finding it was not at all about her but about myself. Bon Dieu what an angel I remember thinking her just twenty-five years ago."[117] "Just twenty-five years ago" would have placed the affair in July, 1829, and borne out the suspicion[118] that it had started when he was en route to Paris after his first term at Cambridge.

But lest anyone get the impression that Thackeray spent that summer sighing his heart out over Sontag, it should be added that a few days after his arrival in Paris, and a week after he had seen that lady let her hair down, he was telling his mother how the ballet of the opera boasts a "damsel yclept Taglioni who hath the most superb pair of pins, and maketh the most superb use of them that ever I saw dancer do before."[119]

[115] The same. Since *La Donna del Lago*, an adaptation of Scott's *Lady of the Lake*, contains no murder of the soprano by a male character, the performance which Thackeray describes was clearly Rossini's *Otello*. The only time Sontag and Donzelli sang that opera together in London, according to Mme. Sontag's anonymous biographer, was on July 25, 1829 when Thackeray was in Paris. The performances in question could not very well have taken place in 1828, though Mme. Sontag gave numerous performances at London during May and June of that year of both the operas mentioned, for Donzelli did not sing with her on that engagement, and Thackeray was ill at Larkbeare at the time. He could, however, have seen the two sing together in *La Donna del Lago* on June 9, 1829, on his way home from Cambridge, where he had completed his term examinations on June 5 (*Letters*, I, 83), and could have seen her with another leading man in *Otello* on July 9 or 11 of that year, en route to Paris, which he reached about July 14 (*Letters*, I, 8). This evidence plus a quotation in a letter of 1854 (*Letters*, III, 379), seems to establish July 1829, as the date of Thackeray's enthusiasm for Mme. Sontag.

[116] *Letters*, II, 666.

[117] The same, III, 379.

[118] See note 115.

[119] *Letters*, I, 85f. For Thackeray's burlesque of Taglioni's Ballet *Flore et Zéphyr*, see below, pp. 67f.

This was the same Taglioni who had been mentioned in "De Juventute."[120] But her reign, too, was short, for in less than three weeks, word went off to the long-suffering Mrs. Carmichael-Smyth that

Mademoiselle Mars is most glorious, and Leontine Fay at the Theatre de Madame the most delightful little creature I ever set eyes on; she has a pair of such lips! out of which the French comes trilling out with a modulation and a beauty of which I did not think it capable.[121]

Two weeks later he has again seen his "little Favorite Leontine Fay" and found her "as usual divine."[122] But there were signs that even Mrs. Carmichael-Smyth's patience was wearing thin. In the first place she shared the scruples of the Evangelical sect on the subject of theater-going, a fact which may have lent it an additional luster in her son's eyes. Certainly a passage in *The Virginians* seems autobiographical:

no wonder George Warrington loved the theatre. Then he had the satisfaction of thinking that his mother only half approved of plays and playhouses, and of feasting on fruit forbidden at home.[123]

Seemingly, the remarks about Taglioni's legs and Mlle. Fay's lips had made uneasy reading in Larkbeare, and there had been protests, for in his next sentence Thackeray goes on the defensive and resorts to rationalizations: "I wonder at your objecting to the Theatregoing, for it gives me the best French possible." Then comes a naïf pretense—whether on his part or his mother's it is impossible to say in the absence of her letter—that her objections to his playgoing were based on the late hour at which the theaters let out: "I am quite enough used to it not to feel the effects of it in the morning, especially as most of the Theatres are closed before 11 o'clock." In the next day's continuation of the letter, however, there is a jocoseness about Miss Fay that may have been meant to put Mrs. Carmichael-Smyth's mind at ease: "I don't know how it is that my love for Leontine Fay should go off but it is not so strong to day as usual."[124]

Yet the string of enthusiasms produced by the summer of enchantment was not over. In 1833 Thackeray was to see his "ancient flame

[120] See above, p. 32.
[121] *Letters*, I, 91.
[122] The same, p. 93.
[123] Chapter 53. *Works*, XV, 661.
[124] *Letters*, I, 93.

Duvernay at the French opera" and wonder how he "could have ever been smitten,"[125] and in 1834 Edward FitzGerald heard from Paris that a mysterious Thérèse "has got a child after 4 years marriage," adding "I don't think I am in love with her any more."[126] If, as is probable, this *amour* dates from before the lady's marriage, it must have occurred in 1829.

But the story was not over yet. Two months more elapsed, and Thackeray stopped off in London on his way back to Cambridge to witness the sensational debut of Fanny Kemble as Juliet. The Paris reprimand had taught him a little caution in writing to his mother, and he only divulged that he had seen "Miss Fanny Kemble and was much delighted with her."[127] Years later, however, that actress repeated a remark by Thackeray that he and all his friends "were in love with you, and had your portrait by Lawrence in our rooms."[128]

Thus a series of romantic infatuations for actresses was a stage in Thackeray's emotional growth. To him these attachments symbolized the illusions of youth, which he was soon to discard when he embraced his "vanity of vanities" philosophy. The denial of illusion which that philosophy entailed meant, however, an emotional loss which he kept lamenting to the point of masochism. In one of the passages of *Philip* where the hero's youth is a copy of Thackeray's own, he described how

the simple young fellow, surveying the ballet from his stall at the opera, mistook carmine for blushes, pearl powder for native snows, and cotton-wool for natural symmetry; and ... when he went into the world, he was not more clear-sighted about its rouged innocence, its padded pretension, and its painted candour.[129]

One cannot help speculating on what might have happened had Thackeray not been so starved for warmth and beauty in the drab purlieus of Charterhouse. Certainly then the London theater would not have seemed so unreally wonderful, and his later reaction to the discovery of its tinsel character would hardly have been so violent. Accordingly, the philosophy that "all is vanity" which was to inform most of his mature writings would have lost an important wellspring.

[125] The same, p. 266. There is a possibility that he could have fallen under this lady's spell in 1832, but the probabilities favor 1829, as Professor Ray has shown in the note to the passage.

[126] The same, p. 276.

[127] The same, p. 105.

[128] Frances Ann Kemble, *Records of Later Life* (New York, 1882), p. 627.

[129] Chapter 4. *Works*, XVI, 40f.

CHAPTER II
College Days and Bohemianism

WHEN her son left for Cambridge at the beginning of 1829, Mrs. Carmichael-Smyth realized how her authority was endangered by the loosening of the bond between them. Like the mother of William Brookfield, her husband's friend-to-be, she undoubtedly "prayed that her William might be able to escape the snares with which he will be surrounded."[1] And she must have been vastly reassured when he established the habit, on arriving at college, of keeping a diary and sending it to her as his weekly letter. The practice does not seem to have irked Thackeray at first; he was apparently as anxious to keep close to her as she was to watch over him. Moreover, the daily writing gave him abundant opportunity to perform before her approving eyes.

The showmanship, inherent in all children and naturally strongest in the gifted, craves audiences of both adults and playmates. In Thackeray's case it had obviously been repressed before the unsympathetic masters at Charterhouse. He had achieved a second-best acceptance among his schoolmates by drawing sketches and making verses, but Mrs. Carmichael-Smyth would inevitably be still his most constant and admiring audience.

This diary type of correspondence was valuable insofar as it enabled Mrs. Carmichael-Smyth to share Thackeray's little sorrows and triumphs. It kept open the channels of candor between them. Consequently their relationship did not suffer from the conventional dummy-like exchange that passes for correspondence between parents and students away from home. Furthermore, the diary-letters to his mother helped develop in Thackeray the habit of baring his heart to sympathetic women. Many years later the wisest of his women friends, Mrs. Bryan Waller Procter, applied to him the description of Paul Emanuel from Charlotte Brontë's *Villette*. This man's tenderness was such that it "bound him to girls and women,

[1] Charles and Frances Brookfield, *Mrs. Brookfield and Her Circle*, 2 vols. (New York, 1905), I, 2.

to whom rebel as he would, he could not disown his affinity nor quite deny that, on the whole, he was better with them than with his own sex."[2] Thackeray himself revealed the other side of this picture when, in 1854, he wrote to his American friend, Mrs. Baxter, and said of her husband: "He mustn't mind my not writing to him. I don't to any man except on business."[3]

In part because of his letter-writing habits Thackeray's style achieved a lack of restraint which often made his books little more than parade-grounds for the "play of the humourous ego." They came to be primarily revelations of his personality rather than narrations of events as he burst out of character for the famous chats with his readers. And it is a striking fact that he was often to visualize these readers as women rather than men.[4] Almost the most important symptom of his boyhood unhappiness was the craving for esteem. It was that which compelled him to exhibit his most trivial thoughts and emotions to a sympathetic audience of women.

In the matter of the diary-letters, however, this candid parade of events and impressions became more difficult. As Thackeray grew into manhood the bond between mother and son was strained by the inevitable divergence of their tastes and attitudes. His confidences to Mrs. Carmichael-Smyth about his stage loves are a case in point. The motivation behind these rapturous disclosures to her was that which has always impelled many young men to make such confessions to their mothers—a sort of show-off bravado, compounded of male vanity and a touch of sadism. By the time he wrote *Pendennis* in 1849, Thackeray had perceived that Helen Pendennis— a thinly disguised version of his own mother—possessed "that anxiety with which brooding women watch over their sons' affections— and in acknowledging which, I have no doubt there is a sexual jealousy on the mother's part."[5]

Thackeray was forced to strange devices in maintaining candor with his mother when he learned the consequences of telling her the whole truth. His best defence lay in the rationalizations and self-exculpations that sprang so easily from his introverted temperament.

[2] *Letters*, III, 231.
[3] The same, p. 357.
[4] See below, p. 128.
[5] Chapter 24. *Works*, XII, 298.

He skillfully rationalized his theater-going, as we have seen, on educational grounds. Later he would do the same when he started card-playing.[6]

Arthur Pendennis was as adept as Thackeray in overriding his mother's protests at his man-of-the-world poses. During his first college vacation he explained that "he was at work upon a prize-poem . . . and could not compose without his cigar."[7] When Helen "read such things" in his French "light literature . . . as caused her to open her eyes with wonder," he "showed her . . . that it was absolutely necessary that he should keep up his French by an acquaintance with the most celebrated writers of the day." And when she was "frightened at the amount" of his wine-bill, he pointed out that "everybody drank claret and champagne now."

The fact that Thackeray, like Pendennis, acquired some man-of-the-world poses at college does not mean that the future novelist was a "blood" during his terms at Cambridge. Such a comfortable generalization emphasizes one side of his character to the exclusion of all others. Like all of his intelligent fellow-students he was racked by three questions: how to benefit by the outmoded curriculum; what to do with himself when he should leave college; and what sort of Divine Power he should believe in. To the uncongenial curriculum, weighted with mathematics, the majority of Thackeray's fellows made a compromise adjustment. They did what was required without too much fuss and feathers, usually by grinding hard before examinations. At other times they relaxed and made their own informal curriculum, reading extensively in the English classics and contemporary literature, trying their hands at writing verses and essays, editing little periodicals, debating, and endlessly discussing things among themselves. The formal curriculum was, nevertheless, of some value to them as intellectual discipline, even though they may not have recognized the fact.

The young men like Thackeray who belonged neither to the aristocratic gentlemen commoners nor to the hard-working sizars at the university, were confused by their ambiguous middle-group position, corresponding to the social level where they would find themselves on leaving college. They were all to some extent victims of the younger son philosophy of the hereditary aristocracy, whatever their

[6] See below, pp. 48f.
[7] Chapter 18. *Works*, XII, 214.

own family histories. Furthermore, they were prone to feel that niches should open for them in one of the gentlemanly professions: law, clergy, parliament, or government service. But the forces of democracy were constantly stepping up the number of non-university competitors in these professions. Surveying the situation, college men often felt as fatuous as did Thackeray's narrator-hero, George Fitz-Boodle, when he wrote:

such is the glut of professionals, the horrible cut-throat competition among them, that there is no chance for one in a thousand, be he ever so willing, or brave, or clever: in the great ocean of life he . . . sinks.[8]

The profession of literature offered a possibility of compromise, for the number of university men with pens skilled enough to sell their writings was proportionally far higher in 1829 than it is today. The compulsory exercises in the classics at school, however onerous, at least brought about that good. But the flavor of Grub Street still clung to earning money by the pen, and the influx of clever non-university men—many of them Scotch and Irish—into London increased competition there. Moreover, the unholy alliance of publishing with politics made it nigh impossible for professional writers to keep their skirts clear of the mud-slinging of political controversy.

The fate of Keats at the hands of the critics was generally known. Furthermore, that fate was about to be repeated in a way at the expense of Alfred Tennyson, the Cambridge student whose literary gift was most indubitable and manifest to his friends. The thin-skinned sensitiveness which Tennyson shared, not only with Thackeray, but with many other undergraduates of their type, was enough almost to drive Tennyson from the field of professional authorship, in spite of his lifetime dedication of himself to poetry. How much more then could it be expected to inhibit the equally sensitive Thackeray, who—unlike Tennyson—did not feel during his young manhood that he had a vocation in literature!

Thus a combination of factors peculiar to young gentlemen in his position had much to do with Thackeray's tackings, veerings, and indecisions during the years from 1829 to 1833, when he lost the remainder of his patrimony. Like all well-bred young men of

[8] "Fitz-Boodle's Professions" (1842), *Works*, IV, 229.

his kind, he started his undergraduate career with the best of studious intentions. Making allowance for a boy's natural tendency to put his best foot forward in his letters home, his diary-letters during his first term at Cambridge indicate a studious effort that is in no sense discreditable. Nor is there any discredit in Thackeray's being ranked, at the end of that term, in the fourth class, where "clever 'non-reading men' were put, as in a limbo."[9] Continuing on that course would have brought him in time an undistinguished degree. Then he would have studied at the bar in a similar inconspicuous way, and spent the rest of his days as a prosaic solicitor or barrister lost in the dust of time.

But circumstances changed all that. In the first place, Thackeray had the drive to succeed that often comes from insecurity and lack of confidence. Added to it was the kind of pride which, having com-competed and lost out, prefers not to compete again. One of his Charterhouse schoolfellows attributes his lack of scholastic success at boarding school to the fact that as a younger boy he

had been ill-grounded and so lost confidence when he came to cope with those who had been better initiated, and gave up the race in which he thought he might fail, for he had plenty of pride and ambition.[10]

The same handicaps still held Thackeray back at Cambridge. The letter-diary contains promises to better his standing at the expense of his fellows,[11] and a failure to surpass them in 1829–30 (a period whose records are nearly all lost) may have driven him to early surrender.

Naturally, Thackeray was most resourceful in excuses to cover his failures. A fortnight's illness just before examination cost him a hundred places in the rankings;[12] his tutor would not review mathematics with him from the beginning;[13] "in every thing but Mathematics" another tutor "is deficient."[14] It should be granted too that the subject of mathematics, then basic at Cambridge, was unsuited to Thackeray's talents. Yet one cannot help feeling that more of

[9] *Letters*, I, 108n.
[10] Boyes, "Thackeray's School-Days," p. 120.
[11] *Letters*, I, 69, 70, 83.
[12] The same, p. 83.
[13] The same, p. 69.
[14] The same, p. 104.

his study hours were spent worrying about his mathematics than in actually doing it.

Possibly a bit of the snobbery that inhibited Pendennis had a share in Thackeray's academic discouragement. That hero, it will be remembered, "gave up his attendance . . . in the lecture-room . . . being perhaps rather annoyed that one or two very vulgar young men, who did not even use straps to their trousers so as to cover the abominably thick and coarse shoes and stockings which they wore, beat him completely."[15] In *The Book of Snobs* (1846) Thackeray was to recall that

we *then* used to consider Snobs, raw-looking lads, who never missed chapel; who wore highlows and no straps; who walked two hours on the Trumpington road every day of their lives; who carried off the College scholarships, and who overrated themselves in hall. We were premature in pronouncing our verdict . . . The man without straps fulfilled his destiny and duty.

Now, we are told, this once despised creature has written a Dictionary or Treatise, joined the Oxford and Cambridge Club, and insinuated himself into a parish where his "parishioners love him, and snore under his sermons."[16]

Yet within the closed circles of undergraduate "sets" there was at all times complete democracy. To these young men, as to most adolescent social groups, one qualified for membership on the basis of what he was, not what his parents were. Unfortunately, the term "what one was" did not apply so much to one's basic character as to one's external marks of prestige. The right manner, accent, clothing, etc. were all-important. This is the criterion neither of the adult world, where rank or money makes one a gentleman, nor of Thackeray's matured philosophy, wherein a subtle compound of morals and innate breeding confers the accolade. It is nevertheless the criterion which Thackeray was applying to the father of one of his closest friends at Trinity when he wrote his mother: "Young's governour arrived to day; I must ask him to breakfast I suppose. Tho he is no favorite of mine, for he is not a *gentleman*."[17]

[15] Chapter 18. *Works*, XII, 212.

[16] Chapter 15. *Works*, IX, 324f. In one of Thackeray's short stories, "Bob Robinson's First Love" (1845), the daughter of a boarding-school proprietor is courted by a fellow and tutor of Maudlin[sic] College named Butts. The latter is despised by the boys because he wore "high-lows and no straps to his trousers" (*Works*, VI, 459).

[17] *Letters*, I, 61.

This application of their own criteria of gentility to those they met naturally made the undergraduates contemptuous of more worldly standards. Particularly offensive to them was the sight of the sycophantic dons and tutors, clinging to the "tufts" with their tongues slavering in expectation of livings. This scorn—in Thackeray's case closely related to his feeling for sycophantic schoolmasters—[18] led to some memorable passages of satire in his writings. In *The Book of Snobs* (1846) he denounces Hugby and Crump, tutors of St. Boniface College, Oxford, for such practices.[19] In *Pendennis* Arthur is invited to a wine-party by his tutor after the latter sees the boy's uncle in a carriage with two Knights of the Garter.[20] Later in the book, the hero accuses the tutors of "truckling to the tufts, and bullying the poor undergraduates in the lecture-room."[21]

The undergraduates' disregard for the outer world's criteria of social standing made it possible for a peer's grandson like Milnes while at the university to accept the leadership of a small-town attorney's son like Brookfield,[22] just as Lord Magnus Charters was glad to attend a dinner in the rooms of Arthur Pendennis, the apothecary's son.[23] And although Thackeray praises that young hero because "he never knew the difference between small and great in the treatment of his acquaintances" and "was only too ready to share his guinea with a poor friend,"[24] one can rest assured that those acquaintances and poor friends were men with straps on their boots.

[18] See above, pp. 28f.

[19] Chapter 14. *Works*, IX, 319–323.

[20] Chapter 19, *Works*, XII, 237.

[21] Chapter 61. *Works*, XII, 796. Cf. "Fitz-Boodle's Confessions" (1842), *Works*, IV, 206, wherein the Christ Church tutor Otto Rose "was as remarkable for his fondness for a tuft as for his nervous antipathy to tobacco." Also cf. *Henry Esmond* (1851–1852), chapter 13. *Works*, XIII, 135: "Doctor Montague, the master of the college, who had treated Harry somewhat haughtily, seeing his familiarity with these great folks, and that my Lord Castlewood laughed and walked with his hand on Harry's shoulder, relented to Mr. Esmond, and condescended to be very civil to him." Also cf. *The Newcomes* (1854), chapter 52. *Works*, XIV, 698. "Princekin or lordkin from his earliest days has nurses, dependants, ... fellow-collegians, college-tutors, stewards and valets, led-captains of his suite, and women innumerable flattering him and doing him honour." See also Thackeray's most finished specimen of the sycophantic college don, the Reverend Baring Leader, in "The Kickleburys on the Rhine" (1850), *Works*, X, 256ff.

[22] Anne T. Ritchie, ed., Biographical Introduction to *The Works of William Makepeace Thackeray* (London, 1898–1899), II, xxx.

[23] Chapter 19. *Works*, XII, 226.

[24] The same, p. 234.

No one saw more clearly than Thackeray the incongruity of the Byronic radicalism affected by these young aristocrats, who damned as "snobs" men with incorrect gloves, yet wrote daring essays in defense of republicanism "*à propos* of the death of Roland and the Girondins." As Thackeray points out, the author of that essay was in time to wear "the starchiest tie in all the diocese, and would go to Smithfield rather than eat a beefsteak on a Friday in Lent."[25] Staunchly conservative elders like Major Pendennis regarded it as part of the tradition that young Lord Magnus Charters should be one of the "most truculent republicans" in the Oxbridge Union Debating Club, because "it sits prettily enough on a young patrician in early life, though nothing is so loathsome among persons of our rank."[26] And as a student Thackeray was to betray the same mistrust of extremes in political and religious questions that he showed in later life. He refused to succumb to the Shelley cult in Cambridge which was then glorifying *The Revolt of Islam* as an epoch-making poem,[27] he signed a petition against Catholic Emancipation,[28] and in the witty mockery which was one of the bases of his later success, he revealed a conservative's mistrust of romantic extremes that later became one of the foundations of his writing.

Of the two recognized avenues of intellectual achievement outside the curriculum, debating and publication, the latter was clearly Thackeray's *forte*. Debating at the Union had the advantage of being the doorway to a political career, but Thackeray lacked both the necessary analytical powers and the self-confidence to succeed there. In the little magazine *The Snob* and its successor *The Gownsman*, he found, however, just the outlet he needed for his embryonic powers of satirical writing. The man who feels inadequate to compete can often make his mark by scoffing at those who do, and in Thackeray this trait had been already so well developed before he left Charterhouse that a schoolmate there is said never to have got over his awe of Thackeray's power of sarcasm.[29] Now at Cambridge there occurred an event of historic irony: Tennyson, destined to be one of the greatest poets of the coming age, won the Chancellor's

[25] Chapter 18. The same, p. 220.
[26] Chapter 19. The same, p. 227.
[27] *Letters*, I, 74.
[28] The same, p. 47.
[29] Boyes, "Thackeray's School-Days," p. 127.

Medal with his serious poem on the subject of Timbuctoo, while Thackeray, its greatest satirist, won a minor success in his own coterie by publishing in *The Snob* a burlesque of the same subject.

Thackeray's connection with these little college magazines gave him a *kudos* which must have raised his spirits for a time, but not for long. The reasons for discontinuance of *The Gownsman* in February of 1830, several months prior to his departure from Cambridge, are unknown. Lack of funds, or subscribers, or both was probably the immediate pretext. Yet in the light of his growing tendency to lose interest in his pursuits and to drop them, one suspects that the periodical may have died in large part because its editor was bored with it.

The little that we know about Thackeray's friendships at Cambridge sheds some light on his development. The diary-letter for April 1, 1829, lists six of his eleven closest friends as being fellow Carthusians.[30] Two weeks later, he and three other Charterhouse men were hard put to it to find six fellow-members for a proposed Essay Club who were not from their old school.[31] About ten months later, John Allen's diary[32] shows that the Essay Club was still operating, that it was roughly co-extensive with his and Thackeray's "set," and that this "set" contained many of the old Charterhouse group of the previous year. These men became good solid citizens, but none of them has gone down as a great name to posterity.

Thackeray certainly knew some of The Apostles like Brookfield, Spedding, and Kemble while he was at Cambridge, but he never knew all of them, and he was never a member of that transcendent set of young intellects. An undergraduate body is a perfect demonstration of the law that fluid rises or falls to its natural level. Thackeray's level did not at that time rest with The Apostles, but with the more mediocre group in which he settled. Here he was a beloved purveyor of merriment, perhaps even a bit of a buffoon.[33]

It was another of Thackeray's ambivalences that he had in him

---

[30] *Letters*, I, 53.

[31] The same, p. 56.

[32] The same, pp. 493–495.

[33] "He had always a flow of humour and pleasantry, and was made much of by his friends. At supper-parties . . . he enjoyed the humours of the hour, and sang one or two old songs with great applause. 'Old King Cole' I well remember to have heard from him . . . It made me laugh . . . from the humour with which it was given." From William Hepworth Thompson, *Memorials*, quoted by Stevenson, The Showman of Vanity Fair, p. 28.

much of the self-tormenting jester—one of those men who force the public to laugh at them and then inwardly bleed because they are not taken seriously. He was too large, ungainly, and unprepossessing with his broken nose to figure seriously as either athlete or charmer. The sense of intellectual inadequacy that Dr. Russell's sarcasm had ground into him disqualified him from consecutive, hard thought. Yet he could burlesque and ridicule the things which he felt were not his to enjoy, and by that ridicule he could win acceptance of a sort. The drawback was that such acceptance failed in time to satisfy him. The ready applause of his set or of the few readers of *The Snob* and *The Gownsman* was eventually little more stimulating than that of the family group at Larkbeare.

So Thackeray's failure at Cambridge was doubtless in part a failure of mediocrity; although highly intelligent, he was too lacking in any one distinction to impress himself on any dominant group. He resented the dons because they took no interest in his welfare, either intellectually or spiritually. Their attitude in fact was worse in some ways than the sarcastic attention of Dr. Russell. Hence Thackeray was never really happy about these dons until he had paid them back by lampooning their interest in young aristocrats. He subconsciously resented also the brilliant young intellectuals because he was not fully one of their group, and he both resented and was fascinated by the aristocratic young men of pleasure.

Within his set, Thackeray seems to have had only two very close friends, both of them talented young men who, like himself, didn't fit into recognized patterns. Each of these friendships was to supply a different need of his nature.

Edward FitzGerald, later to be famous as translator of *The Rubaiyat of Omar Khayyam*, was a younger son of a landed family of considerable wealth. In certain respects, he was the opposite of Thackeray. Whereas the latter's worldly, pleasure-loving side partly compensated for the protective watchfulness of a saintly mother, FitzGerald's temperament shunned polite society to protest against the neglect of his worldly, fashionable mother. That anti-worldliness on the part of his friend was to be, however, of great value to Thackeray in formulating the main ideas behind his more famous books.

Thackeray's selection of FitzGerald as his most intimate friend, and the strength of their attachment for several years is significant. It represents to a large extent the clinging together of two similarly confused spirits in a world which seems to have no place for them. Their time together at Cambridge was short, for they did not meet until the autumn of 1829 and FitzGerald was graduated in January. Yet Thackeray sensed in the other what he apparently missed in the shallower group with which he had until then associated—emotional depth and intelligence without the depressing intellectuality and earnestness of The Apostles.

Thackeray's other close friend, John Allen, was the son of an Anglican minister. Preparing himself for the clergy by the hardest sort of spiritual and intellectual exercises, he was the type of reading man who would normally have been avoided by Thackeray and his more pleasure-loving set. Yet Allen relieved, by affection and geniality toward his friends, the austerity which he demanded of himself. His other-worldly, impractical ways must have reminded them of the beloved fictional characters, Dr. Primrose and Parson Adams. In time he was to become an Archdeacon and to provide some of the traits for Dobbin in *Vanity Fair*.[34] While they were at Cambridge together, however, Allen's function was that of unofficial chaplain, to offer the spiritual food which the preoccupied dons failed to provide.

The entries in Allen's diary for February 3-4, 1830, disclose the fact that "Thackeray came in, we had some serious conversation when I affected him to tears he went away with a determination tomorrow to lead a new life, Prayed for him FitzGerald and myself afterwards in tears . . . went to morning chapel, called Thackeray, *prayed*." Three days later, "Thackeray came up—expressed some doubts of Christ being equal with God, read over St. Matthew together and he was convinced thank God for it."[35] In other words, Thackeray, FitzGerald, and Allen had formed one of those deeply attached coalitions of undergraduates that one meets in all colleges, but which seemed to flourish especially in the English universities during the last century.

Clearly Thackeray was experiencing at that time a moral and spiritual crisis. It is characteristic of the age that both came to him at once, for since the moral law rested on a theological foundation, the shaking of that necessarily undermined the bases of conduct.

[34] *Letters*, I, lxxxi-lxxxiv.
[35] The same, p. 493f.

Also significant is the raising of Thackeray's theological crisis not over the issue, so basic today, of the existence of a personal God. Rather it centered on the trinitarian issue, which was part of the larger question of Biblical infallibility. In other words, his faith in the literal inspiration of the Bible was shaken and with it his faith in the theological and moral order, of which his mother was to him the high priestess, and John Allen her vicar. In truth, Thackeray was at this time far from being the happy-go-lucky youth that some have pictured him. For as the theological foundation of his morality crumbled, the winds of temptation were blowing hard upon its super-structure.

During his studious, virtuous first term at Cambridge, Thackeray had been rather a prig, writing contemptuously of another man up from Charterhouse "who swears in such an impertinent disgusting way, that three men (myself included) have cut him."[36] And the same priggish note creeps into his description "of receiving a drunken man in my rooms, whom I persuaded my name was Jenkins, and dismissed."[37]

Quite naturally, Thackeray became as skilful a tightrope walker in writing home about his drinking as he was in confiding his love affairs. It was impossible for his honest and confiding nature to lie to Mrs. Carmichael-Smyth and say he never went near one of the wine parties which were then a feature of Cambridge life. On the other hand, he was at pains to make clear the fact that they were a bore,[38] that he gave them only to pay off social obligations,[39] and that when he attended them he was a noted pillar of abstemious-ness.[40] To make his case more plausible, Thackeray was occasionally willing, like Pope's Atticus, to "hint a fault." "I had a head ach [sic] or two when I first came up. I did not live temperately enough, but I am now as well and cool as possible."[41] "Two other men carried me off to the Bull, where they gave me some milk punch and have sent me home in a great state of comfort to baid [sic]."[42] "I now

[36] *Letters*, I, 65.
[37] The same, p. 77.
[38] The same, p. 37.
[39] The same, p. 50.
[40] The same, pp. 52, 53, 66, 82.
[41] The same, pp. 64f.
[42] The same, p. 66.

(although I have only drunk two glasses of wine this day . . .) feel half drunk."[43] During the following year Allen's diary tells of an evening when "Thackeray got a little elated."[44] In truth the future novelist acquired at Cambridge the habit of conviviality which was in time to become part of the Thackeray legend when he was proud of being a two-bottle man who did not show his liquor.[45]

The causes for that pride are allied to the reasons why Thackeray became a gambler during his young manhood. Since he could not be an athlete, a brilliant scholar or debater, a Byron or Don Juan in the drawing room, he could at least model himself on one type of hero: the great man who never quails or betrays emotion in the face of circumstances. Such men fascinated him; his writings express a deep admiration for Wellington, George Washington, Charles James Fox, and others who possessed the all-essential coolness. And in spite of the mask of irony assumed by Thackeray in narrating the career of Barry Lyndon, a note of genuine admiration often permeates the irony because that gentleman had such imperturbable *sang froid* during his palmy days.

The truth is that Thackeray's inward feelings of inadequacy craved the protection of such an outer shell of resolution and stoicism as he believed Fox and the others to have possessed. So the glory of being a two-bottle man and not showing it was one way of emulating his heroes; another was losing large sums at the gaming table with unaffected mien. In a mock-heroic passage in *The Kickleburys on the Rhine* (1850), during a run on the bank at the casino of a German watering-place, Thackeray's ironic pose cannot conceal his real admiration for Lenoir, the casino proprietor, whose coolness he compares to that of Ney at Waterloo, Washington before Trenton, Miltiades at Marathon, Wellington at Waterloo, and Elizabeth at the time of the Armada.[46] At the gaming-table Thackeray was defying most completely the maternal authority, suffering the greatest inward quakings of guilt and fear, and yet by maintaining an outwardly calm front, feeling himself most impressive in the eyes of the world.

The young Trinity man's first gambling experience took place in

[43] The same, p. 77.
[44] The same, p. 494.
[45] Stevenson, *The Showman of Vanity Fair*, p. 375.
[46] *Works*, X, 275f.

that same summer vacation of 1830 which saw the delightful series of infatuations for actresses.[47] In the case of the gaming as in that of the *amours*, his candor with Mrs. Carmichael-Smyth was maintained. At Frascati's fashionable gaming house in Paris, the young Thackeray confessed:

The interest in the game Rouge et Noir is so powerful that I could not tear myself away until I lost my last piece—I dreamed of it all night—and thought of nothing else for several days, but thank God I did not *return* ... I hope I shall never be thrown in the way of the thing again, for I fear I could not resist.[48]

Perhaps he expected a shocked protest from home; certainly he must have received one, for his knack of devising excuses that had served him so well in the matter of the theater-going was called into play in his rebuttal:

I have learnt the full extent of the evil. I have discovered my temperament and inclination with regard to it ... In what then am I so blameable? I so went with *no* bad motive, no desire for gain. Mother, I came out with a knowledge of my own weakness ... to resist a crime on which I could before descant with all the knowledge of ignorance.[49]

But this casuistry was really sprung from the need of excusing himself, as is shown by the sequel. Instead of using the self-knowledge of which he had boasted to avoid his weakness, Thackeray was to gamble all the more heavily. At some time in the following spring, during his last term at Cambridge, two gamblers took lodgings opposite his for the specific purpose of plucking him, which they did to the tune of £1,500.[50] Nor did his gambling cease until long afterward, when the last of his patrimony was dissipated in the Indian bank failure of 1833.

Although nearly all of Thackeray's letters to his mother during this last college year have been lost, it is a safe guess that the candor of their relationship broke down considerably, if not entirely. And probably the breakdown had much to do with the tears that Thackeray shed while on his knees in Allen's chambers. Ostensibly, he wept because of penitence at the state of his soul, but really because such penitence was a cheap way of atoning for his feelings of guilt.

[47] See above, pp. 32ff.
[48] *Letters*, I, 90f.
[49] The same, p. 97.
[50] The same, p. 506.

Furthermore, the rationalism that he was assimilating at Cambridge had deposed his mother's own God and with Him went much of her authority as her son's personal goddess. Thackeray had learned that doing the things he wanted most to do and then writing home candidly and proudly of them—as had been the case with his boyhood exploits—brought back only tearful expostulations. Concealment was becoming necessary, with concealment the feelings of guilt increased, and yet the things he wanted to do became more, rather than less, attractive as he fought the temptation to do them.

The whole situation came to a head during the Easter holidays, when FitzGerald invited Thackeray to come to see him in Paris. Mrs. Carmichael-Smyth would not take gladly to such a trip, yet it was necessary to tell his otherwise indifferent tutor Whewell, who stood *in loco parentis*, where he planned to spend the holidays. So Thackeray lied to Whewell, and atoned for the lie by agonies of remorse. Thirty years later, he was preparing for his impending death. Part of the preparation was confessing to his public in *The Roundabout Papers* all manner of old guilts and miseries. This escapade was then disgorged from the depths of his recollection. He tells us that there was

only half a crown left, as I was a sinner, for the guard and coachman on the way to London! And I *was* a sinner. I had gone without leave. What a long, dreary, guilty, forty hours' journey it was from Paris to Calais, I remember ... Guilt, sir, remains stamped on the memory, and I feel easier in my mind now that it is liberated of this old peccadillo.[51]

The episode is symbolic, not only of the conflict at this time between the outer and inner Thackeray, but of the beginning of a new theme in his life—the flight motif. Whenever circumstances became too much for him in one milieu, he had now learned a way out—to go somewhere else. Cambridge no longer had any fascination, scholastic ambition was gone, his circle of friends had ceased to provide new stimulus, home was the citadel of an outworn theology with its guilt-producing restraints. But London and Paris represented freedom, gaiety, Bohemia. Thackeray was doubly ready for the gamblers that invaded Cambridge to pluck him soon afterward because they were emissaries from that fresher, greener world. And the fact that he had once deserted his post briefly without detection made it easier to do so again, and again.

[51] "Dessein's," *Works*, XVII, 617.

Thackeray's departure from Cambridge to Weimar in the summer of 1830 is the first of those major changes of direction which marked his life during the early 1830's. The months in Weimar themselves were an idyllic interlude of which biographers have made much: The young author-to-be broadened himself by travel; he learned German, he picked up a veneer of German literature, which wore thin in later years; and he met Goethe. More important, however, from the standpoint of his inner life, is the climax which those months brought about in his relationship with his mother.

Much as Mrs. Carmichael-Smyth continued to concern herself thereafter with her son's personal morals, she was more worried about his aimless life. He was in the tight grip of that dilemma then as always so perplexing among young university men—the finding of a career. The problem was worse in Thackeray's case because of his self-indulgence, his rationalizations, his self-exculpation, and his easy, facile repentance.

One can not fully account for Thackeray's self-indulgence by merely saying that he regarded himself as a gentleman, that he had a small patrimony, and that there was therefore no need for him to work until he had squandered his capital and taken to himself a wife. The mere fact of his being a gentleman and one who always expected to marry, meant that he must acquire by labor—unless he should marry money—a considerably greater income than he had inherited. Otherwise he could not maintain the position expected of him. Moreover, the Thackeray family tradition was one of aristocratic diligence, not aristocratic indolence. The novelist's father had risen to distinction in the Indian Civil Service, and prior to him there had been an impressive array of ancestors in most of the short roster of gentlemanly professions: church, army, and government service.

Possibly Thackeray's indolence and lack of purpose was, at least in part, a subconscious rebellion against these ancestors. The family tradition of following in their footsteps was so strong that even in his boyhood it appalled him. No doubt it had been held up as a responsibility before Thackeray's boyish eyes by his mother, who was also the one to hold up to him her ideals of piety and joyless hard work. The reaction was inevitable.

Probably the Weimar trip was undertaken with the vague thought of a career in diplomacy. But from the little German principality

Thackeray wrote Mrs. Carmichael-Smyth, pointing out that his brief stay there had cured him of a hankering for foreign service: "the profession is interesting enough but the town is so dull."[52]

This is the defense of a man with aristocratic prepossessions. It comes from that article of the aristocratic code which states that any evil is better than boredom. And boredom is merely another word for responsibility, which above all things Thackeray was at that moment anxious to avoid. But he was not yet ready to repudiate altogether his dedication to duty as long as the repudiation could be put off until his return to England. So the letter continues: "I must drudge up poor and miserable the first part of my life, and just reach the pinnacle . . . These are the pleasures of the law—and to these I fear I must dedicate myself—As I have thought a great deal on the profession I *must* take; and the more I think of it the less I like it." This is hardly an encouraging start for a brilliant legal career.

The same letter announces that "a clergyman I cannot be," and for this statement the reasons are obvious, as was the decision not to become a physician.[53]

Lastly Thackeray rejects the army, which "a little time ago . . . would have done, but now I suppose there will be no war and no advancement." In other words, during the recent Napoleonic Wars, a military career would have been conceivable, but such is no longer the case. A career is unthinkable to a man with an aristocratic bent unless it leads to the top; otherwise he who follows it will be unworthy of his forbears. With this ancestor-reverence was bound up Thackeray's hero-worship of certain great military leaders of the eighteenth century and Napoleonic Wars: Webb, Wolfe, and Wellington. But all these men had won glory in wars that revealed their shining talents. The prospects of war were dim in 1830. Hence there was no chance that a General William Makepeace Thackeray would be catapulted to a place beside Wolfe and Wellington in England's Pantheon of military heroes.

But Thackeray was still too worried about Mrs. Carmichael-Smyth's good opinion to surrender altogether the struggle to "make something of himself." Yet any profession must offer rapid advance-

[52] *Letters*, I, 136f.
[53] The same p. 137.

ment to the top of the ladder and entail little boredom and drudgery for the climber who is still on the bottom rungs. But, as a practical matter, no profession meets those requirements, least of all the law.

The legal profession, moreover, was an area where the humbly born, with his capacity to devote himself single-heartedly to the business in hand, could run rings around the gentleman. One recalls how Thackeray, in the guise of Pendennis, had refused to compete for academic advancement because his "inferiors," the men with no straps on their boots, could excel him. Now the story was to be repeated in the Inns of Court. Thackeray's feelings on this subject were later to be revealed by a bitter attack on the Inns-of-Court grind, Paley, in *Pendennis* who is praised by everyone for his industry, although

he could not cultivate a friendship or do a charity, or admire a work of genius, or kindle at the sight of beauty or the sound of a sweet song—he had no time, and no eyes for anything but his law-books.[54]

One of Thackeray's narrator-heroes, the fatuous George Fitz-Boodle, is the comic incarnation of the self-belittlement that accompanied his creator's search for a profession. Fitz-Boodle rejects the bar because Sergeant Snorter, "a butcher's son with a great loud voice," a sizar and wrangler at Cambridge, who "has never been in decent society in his life,"[55] and drinks *port rather than claret*, knows more law and will be a better advocate than he.

Whereas Fitz-Boodle solved his problem by becoming an auctioneer, Thackeray was more prone to "lie on a sofa with a novel," a pastime which recurs constantly in his works as a symbol of idleness. For his ultimate profession this slothful practice was better training than the study of mathematics at Cambridge or law in the Middle Temple. In fact the novelist-to-be had a vague sense that some good would come from this drifting when he wrote from Weimar: "In my reading and my pursuits here I have had a freedom which I never enjoyed in England—and I hope you will feel the benefit it has done me."[56] But this little bit of defiance did not gain the writer its measure of freedom without exacting in return some remorse: he had become afraid to open his mother's letters. Even

[54] Chapter 29. *Works*, XII, 368f.
[55] *Works*, IV, 234.
[56] *Letters*, I, 139.

when they contained no reproaches, he dreaded facing "the misery which not the words but the tenor of them conveys."

Thackeray was afraid, in part because he had failed to free himself from his mother's domination, but also in part because he suspected that many of his proud words were rationalizations and not the fruits of genuine insight. That insight was to come, but only slowly. It had arrived years before the end of his life when he drew the portrait of Philip Firmin, who is the serious mirror of the Thackeray trying to find his niche in life, as Fitz-Boodle is the comic portrait.

To the remonstrances of old friends he [Philip] replied that he had a right to do as he chose with his own [life]; that other men who were poor might work, but that he had enough to live on, without grinding over classics and mathematics.[57]

Or again: "What call had *he* to work? Would you set a young nobleman to be an apprentice? . . . In fact Phil, at this period, used to announce his wish to enter the diplomatic service," hoping that his uncle, an earl, would get him appointed as secretary to an ambassador.[58]

Thackeray, in the days of his later insight, was to pour into Philip not only his own youthful grandiose ambitions but also his sensibility and the beginnings of his satiric power, as well as his inconstancy, his indolence, and his penitence.

He [Philip] had a childish sensibility for what was tender, helpless, pretty or pathetic; and a mighty scorn of imposture, wherever he found it. He had many good purposes, which were often very vacillating, and were but seldom performed. He had a vast number of evil habits, whereof, you know, idleness is said to be the root. Many of these evil propensities he coaxed and cuddled with much care; and though he roared out *peccavi* most frankly, when charged with his sins, this criminal would fall to peccation very soon after promising amendment.[59]

The history of Thackeray's legal career was, under the circumstances, foreordained. At first there were occasional faint pretenses in letters home that the work was interesting. But the journal, which was kept at intervals during this year 1831–1832, says nothing of law studies at the Middle Temple, everything of social life, gambling, play-going, and fiction reading. By April of 1832 he admits to long

[57] *Philip*, Chapter 5. *Works*, XVI, 59.
[58] The same, pp. 77–78.
[59] The same, p. 80.

absences from the office,[60] by May he is noting down when he goes there as if the act were exceptional, and by June he seizes the excuse to go electioneering in Cornwall with his friends the Bullers. Finally in July he comes of age, becomes master of his inheritance and his fate, and executes another major flight—this time once more to Paris.

During these months in London Thackeray had cherished no illusions that he was a diligent young man. He revelled in his idleness and in the cheap way he could pay for it by occasional fits of expiatory remorse. He was hurting his mother by his indolence, and lacerating his own sensibility by so doing. The persistence of this state of mind is shown in a diary which the young prodigal was keeping at that time.[61] It abounds in such phrases as "idle and vicious as I am,"[62] or "was not at Taprell's,[63] and have not read a syllable of anything for 3 days. I must mend, or else I shall be poor idle and wicked most likely in a couple more years."[64]

Thackeray was now gambling heavily and frequently. In fact he was clearly a victim of what is now called "neurotic gambling," whose most striking symptom is that the "gambler *wants to lose*."[65] Certainly Thackeray's self-portrait of himself as weak and inadequate must have been confirmed within him as he saw himself voluntarily throwing away his patrimony. Moreover, neurotic gambling can be traced "back to childhood rebellion against authority." The patient, now grown up, "finds in gambling a means of carrying on his revolt." Certainly Thackeray was at this time a rebel. He had showed again and again a latent opposition to his mother's efforts at controlling his life. He had left Cambridge without a degree; he was neglecting his law studies and preparing to abandon them as soon as possible; he was to embrace the dubiously genteel life of Bohemia, and to undertake the career of a satirical—i.e., a rebellious —author.

Furthermore, Dr. Edmund Bergler tells us, "the neurotic gambler

---

[60] *Letters*, I, 188, 190.

[61] The same, pp. 185–238.

[62] The same, p. 209.

[63] Thackeray was ostensibly studying in the office of Taprell, a special pleader of the Middle Temple.

[64] *Letters*, I 190.

[65] Philip Harkins, "Gambling is a Disease", *This Week Magazine* (December 31, 1948), p. 5.

feels guilt about this rebellion. His feeling of guilt is relieved by his gambling losses."[66] Thackeray was extremely remorseful and secretive about these losses. It was his wont to go alone to the "gambling hells" that then infested London. On his return he would communicate the results only to his diary, often in German to conceal his remorse. "Spielte und verlierte acht pfund . . . des abends spielte ich, und bekommte fünf pfund . . . spielte und winnte eighteen pence . . . spielte und verlierte zehn pfund . . . spielte und verlierte ein pfund . . . spielte und wie gewohnlich verlierte . . . spielte und winnte fünf pfund."[67] So goes the refrain, with the losses of course exceeding the winnings.

Although gambling was an outlet for Thackeray's aggressive reaction to authority, that other "man of the world" affectation, sexual license, had at this time little appeal for him. Moreover, the gambling and the neglect of his law studies made him feel guilty enough toward his mother. It would be going too far to spatter her pure image by his own unchastity. In any case, he was repelled rather than charmed by the flyblown beauties of the London streets. A passage from the diary dated April 29, 1832, describes how Thackeray found a friend, Kinderley, "tipsy with a common beast of the town, and took him away from her, and home to bed—much to the Lady's disgust and Kinderley's advantage."[68]

Thackeray's neglect of his law studies and his addiction to gambling during this period as a student in the Temple had only this permanent effect on his character: to fix in his mind a weak and indolent self-portrait. Had he possessed more insight, he might well have seen it as a time of strong-willed driving toward the true path which fate had laid down for him. This drive was aided most particularly by a number of stimulating new friends.

During the first few months after Thackeray's return from Weimar, his sentimental friendship with FitzGerald had reached its climax. Long and tender letters were exchanged. Thackeray, obviously fearing lest his friend's skepticism endanger his own faith, crossed foils with him over matters of doctrine. On taking up his chambers in London, Thackeray got FitzGerald to visit him and

[66] The same.
[67] Letters, I, 200–208.
[68] Letters, I, 195.

wept after his departure.[69] Yet this flowering of their friendship was obviously the result of mutual loneliness. Essentially their temperaments lay in opposite directions. FitzGerald was a recluse like his friend, Alfred Tennyson. To them the good life lay away from London, in secluded spots where they could invite selected friends or whence they could sally out on visits to those friends. Thackeray was always a cosmopolite. Such happiness as his restless temperament could find was to lie in London, where he could crowd his life with a kaleidoscopically varying host of friendships. When he escaped, his flight most often took him to colonies of London, like Brighton, or to expatriate groups on the continent.

During the winter of 1831–1832, Thackeray made so many stimulating new friends in London that by May 14 he could confide to his diary, on hearing from FitzGerald:

what a short lived friendship ours has been; The charm of it wore off with him sooner than with me but I am afraid now we are little more than acquaintances, keeping up from old habits the form of friendship by letter.[70]

Actually the severance was not as complete as that; FitzGerald was to remain Thackeray's official-best-friend for the rest of the novelist's life. He was to discharge such formal obligations of that office as lending Thackeray money at the time of his marriage and of his wife's illness. Still later he undertook the care of Thackeray's family and the responsibilities of his literary executorship should the novelist fail to come back alive from America.[71]

As things turned out, Thackeray's future was shaped far less by FitzGerald than by two groups with whom he became intimate during the winter and spring of 1831–1832. One was the coterie of brilliant young men, recently down from the universities, many of whom were also ostensibly studying law. The other was the professional journalists represented by William Maginn. The influence of the first was primarily political, the second largely literary. From both, however, Thackeray acquired the habit of regarding most existing institutions as hollow shells. These it was the responsibility of right-thinking young men to puncture and expose.

[69] *Letters*, I, 172.
[70] The same, p. 200.
[71] See below, p. 175.

Thackeray often dined in Hall with his young intellectual friends, less often in taverns, which they eschewed because of expense.[72] And by the spring of 1832, when he had become accepted in their group, he spent many more evenings with them than he devoted to gambling or to his beloved theaters.[73] With some of this group, such as John Mitchell Kemble, Thackeray had been acquainted at Cambridge; others he was coming to know for the first time, notably such former "Apostles" as Arthur Hallam and Charles Buller. Buller was both a "radical" and a Member of Parliament, and Thackeray's close association with him came during the agitation for the First Reform Bill. Inevitably, Thackeray became deeply interested in politics. "Three years before, during the almost equally bitter crisis over Catholic Emancipation, he had parroted the prejudices of his caste. Now, however, the enthusiasm of Buller and the general idealism and humanitarianism among the radicals won him over."[74]

Never until 1857, when he himself stood for Parliament, did Thackeray show such political enthusiasm as sent him to Devon and Cornwall electioneering for Buller in June of 1842. Yet the fact that he was always to be a shrewd observer of the political scene has escaped the notice of posterity because his witty political squibs are buried among his *Punch* contributions and other ephemera. Unlike Disraeli and Trollope, he felt that politics did not belong in the sphere of the novel.

More important than politics, however, were the ideas that Thackeray absorbed from Buller on the subject of opposition to cant and hypocrisy. Some of these were concepts which Buller would have absorbed from his former tutor, Thomas Carlyle; others he would have assimilated from the prevailing air of "radicalism."

Enmity to cant and hypocrisy was also a fetish with William Maginn, Thackeray's other mentor during the early part of 1832. Although still a mainstay of *Fraser's Magazine*, Maginn was far gone in drink and insolvency when Thackeray first met him on April 16, 1832, and liked him "for his wit and good feeling."[75]

[72] *Mr Brown's Letters to His Nephew*, chapter 3. *Works*, VIII, 298.

[73] Professor Stevenson has pointed out that Thackeray went on a "theatrical debauch" when he first came to London which had worn itself out by the end of 1831. Thereafter "he seldom went more than once a week" (*The Showman of Vanity Fair*, p. 44).

[74] Stevenson, *The Showman of Vanity Fair*, p. 48.

[75] *Letters*, I, 191f.

On May 2 of that year the Irishman whetted the younger man's interest in journalistic affairs by taking him to the offices of the *Standard* (not the one that Thackeray was to own) and showing him "the mysteries of printing and writing leading articles."[76] Two days later they went together to dinner with "a dull party of low literary men," and on May 12 Maginn introduced Thackeray to James Fraser, the editor of *Fraser's Magazine*, but—curiously—not the Fraser for whom it was named. *Fraser's* had by now replaced *Blackwood's* as Britain's most daring organ of swashbuckling political and literary controversy, and Thackeray's introduction to Fraser was the first step on the road which led to the young author's later role as foremost of the Fraserians.

Thackeray found Fraser "neither clever or good very different to hearty witty Maginn, who is a very loveable man."[77] Any social prejudice against Maginn that may have lingered in his young friend must have vanished when the latter discovered the superiority of the Irishman's formal education to his own. After they had passed a Sunday morning together, Thackeray reported that Maginn "read Homer to me and made me admire it, which I had never done before moreover he made me make a vow to read some Homer every day."[78] Thackeray knew himself well enough to add that he doubted whether he should keep the vow. Nevertheless Maginn's remarks on Homer "were extraordinarily intelligent and beautiful mingled with much learning a great deal of wit and no ordinary poetical feeling."

If Thackeray saw the sublime side of Maginn on that Sunday, he saw the reverse on the next Sabbath day when they went together to a brothel. There, says the diary,

I left him, very much disgusted and sickened to see a clever and good man disgrace himself in that way ... Thank God that idle and vicious as I am, I have no taste for scenes such as that of last night.[79]

The dilemma of the younger man's life at the time is summed up in that excerpt. He can follow Maginn as an intellectual mentor, but Mrs. Carmichael-Smyth's influence made it impossible for him to stomach the Irishman's morals. Hence Thackeray wavered helplessly

[76] The same, p. 197.
[77] The same, p. 200.
[78] The same, p. 207.
[79] The same, p. 209.

at a mid-point between the two influences and tortured himself for his indecision with the conviction that he was "idle and vicious."

Seemingly Maginn's personal influence over Thackeray waned thereafter, though the younger man paid tribute of a sort to his elder when he drew Captain Shandon in *Pendennis* partially, at least, in the likeness of Maginn. The connection, however, had already served its purpose; it had enabled the younger man to attach himself, even if temporarily, to a first-rate satirist. Maginn was poles removed from the amateur undergraduates who had edited *The Snob* and *The Gownsman*. Thackeray could not at the time see how the discontent behind the Irishman's slashing articles stemmed from his poverty and position in a truculent national minority. The young Englishman had no special reason to quarrel with the existing order, except that at Charterhouse, at Cambridge, and now in London it seemed inclined to go jogging ahead in blissful ignorance of a young man named Thackeray. The combativeness aroused by that neglect had never found the usual undergraduate outlet in the beating up of bargemen. Now it at last found a place where it could have play—in controversial journalism.

To be sure Thackeray did not at once fully avail himself of the connection at *Fraser's*,[80] but after his marriage it became, if not the most lucrative, at least the most dependable outlet for his wares. Moreover it was then to bear greater results for his unfolding career than any magazine until he joined the staff of *Punch*. The spirit of satire was in the air in *Fraser's* publishing rooms, and its breath whetted Thackeray's satiric zeal toward ever-higher achievements. Starting with *The Yellowplush Papers* (1837–1840) the progress continued through *Catherine* (1839–1840), *A Shabby Genteel Story* (1840), and *The Great Hoggarty Diamond* (1841), to *Barry Lyndon* (1844).

But back in 1833 the chief fruit of Maginn's influence, direct or indirect, was the discovery of a way for Thackeray to circumvent the bottom rungs of the journalistic ladder and buy his way at the outset to a position near the top. In May of that year, possibly aided by some of his stepfather's capital,[81] the fledgling journalist pur-

---

[80] H. S. Gulliver suggests (*Thackeray's Literary Apprenticeship* [Valdosta, Georgia, 1934], p. 68) that certain articles in *Fraser's Magazine* from 1831 to 1835 might have been by Thackeray. If the story *Elizabeth Brownrigge*, which appeared in that magazine in 1832, were by Thackeray, it would materially increase his canon of early writings. But his authorship of that apocryphal book is generally discredited.

[81] See Gulliver, p. 39.

chased a weekly newspaper, *The National Standard and Journal of Literature, Science, Music, Theatricals, and the Fine Arts*. Legend has it that he gave Maginn £500 to edit this periodical for him.[82] Certain it is that the Irishman had that much from him about this time.[83] Of course, the paper's sales were much less than the young proprietor expected and its losses much greater; in fact, he was able to write before many months that he expected to "be ruined before it succeeds"[84] and, of course, he soon "tired of his new toy."[85] By the end of the year *The Standard* stopped publication, almost simultaneously with the Indian bank failure which took away nearly all that was left of the young journalist's little fortune.

As always, Thackeray was long afterward to salvage and make literary capital of this shipwrecked early venture. In *Lovel the Widower* (1860) the narrator is a man named Bachelor, a thinly disguised mouthpiece for Thackeray himself. He similarly acquired a magazine after coming to London from Oxbridge and embarked on its publication with fantastically ambitious schemes:

I dare say I gave myself airs as editor of that confounded *Museum*, and proposed to educate the public taste, to diffuse morality and sound literature throughout the nation, and to pocket a liberal salary in return for my services. I dare say I printed my own sonnets, my own tragedy, my own verses (to a Being who shall be nameless, but whose conduct has caused a faithful heart to bleed not a little). I dare say I wrote satirical articles, in which I piqued myself upon the fineness of my wit, and criticisms, got up for the nonce, out of encyclopaedias and biographical dictionaries ... I dare say I made a gaby of myself to the world: pray, my good friend, hast thou never done likewise?[86]

A more mundane outlet for both Thackeray's energy and part of his diminishing patrimony at this time was a bill-broking establishment in which he invested,[87] apparently most secretively. Such naïf hopes could only have been raised in him by one of the shady gentlemen who customarily conducted such businesses. In Thackeray's case financial loss was the inevitable outcome.

In later years, one of the reasons for the novelist's purblind rage

[82] On the evidence of "Father Prout," another Irish journalist in London. See *Letters*, I, 260.

[83] The same, p. 508.

[84] *Letters*, I, 270.

[85] See Stevenson, *The Showman of Vanity Fair*, p. 52.

[86] Chapter 1. *Works*, XVII, 74.

[87] *Letters*, I, 504f.

against the critic Keane[88] was the latter's digging up of the bill-broking episode from his past. In fact, Thackeray was always to display
a hatred of moneylenders more violent than was usual, even in a
time when the literary profession's chronic war with them was rag-
ing feverishly. In stooping to a business detestable both to authors
and to gentlemen, Thackeray acquired one of those "skeletons in
the closet" which were to be a recurring theme in his books. Since
his own later financial reverses never drove him into the hands of
moneylenders, his hatred of them has no personal basis in those
experiences. Clearly he added, to the conventional man of fashion's
dislike of the usurer, the venom of an author's enmity, plus the
reactive emotion that came from his brief flight into the bill-dis-
counting business.

As Thackeray grew tired of *The National Standard*, his editorial
chores were increasingly felt as the fetters of bondage, and alluring
Paris stood for freedom. Mrs. Carmichael-Smyth's voice was now
less insistently the voice of duty, and thus she became again more
of a confidante. Meanwhile the escape across the English Channel
developed into a motif in the young author's life which ever increased
in frequency. In time it was to broaden and vary until any place
that would draw him from his desk was a haven of escape.

As early as July, 1833, Thackeray had rationalized this personal
necessity on grounds of business need: "It looks well however to have
a Parisian correspondent; and I think that in a month more I may get
together stuff enough for the next ten months."[89] In the next breath
he confides:

I have been thinking very seriously of turning artist—I think I can draw better
than do anything else and certainly like it better than any other occupation why
shouldn't I?—It requires a three years apprenticeship however, which is not agreeable—but afterwards the way is clear and pleasant enough; and doubly so for an
independent man.

Thackeray's career as an art student would also have palled before long had his inherited income remained as a constant temptation to idleness. But all was changed by the loss of that patrimony
in the autumn of 1833. Yet this blow was not immediately crushing.
He must have foreseen that his gambling losses would eventually

[88] *Letters*, II, 103ff.
[89] *Letters*, I, 262.

complete a process which the Indian bank failure only speeded up. Moreover he had a quality common in those who have been reared in luxury—a delight in the *beau geste* of stoically accepting disaster at the time, only to have adversity—when its realities are fully understood—gnaw away the fragile foundations of his inward peace. As Thackeray wrote in *The Newcomes*, over twenty years after the loss of his patrimony: "the great ills of life are nothing—the loss of your fortune is a mere flea-bite. . . . It is not what you lose, but what you have daily to bear that is hard."[90]

At the time of his calamity, however, Thackeray was able to write casually to his mother: "I believe that I ought to thank heaven for making me poor, as it has made me much happier than I should have been with the money."[91] But the state of mind he described was only the fun of thinking about being poor; it was far removed from actually being poor. A passage in *Philip* shows us again the later insight that came with experience: "A young man ruined at two-and-twenty, with a couple of hundred pounds yet in his pocket, hardly knows that he is ruined . . . Philip seemed actually to enjoy his discomfiture."[92]

Thackeray may or may not still have had two hundred pounds, but he had something better, the faith that his parents could and would support him. The letter announcing his poverty continues: "I must now palm myself on you and my father, just at a time when I ought to be independent, and no burthen to you." The young man's temperamental pendulum, having swung him into the world of freedom, where he had lost his patrimony, could now—conveniently—swing him back into the security of his mother's and step-father's little income. Even better, that security need not carry with it imprisonment under their roof; he was to be physically free in that freest of all possible worlds—the artistic circles of Paris.

Allowing for the usual nostalgia with which the latter-day Thackeray wrote about his youth, his description of these days in a letter of 1849 is accurate enough. Writing to Mrs. Brookfield from Paris, he said:

I went to see my old haunts when I came to Paris thirteen [actually fifteen] years ago and made believe to be a painter—just after I was ruined and before I fell in

[90] Chapter 40. *Works*, XIV, 529.
[91] *Letters*, I, 271.
[92] Chapter 15. *Works*, XVI, 202.

love and took to marriage and writing. It was a very jolly time. I was as poor as Job: and sketched away most abominably, but pretty contented: and we used to meet in each others little rooms and talk about Art and smoke pipes and drink bad brandy and water. That awful habit still remains; but where is Art that dear mistress whom I loved though in a very indolent capricious manner but with a real sincerity?[93]

The one immediate drawback to the situation was the partial loss of Thackeray's cherished status of gentleman. Painters were then only on the fringe of gentility. But he could afford to sacrifice a little of his aristocracy; there was enough left to protect him from any really degrading occupation—for example, trade. Rather than drive him to such a fate, the code would certainly sanction his acceptance of a parental allowance. Hence the loss of prestige in becoming an artist was endurable.

Later in life Thackeray was to foster in his books the legend of a great freemasonry and democracy among artists. Probably he did this to justify some inward fear that his art career had lowered him in the social scale.[94] To be sure he created some artist characters who were unmitigated snobs like Pinkney in *Our Street*, or Smee and Gandish in *The Newcomes*, but the same book contains the Damon-and-Pythias-like friendship between Clive Newcome, the well-born young artist who is in part Thackeray himself, and J. J. Ridley, the butler's son.

Certainly the selection of Paris as the site of Thackeray's proposed art studies had more to it than the French city's reputation for pleasure and freedom. Living was cheaper there, the art schools were better, and—most important—the artist enjoyed a higher position in the social scale. As Thackeray was to put it six years later in an essay, *On the French School of Painting*, the art students of Paris looked down upon the merchant class

with the greatest imaginable scorn—a scorn ... by which the citizen seems dazzled, for his respect for the arts is intense. The case is very different in England, where a grocer's daughter would think she made a misalliance by marrying a painter.[95]

Thackeray's Paris years provided too one of those comic episodes which sometimes parallel as *leitmotif* the more serious themes of his

[93] *Letters*, II, 503.
[94] See below, pp. 206f.
[95] "The Paris Sketch Book," *Works*, II, 44.

life. In the autumn of 1834, Mrs. Carmichael-Smyth's mother, Mrs. Butler, moved to the French capital. An agreement was made whereby she—the only close relative with a comfortable income—was to pay her grandson's expenses at her *pension* in return for his companionship.

La grandmère was the chief prototype of the famous dowagers in her grandson's novels. These old women shared, in some degree, her eighteenth-century attitude toward life. They commonly enjoy the minor vices of gluttony, liqueur-drinking, card-playing, pampering their poodles or spaniels, and bullying their maids or companions. Usually they have young kinsmen like Rawdon Crawley, Henry Esmond, Lord Kew, or Harry Warrington corresponding to Thackeray himself. The dowagers caress, browbeat, and give money to these young men. More important, they *form* them—in other words, indoctrinate them into the life of men-about-town. Mrs. Butler's literary portraits include Lady Pash of *Men's Wives*,[96] Miss Crawley in *Vanity Fair*, Great Aunt McWhirter in *Mr. Brown's Letters*,[97] the dowager Lady Castlewood of *Henry Esmond*, Lady Kew of *The Newcomes*, and Baroness Bernstein of *The Virginians*.

Mrs. Butler's companion in 1834 was an unfortunate creature named Miss Langford who dropped her "h's" all over the *pension*. She is transmuted into literature as a whole series of browbeaten dependents: Miss Crawley's Briggs, Lady Kew's daughter Julia, Bernstein's niece Maria, and the anonymous companions who minister to the dowager Lady Castlewood.

Thackeray and his grandmother had been domiciled together barely a fortnight when he wrote his mother: "several of the inhabitants of Mme. Durand's house can bear witness to the extraordinary eloquence of the grandmother, and the dutiful resignation of the grandson."[98] Then follows the note of pious determination, the saying of the expected thing, comparable to the earlier stoic acceptance of poverty at its outset: "But I am ready to bear any reproofs of this kind, for . . . I see how very kind and good she is." Yet even this worthy resolve was to fail like Thackeray's others, and nine months later he is confiding to Mrs. Carmichael-Smyth: "It hurt me very much to be obliged to leave her, as I have done,

[96] *Works*, IV, 331f.
[97] The same, VIII, 281.
[98] *Letters*, I, 273.

and to reject the stipend which she made me for a while." Again comes that self-exculpation which is simultaneously a rationalization of weakness, an assertion of his independence, and a step toward finding his true place in the world. The letter goes on: "I am sure I was right in quitting her."[99]

By this time Mrs. Carmichael-Smyth had grown reconciled to her son's new career. The role of guardian angel and comforter was again hers, while Mrs. Butler had become the obstructionist, pouring cold water on her grandson's hopes when he most needed encouragement. That was the final cause of the break with the old lady as Thackeray wrote his mother:

a man does not forget his best friend and his greatest consolation, when he is alone, and neither very well nor very cheerful.—not after a bitter and fruitless day's work, such as is every day's work now, or a scene with a certain old lady, you may suppose that I think about home and the dear Mother who would sympathize with my failures and hasten, I think, my successes, and would not hurt me with bad words, such as with a wonderful eloquence and ingenuity are rung into my ears by G.M.[100]

Clearly Thackeray's pendulum had now begun to swing away from an art career as the ideal life. His talent for caricature had not developed, as he had hoped, into a genius for serious easel-painting. In effect, the hours of law-reading at Taprell's had only been replaced by hours of copying at the Louvre, and in both careers such hours were endurable only if they could guarantee rapid glory. Yet art like law withheld that guarantee. Inevitably despair resulted, and a letter of April, 1835, tells of "enough torn-up pictures to roast an ox by":

In these six months, I have not done a thing worth looking at. O God, when will Thy light enable my fingers to work, and my colours to shine?—if in another six months, I can do no better, I will arise and go out and hang myself.[101]

Not surprisingly, the letter concludes with the news that the young Raphael-to-be has spent the last month "lying on sofas reading novels, and never touching a pencil."

The pendulum of Thackeray's vocational life could no longer

---

[99] The same, p. 289f.

[100] The same, p. 289. Thackeray habitually refers to Mrs. Butler as G.M. [grandmère] and to Major Carmichael-Smyth as G.P. [grandpère].

[101] The same, p. 279.

swing back toward a respectable career in something like law or diplomacy; hence it moved in a direction which he had hitherto not considered too seriously—authorship. He had never been without vague aspirations to achieve some major piece of writing, particularly when he contemplated with scorn the tinsel successes of Edward Bulwer. In fact the latter's *Eugene Aram* had once prompted Thackeray to confide in his diary: "The book is in fact humbug, when my novel is written it will be something better I trust."[102] And two months later he was tempted by the thought of writing a comedy, adding characteristically: "I wish I had perseverance to try—Amen says my mother and so do I from the bottom of my heart."[103]

But to anyone revelling in the consciousness of indolence, as Thackeray had then been (it was the period of flagging attendance at Taprell's), the sustained effort of a novel or comedy was unthinkable. Proficiency in painting had looked much easier of attainment. Yet now after three years, with the drawbacks of the artist's life all too evident, the remoter hills of writing had again turned green. So five days after the threat to hang himself, Thackeray had forgotten the six months of final probation at painting which he had promised himself.[104] He was applying for a job as *The Morning Chronicle's* Correspondent to Constantinople. The application did not succeed, but by October of that year, 1835, we hear of efforts at hack journalism for an English paper in Paris,[105] and in April of 1836 there appeared *Flore et Zéphyr*.

This series of drawings, which was issued under the name of Théophile Wagstaff, was published in both Paris and London. It is a burlesque of the ballet in general, of Thackeray's old flame Taglioni[106] in particular. With its brilliant caricatures and their ironic French captions, *Flore et Zéphyr* contains in embryo the theme of most of his later satire—the discrepancy between outward glamor and inner sordid reality. After seven drawings of the hero and heroine of the ballet striking their incredible attitudes on the stage, another print is devoted to "la retraite de Flore." The now wilted

[102] The same, p. 198. Written in May, 1832.
[103] The same, p. 216.
[104] See above, p. 66.
[105] *Letters*, I, 297. See also I, 295, n. 49.
[106] See above, p. 32.

Taglioni is seen in her dressing room, chaperoned by an ogre of a mother and flirting with a Paris dandy and a fat plutocrat. A companion drawing, entitled "les délassements de Zéphyr," depicts the hero—half-dressed and profoundly bored—taking snuff in his *retraite* while a valet brushes his wig and a boy from the café stands by with a tankard of beer.[107]

If the ballet dancers of Paris lost their appeal for Thackeray, still less was he attracted by that famed Latin quarter type—the *grisette*. *The Paris Sketch Book* (1839) has a prose portrait of "a dirty student, sucking tobacco and beer, and reeling home with a grisette from the chaumiére, who . . . will hiccup, to such as will listen, chapters of his own drunken Apocalypse."[108] This revulsion was certainly involved to some extent with Thackeray's conviction that he was a failure at his art studies. That feeling, moreover, might never have existed had he not started those studies with inflated ambitions and notions of his own deserts. Certain aspects of French life: the tattered remnants of its romantic movement in art and literature, its dirtiness, its sexual license, and the sordidness of its *grisettes*—all become objects on which he vented the anger of his own disillusionment. Had he continued in England, comparable English institutions would have roused the same ire, as they were later to do.

Inevitably Thackeray's emotional pendulum began to swing back to things English. Circumstances had not yet made it feasible for him to live again across the channel. Yet he did the next best thing when he fell in love with an English girl of the type most diametrically opposed to the Parisian *grisette*. Clearly new forces were soon to make themselves felt in the life of the fledgling artist-journalist-author.

[107] *Works*, I, 64f.
[108] *Works*, II, 228.

CHAPTER III

Marriage and Struggle

THACKERAY'S wife-to-be, Isabella Shawe, was of an Irish family. She lived with her mother, an officer's widow, in the colony of expatriate Britishers in Paris, where they could maintain shabby gentility on a small income better than they could at home. Thackeray was deeply in love with Isabella from the start, and he continued until the end of his life to love her in one way or another.

One is not surprised to find in Isabella Shawe an ideal bride-to-be of the type favored by the sentimental, early-Victorian bourgeoisie—a "pure young girl" with no particular education or aptitude for marriage. Such girls' chief asset was their carefully shielded innocence in matters of sex. This naïveté was presumed to insure their chastity after marriage, although such chastity was almost guaranteed already by the terrible social punishments visited on unchaste wives. Even at that, however, innocence in the life partner was a sort of extra lock on the door of domesticity. Psychologically, the argument for marrying immature girls was the belief that they would make more docile, and—presumably—more devoted wives, ready to give their husbands an extra measure of idolatry. Now Thackeray's ego craved such idolatry to replace that which he had received from his mother.[1] Hence he visualized his life partner as a girl who would idolize him. Moreover, his phobia against any sort of affectation demanded that she have the much-prized quality of "artlessness," which is a form of immaturity.

There is no more than substantial truth in a letter which Thackeray wrote many years afterward to an impecunious young bridegroom. After raising the subject of financially imprudent marriage, he confesses:

I made such a marriage myself. My means being 8 guineas a week (secured on a newspaper which failed 6 months after.) My wifes income 50£ a year promised by her mother, and paid for 2 quarters, since which (1837) I have received exactly

[1] See above, p. 17.

10£ on account. And with this fortune, I have done so well, that, you see, I am not a fair judge of early marriages, but always look upon them, and upon imprudent young people *qui s'aiment* with a partial eye. In the first 6 months, *I saved money.*[2]

The letter was written in the nostalgic mellowness of the later years, when the pain of old sufferings was largely gone. Furthermore, Thackeray's situation at the date of his marriage was not too desperate, since he and Isabella expected to share an income on which they could live in Paris respectably if not luxuriously.

Anyone critical of the budding author's heroism could further point out that the newspaper job which provided his eight guineas a week, that of Paris correspondent on the new ultra-liberal *Constitutional and Public Ledger*, was largely subsidized by his stepfather. In fact, one of the old soldier's motives for risking a large part of his wife's and his own financial security was the desire to purchase a job and a career for his stepson.[3]

But even if the position which made the marriage possible were subsidized, Thackeray announced clearly to Isabella his intention of going ahead with or without it: "So look out and be ready dear Puss to marry me soon, for I am determined to do it, whether the Constitutional should come out or not."[4] And when the paper failed, in less than a year, he was forced to swim by himself. He did so manfully and with an effort that carried him eventually to the top of the literary world. The streak of fortitude which he displayed was hitherto unsuspected, even by his schoolfellows. One of them wrote: "not one of us would have given him credit for that 'stalk of carl hemp' with which he met subsequent misfortunes and difficulties."[5]

The chronicle of Thackeray's courtship and marriage is largely

[2] *Letters*, IV, 145.

[3] See *Letters*, I. 305: "My father's conduct to me in this Paper business has been very noble, he was offered a very handsome remuneration for his services as Director (£200 a year)—but he refused, all he wanted was he said that I should be employed on the Journal." Again on p. 321: "P. A.'s [Major Carmichael-Smyth's] last speaks rather gloomily of it amen. I am sorry for him, and his risk and loss for my sake." Finally, on p. 341, in a letter addressed "to the Directors of the Constitutional" just before the paper's collapse: "the paper would long since have stopped, had not these deficiencies been met as they occurred, by one of the Directors the only one who has remained at his post, and whose extraordinary exertions and sacrifices, have maintained the Constitutional hitherto—Major Smyth."

[4] *Letters*, I, 315.

[5] Boyes, *Memorial*, p. 120.

the history of his feud with his mother-in-law, which in turn gave rise to the greatest hatred in his life. Both events and differences of temperament brought about the antipathy that, at the outset, had inspired Mrs. Shawe to impede the marriage as long as possible. To this hostility she was driven in part by Thackeray's poverty, in part by the fact that—like his fictional counterpart, Philip—he must have imperfectly cloaked his scorn of her ways and those of her circle. Moreover, she—like her counterpart, Mrs. Baines—may have aspired to a better match for her daughter. Worst of all, she seems to have been hag-ridden by that domineering maternal quality so common in Victorian annals and so much discussed in the popular psychology of today. Mrs. Shawe did not want to lose any of her children; she tried to reduce them to complete subservience, and in general, she gave them such an upbringing that, as Professor Ray points out, only "two . . . were entirely normal. Henry was a dipsomaniac, Jane pitifully neurotic, and Isabella . . . lost her mind not long after the birth of her third daughter in the summer of 1840."[6]

The tactics used by his mother-in-law in trying to break up the match were certainly in Thackeray's mind when he wrote *Philip*. Charlotte never told her husband

of those painful nights when *her* eyes were wakeful and tearful. A yellow old woman in a white jacket, with a nightcap and a night-light would come, night after night, to the side of her little bed; and there stand, and with her grim voice bark against Philip. That old woman's lean finger would point to all the rents in poor Philip's threadbare paletot of a character—point to the holes, and tear them wider open.[7]

But Thackeray, like Philip, seems at this time to have been unaware of all his future mother-in-law's schemings against him. The full extent of his grievances only unfolded gradually during the course of his married life. Mrs. Shawe paid almost none of the allowance that she had promised her daughter. And when the latter lost her mind and was taken by her husband to the Shawe household, Mrs. Shawe not only abjured all responsibility for her daughter's care; she accused her son-in-law of causing his wife's condition.

Yet in spite of these manifold causes of complaint, one cannot help feeling that Thackeray's feud with Mrs. Shawe was more a

6 *Letters*, I, clxiv.
7 Chapter 23. *Works*, XVI, 337.

matter of temperament than anything else. His sensitive soul feared bores, hated the self-deluded, and dreaded anyone's dislike. Now fate forced him into close dealings with a tedious, self-deluded woman who hated him. The progress of his reactions may be traced step by step through the *Letters*.

Back in September of 1836 during the honeymoon, Thackeray was trying manfully to like Mrs. Shawe, but her affectations, her garrulity, her stupidity, and her boastful snobbery were already getting on his nerves. Describing a social gathering he confided to his own mother: "My Mother in law who was present talked as big as St. Paul's: she is a singular old deevil, and has become quite civil of late. I don't know why I dislike her so much."[8]

By March of 1840, when Isabella was approaching that third lying-in which precipitated her insanity, a more disillusioned Thackeray again wrote to his own mother. His increased tension now found refuge in savage humor:

the old lady is stark mad and so seems to be the best of the family. They are all hated in the county to a wonderful degree, vulgar, stingy, extravagant, bad landlords, bad neighbours, and the juice knows what.[9]

Then, when the question of this she-dragon's presence at Isabella's confinement arose: "If I ask Mrs. Shawe, storms, whirlwinds, cataracts, tornadoes will be the result."[10] Soon she is simply the "nightmare of . . . [a] Mother."[11]

Last came the terrible trip to Ireland. Isabella tried to commit suicide on the voyage over. When her husband had settled her in Cork her mother's presence made her condition worse. In these darkest days of his life, Thackeray's burden of suffering was increased by the strain of enduring without retaliation the tongue-lashings of Mrs. Shawe. Suddenly he received from his own mother an offer to take care of his wife and children. His answer is eloquent:

I have been half tempted to fling it in Mrs. Shawe's face, and say there Madam you who prate about self-sacrifices, you bragging old humbug see the way in which my mother welcomes your daughter, and think how you have received her yourself. But the woman is mad that is the fact or so monstrously unreasonable that

---

[8] *Letters*, I, 321.
[9] The same, p. 424.
[10] The same, p. 433.
[11] The same, p. 444.

it is in vain to talk reason to her, she never speaks but to brag and to lie, and doesn't know truth from falsehood.[12]

This contrast between his mother as a principle of good and Mrs. Shawe as a spirit of evil was to bear fruit constantly in Thackeray's novels. Time healed outwardly the scars of this bitterness. After Isabella's recovery was despaired of and she had been put in custody, her husband again began alluding to his mother-in-law with the restraint befitting a gentleman. But at times the demon of hatred would rise in his soul, and he would exorcise it by adding another figure to the terrible row of mothers-in-law that stalks through his books like the dumb show in *Macbeth*. He started drawing these women back in 1837 with Mrs. Shum of *The Yellowplush Papers*, who—like Mrs. Shawe and all the succeeding members of the series—tries to poison a daughter's mind against her own husband.[13]

In 1843, three years after the climax of Isabella's tragedy, Thackeray drew the likeness of Mrs. Gam in *Dennis Haggerty's Wife*. And after a quarter-century, when one would have expected the scars to be well healed, there came the most diabolic portrait of all, that of Mrs. Mackenzie, 'the Campaigner' of *The Newcomes* (1854–1855).

The strongest dramatic climaxes in all Thackeray's books are those when the novelist most freely casts off his gentlemanly avoidance of powerful emotion and, taking a fictional son-in-law as mouthpiece, disgorges his soul to these old harridans. Altamont thunders at Mrs. Shum as he orders her from his house, imputing to her the same charge of madness which Thackeray ascribed to his mother-in-law:

you lazy, trollopping, mischief-making, lying old fool! Get up, and get out of this house. You have been the cuss and bain of my happyniss since you entered it. With your d——d lies, and novvle reading, and histerrix, you have perwerted Mary, and made her almost as mad as yourself.[14]

Of all the sons-in-law, Clive Newcome performs best in the role. In fact, his final words to Mrs. Mackenzie over the prostrate Rosy can be called the answer Thackeray could not make in the presence

[12] The same, p. 482.
[13] *Works*, I, 182f.
[14] The same, p. 184.

of the stricken Isabella to Mrs. Shawe's diatribes during the awful days in Cork:

> Mrs. Mackenzie, I can bear you no more . . . I will never, so help me God! sleep under the same roof with you; or break the same crust with you; or bear your infernal cruelty . . . or listen to your wicked pride and folly more. There has not been a day since you thrust your cursed foot into our wretched house, but you have tortured one and all of us.[15]

After that the demon in Thackeray's soul was partly exorcised. The next savage mother-in-law, Lady Baker of *Lovel the Widower* (1860), is toned down, and the dualism between her and Thackeray's own mother is comically realized.

Mrs. Carmichael-Smyth has now stepped down from her saint's niche to become the ultra-pious Mrs. Bonnington, a foil to Lady Baker. Yet Lady Baker too must endure the climactic tongue-lashing. Significantly it comes, not from her son-in-law Lovel, but from his friend Bachelor, who is Thackeray's counterpart in the book. He tells Lady Baker that, since Lovel's widowhood, "you have never given the poor fellow any peace. You have been for ever quarrelling with him. You took possession of his house; bullied his servants, spoiled his children."[16]

For the last mother-in-law of the series, Mrs. Baynes of *Philip* (1861–1862), Thackeray felt traces of compassion, particularly when she forfeits her daughter's love:

> That sad, humiliated deserted mother goes out from her daughter's presence, hanging her head. She put on the poor old bonnet, and had a walk that evening on the Champs Elysées with her little ones, and showed them Guignol: she gave a penny to Guignol's man . . . That stricken old woman, then, treated her children to the trivial comedy.[17]

Yet these female tyrants have literary as well as real life counterparts. The rising feminist movement had put men more than ever on their guard against aggressive women like Mrs. Shawe and the Campaigner. The writing profession played its part in the male counterattack by saturating its fiction with dominating women. Douglas Jerrold's Mrs. Caudle, Dickens's Mrs. MacStinger, George Eliot's Aunt Glegg, and Trollope's Mrs. Proudie are all variations

[15] Chapter 79. *Works*, XIV, 993f.
[16] Chapter 6. *Works*, XVII, 187f.
[17] Chapter 28. *Works*, XVI, 415.

of the type. Certainly Mrs. Mackenzie will always hold her own in this redoubtable company, bearing the label placed on her by her creator when he told a friend: "That's my she-devil of a mother-in-law."[18]

This authenticated similarity between Mrs. Shawe and the Campaigner should not delude anyone into taking Isabella for an exact likeness of the insipid little Rosy Mackenzie, though the two share some traits. Rosy had no mind of her own and would never have married Clive Newcome had her mother not ordered her to do so. The more accurate picture of Thackeray's courtship is that in *Philip*, and here Charlotte Baynes seems to be a closer counterpart of Isabella. Both had much of Rosa's "artless"[19] childishness, but Charlotte possesses a vein of steadfastness against her mother's pressure which is notably lacking in Rosy.

It must have taken some courage on Isabella's part to marry the man of her choice, though here the impetuousness of Thackeray's wooing seems to have been decisive in turning the tide. Both Mrs. Mackenzie and Mrs. Baynes succeeded for a time in breaking off their daughters' engagements, but whereas the latter did so by ordering her subservient husband to forbid the match, the former apparently got her way by persuading Isabella that Thackeray had "improper desires which might create [in her] . . . disgust."[20] Thackeray had to promise that he would purge himself of such desires by prayer before he could win his bride.

More serious, he had to give a promise which it would have been folly to keep—that he would not attempt to loosen the bond between Isabella and her mother:

What a scoundrel should I be were I to endeavour to weaken such a tie as exists between you two . . . If you are my wife you must sleep in my bed and live in my house—voila tout—I have no latent plans—no desire for excluding you from those whom I should think very meanly of you, were you to neglect.[21]

---

[18] *Letters of James Russell Lowell*, ed. Charles Eliot Norton, 2 vols. (New York, 1894), I, 239.

[19] Writing to his sister-in-law in 1848, Thackeray refers to his wife as an "artless sweet creature who charmed us both so" (*Letters*, II, 431). Pendennis, the ostensible narrator of *Philip*, says: "we all treated Mrs. Charlotte more or less like a child" (*Works*, XVI, 564). Her letters are described as full of "sweet secrets and loving artless confessions" (The same, p. 248). Another of Thackeray's fictional heroes, George Warrington, describes his wife Theo as an "artless, innocent creature" (*The Virginians*, chapter 83. *Works*, XV, 874f).

[20] *Letters*, I, 319.

[21] The same, p. 309.

Thus Thackeray embarked on matrimony with the burden of dangerous commitments made to an immature girl who was only partly weaned away from a neurotic and possessive mother. She was obviously less sure of her love than he of his. During the betrothal his passionate love letters kept chiding her for the relative scarcity and brevity of her answers[22] and for her chariness in oral expressions of love.[23] Apparently, Isabella's pliability made her coy during the period of her engagement so that she might not run counter to her mother's disapproval of Thackeray. Yet the same trait aided her in transferring her whole devotion to him after the marriage. Thus her impressionable temperament was an asset in the early years of marriage, though in the long run it may have contributed to the tragedy of the young wife's madness.

The first two or three years of the marriage were an ecstatic honeymoon period. Its high-water mark came during a short separation. Thackeray had returned from London to Paris in March, 1838, and sat down to tell Isabella that it was almost a blessing for him to have come away, since absence intensified his love: "Here have we been nearly two years married and not a single unhappy day."[24] With a tragic irony reminiscent of Othello's first greeting to Desdemona in Cyprus, the writer trembled lest their happiness diminish. With an obvious eye on Mrs. Shawe, he prays that their "love is strong enough to stand any pressure from without." To this prayer he adds another that their love may be "superior to poverty or sickness or any other worldly evil with which Providence may visit us." Anticlimactically this series of letters to Isabella concludes: "Your Ma and I are on the best terms possible, and have not had the shadow of a row."[25]

Thackeray's Victorian biographers were usually compelled by the proprieties to describe his wife's insanity merely as "an illness," with the implication that it was a visitation from God and nothing further could be said on the subject. Hence the first acceptable medical diagnosis of her case, so far as I know, is that by Dr. Stanley Cobb in an appendix to the *Letters*. He diagnoses the illness as schizophrenia, of a type that often begins with depression and

[22] The same, p. 309.
[23] The same, p. 319.
[24] The same, p. 354.
[25] The same, p. 364.

ideas of unworthiness, a few weeks after childbirth.[26] Dr. Cobb blames, as contributing factors, Mrs. Shawe's unstable temperament, the emotional complications of the courtship, the three pregnancies, the death of the second child in infancy, and the adjustments to marriage. He finds "no evidence that Thackeray himself was a cause of trouble" and concludes "that he seems to have made a positive contribution toward happiness." Granting that Thackeray's contribution toward Isabella's happiness was great, it is nevertheless highly probable that some of his habits were contributing, although not principal factors in precipitating the calamity.

One of Thackeray's more recent biographers, G. U. Ellis, conjectured that Isabella's insanity might have prevented another tragedy implicit in an incompatibility between her and Thackeray "as it also saved her from criticism, by arousing pity."[27] This suggestion—for which there is much support in the evidence—should not, however, suggest any lurid pictures of the two Thackerays ending their marriage in a sordid drama of the divorce courts. The code of the day demanded that married couples present an unbroken façade to the world, even when the love that was assumed to thrive behind that façade had crumbled to dust. Thackeray's and Isabella's love was far from crumbling to nothing in 1840, but there are signs that such a process had begun. And it is my belief that Isabella's intuitive perception of that fact was a contributing cause of her insanity. For the marriage had passed into the stage of humdrum reality which imposes a strain on hitherto romantic young lovers.

Thackeray's feeling for Isabella was compounded of passion and paternal protectiveness; in fact, she was to some extent a new toy such as *The National Standard* and the art career had each been in its turn. Inevitably her immature charm, like those earlier playthings, would some day pall on him. The Thackerays faced a twofold program in preserving the happiness of their marriage, once Isabella's pretty, babyish ways had ceased to fascinate her husband. The soft spot at the core of his ego would keep exacting from her the clinging devotion which she had transferred to him from her mother. Yet his high intelligence would expect a greater degree of companionship. And the extent to which she could supply such companionship would rest on her ability to cure her weaknesses.

[26] The same, p. 520.
[27] *Thackeray* (New York: Macmillan, 1933), p. 40.

She must decrease the intellectual gap between her husband and herself; in short—using the cliché of that day—to "make herself worthy of him." Such expectations are implicit in some of his letters to her prior to their marriage. Traits inherited from Mrs. Carmichael-Smyth crop up in the catechism he urges her to make for herself. She is urged to ask herself whether he might not feel "hurt at any conduct" of hers which has "an appearance of neglect." Then he begs her to "see whether you . . . have not some other little conjugal duties to perform, one of which (and not the most easy) is the duty of affection."[28]

In the next letter Thackeray hopes that his "little Trot" may overcome "two lazinesses that beset her, not writing letters, and lying abed."[29] The peroration to that letter might have been written by Thomas Arnold, or even Tennyson's King Arthur:

I think I know of a better plan, dearest . . . to cure these evils, and for this you must have recourse to me, you must love me with a most awful affection, confide in me all your hopes and your wishes your thoughts and your feelings; for I want you to be not a thoughtless and frivolous girl, but a wise and affectionate woman, as you will be, dearest Puss, if you will but *love* enough.

Apparently Isabella did not consciously resent this tone. The temporary rupture of her engagement to Thackeray shortly afterward had other causes, as we have seen. Moreover, the surviving letters of the actual married period do not maintain this tone of awful high seriousness. There was no reason why they should. Thackeray had effectually put his wife in her place before the wedding.

So began the happy years from 1836 to 1839. Not until after the death of their second child in March of 1839 did Thackeray drop clues that the frosting on the wedding cake was losing its flavor. Then he said of the dead baby: "I woud not ask to have the dear little Jane back again and subject her to the degradation of life and pain."[30] This passage was not bitter primarily because Thackeray was bitter over his home life; it is the *cri de coeur* of a very affectionate father just robbed by death of a child. But it also contains some of the underlying bitterness that had been infecting his writing for more than a year.

[28] *Letters*, I, 310f.
[29] The same, p. 316.
[30] The same, p. 380.

In *Fraser's Magazine* during the early summer of 1838, Thackeray had savagely chastised his old enemy, the professional gambler, when he wrote "Mr. Deuceace at Paris."[31] At the same time he was creating, in *Stubbs's Calendar; or, The Fatal Boots*,[32] a self-deluded, amoral, young egotist who has all the viciousness and none of the charm of the later Barry Lyndon. Two months after the death of Thackeray's child, the most deliberately sordid of his stories, *Catherine*, began to appear in *Fraser's*. The much-maligned "bitterness" of *Vanity Fair* was but the last faint taste in the mouth after the outpouring of bile which Thackeray had apparently experienced back in 1838–1839.

The depth of satire in this writing can not be entirely attributed to the exuberance of a young writer who had just been taught to throw mud and to write "slashing articles" in the lusty school of controversial journalism. Thackeray had passed that stage of his development some time before in the days of *The National Standard*. There is a wave of disgust in this writing between 1838 and 1840 which is the natural effect on a sensitive and aristocratic man of finding himself down in the street. He is fighting the battle of life successfully against the mob, yet he loathes himself for the means by which he is winning the fight. He has learned to use controversial journalism as a means of livelihood and not a sport; he has forced himself to haggle with publishers over fees; he has dunned them for those fees; he has rubbed elbows with "snobs"[33] and other persons outside the pale of his undergraduate set, and he has learned to watch pennies and maintain a family in an atmosphere of shabby gentility. But these lessons have exacted a toll.

Yet Thackeray had compensations for the growing melancholy and nervous irritability that marked these hard years. For one thing, as the tone of his books grew more bitter, their range and power simultaneously grew, and likewise their popularity, so that he began to taste small sips of the heady wine of success. For a time the letters to his mother display a pride in the conquest of the earlier indolence and indecision which she had so deplored. Yet in writing to her Thackeray was, like most sons, inclined to maintain a cheerful pose

[31] "Mr. Deuceace at Paris," *Yellowplush Papers. Works*, I, 230–300.

[32] *Works*, I, 417–484.

[33] The reader is reminded (see above, p. 29, n. 103) that the word "snob" in quotation marks has throughout this book its older meaning of anyone not a gentleman.

except when accumulated misery would suddenly spew itself over the pages of a letter. Hence in these exultant passages of the 1839 correspondence, one wonders if he may not to some extent have been whistling to keep up his courage. In November, still flushed with the pleasant memories of a trip with his family to Paris, he writes:

You must not go for to alarm yourself about my infinite struggles hardships and labours every one of them do good—and a man's mind would get flaccid and inert if he were always to have others caring for him, and providing his meat and drink . . . look how every body is pushing forward and looking onward, and anxiously struggling—amen by God's help we will push on too: have we not long legs (I mean of mind and body) and why should we lag behind?[34]

Thackeray was reading Carlyle about that time, and both the style and sentiment of the passage suggest that he is masquerading in the great Scotsman's clothes. Another letter a month later is in the same mood but a different style: "O this London is a grand place for scheming, and rare fun for a man with broad shoulders who can push through the crowd." And two weeks later still: "It seems to me often quite wrong to be happy when . . . I should be perfectly cast down at my gloomy condition and poverty."[35]

Then the optimism in the letters gives way to melancholy and nervous irritation. The begging appeals of a destitute kinsman dying of tuberculosis grow bothersome. Thackeray undergoes a period of religious despair; the Chartist riots alarm him; he must open his house to the old family butler, who is dying of an incurable disease; he attends the hanging of the notorious Courvoisier and the sight sends him into acute depression; finally there is the constant threat of a visit from Mrs. Shawe.

Many a man has found in his home a refuge of affection and tenderness at the same time that it was a hornet's nest of vexations. Such was the case with Thackeray at this time. It boded ill for Isabella's happiness, however, that the tender passages evoked in her husband's letters by home associations were no longer inspired by herself but by one of her children. By 1839 Thackeray was mentioning his wife in the perfunctory way of husbands married for three years. When he has occasion, however, to write of his infant daughter Anny, the tone of fatigue lifted from his letters: "She is a

[34] *Letters*, I, 391f.
[35] The same, pp. 397 and 398.

noble little thing, and a perpetual source of pleasure." "Our dear
little woman is wonderfully well thank God and improves daily
having . . . a fine frankness and generosity of character." "My dear
little Missy as gay as a lark God bless her." "The fact is my dear
little Pussy has grown to be more delightful than ever." "She is a
noble little girl . . . and is not made too much of."[36] Unquestionably
Thackeray had transferred to his child some of his tenderness for
the small and helpless which had accounted for much of Isabella's
hold on him.

For obvious reasons Thackeray was never guilty of disloyally
criticizing his wife to his mother. Direct knowledge of Mrs. Carmichael-Smyth's feeling about her daughter-in-law is lost, but one
can surmise. Her literary counterparts, Helen Pendennis and Rachel
Castlewood, are both angelic mothers, but their beatitude is slightly
tarnished by pronounced jealousy toward their sons' love objects.
And as late as 1852 Thackeray was to explicitly accuse his own
mother of such emotion. "It gives the keenest tortures of jealousy
and disappointed yearning to my dearest old mother . . . that she
can't be all in all to me, mother sister wife everything."[37] Even if
she refrained from active criticism, Thackeray's abnormal sensitivity
to hostile emotion would wince under an oblique censure of his wife
by his mother. Apparently such criticism was given on the score of
Isabella's household management. It was none too good, if one may
judge by the housewifery of her counterpart Charlotte Baynes, who
used to say: "I can't understand, my dear, how the grocer's book
should mount up so; and the butterman's, and the beer." Charlotte
used to sit with her "pretty little head bent over the dingy volumes,
puzzling, puzzling."[38]

One of Isabella's letters to her mother-in-law betrays the anxiety
of a typical anxious bride who is restive under the disapproving eye
that scans her household management. In the middle of discussing
a quite different topic, she suddenly leaps to the defensive: "I assure
you I keep my account very right and W complains how little
money he is allowed to spend."[39] About a year later, Thackeray
makes a similar defense after admitting to some exorbitant house-

[36] The same, pp. 400, 411, 422, 424, 445.
[37] The same, III, 12f. See above, p. 17.
[38] Chapter 39. *Works*, XVI, p. 588.
[39] *Letters*, I, 382.

hold bills: "I think you are inclined to be hard upon—but never mind what."[40]

On another growing source of difficulty he is more candid:

We are having the house painted outside as per lease and there is at this minute such an infernal clattering scouring tramping door-banging that I dont know what I write. Missy's little voice I can hear carolling in the parlor. Isabella comes to pay me a visit every ½ minute or so, and I'm not as angry as I ought to be.[41]

Two months later his tone is sharper:

there has not been five minute's cessation of knocks and bell-ringing this blessed day: and between times my wife comes in with the prettiest excuses in the world. I must go to the garrets that's positive or O for a lodge in some vast wilderness— the Jack Straw at Hampstead for instance, where I could write and not be half wild with waps (sic) and wings as at this present-ramping...I...have been for a fortnight in the pains of labor: horrible they are: and dreadfully cross to my poor little wife in consequence.[42]

Thackeray was at this time turning out an incredible amount of copy for a large variety of publishers. The fact that he was doing so at home under constant interruption is, in view of his temperament, almost miraculous. And his wife, instead of protecting him from interruption, added to it. Thus with no sentinel to keep petty cares out of his life, one of his earlier psychological patterns reasserted itself. Home became a successor to Charterhouse, to Taprell's office, and to the other prisons from which he had escaped, while travel was again the best avenue to freedom. But the pattern of escape was now complicated by the presence of a third factor, writing. This was a bondage compared with pleasanter occupations, yet it afforded an escape from greater vexations and a justification for little physical flights.

In July 1839, Thackeray went to Greenwich "to write something in peace and quiet."[43] Seven months later, with his wife well advanced on her third pregnancy, he is yearning, as we have seen, for the Jack Straw at Hampstead, complaining that his "poor little wife . . . had much better let me go away on these occasions but she

[40] The same, p. 443.
[41] The same, p. 398.
[42] The same, pp. 420, 421.
[43] The same, p. 389.

won't."[44] A month more, and he had contrived to spend an April week in Ramsgate with a friend. During the first week in May, less than a month before the confinement, he is passing evenings at the Garrick Club, writing until a late hour,[45] and four days before the child was to be born in London, its father is in Leamington, rapturously describing by letter to Mrs. Procter the beauties of Warwickshire in the spring.[46]

Thackeray did get back to London in time for the *accouchement*, but three days after it he is writing his mother from the Reform Club, where he was apparently doing much of his work. On July 30 he has just returned from three days in Dorking, and about the first of August he has left for Belgium, ostensibly to see some pictures and collect material for a series of articles. On his return he finds Isabella in the state of depression which gradually turned to insanity.[47]

Thackeray's excursions, however, were by no means effected with peace of mind. Just as he had once substituted remorse for the reform of his old indolence, so now he substituted it for a genuine effort to stay at home. On the trip to Leamington he wrote to his mother:

The time at Warwick was delightful, only not quite easy in mind enough, for I was always afraid of Isabellas being confined in my absence: and the dear little woman is so good and uncomplaining that I can't bear to think of any neglect.[48]

The situation is expressed here in a nutshell. Isabella's natural woman's fear of being deserted by her husband during pregnancy was accentuated by a helpless, dependent character. She defended herself by an air of uncomplaining pathos, her most effective weapon against Thackeray because of his notorious sensitivity to the pathetic. A wife who is pitied has nevertheless been lowered in her husband's scheme of values, and the phrase "poor little wife," by which Thackeray has now begun alluding to Isabella is highly significant, for that is the way in which he was to designate her constantly during her insanity. In the summer of 1840, however, he could not let himself surrender to the appeal of this pathos, for he was too restless and eager to get away from the home which

[44] The same, p. 421.
[45] The same, p. 444f.
[46] The same, p. 445f.
[47] The same, p. 462f.
[48] The same, p. 446f.

failed to satisfy so many facets of his temperament. He found a partial outlet for this restlessness in bachelor gatherings with his friends and defended these evenings to his mother: "as for jollifying after a day's work I cant help that, and should be good for nothing without it."[49]

Isabella was clearly not the sort to be at ease in the society of men as brilliant as FitzGerald, John Mitchell Kemble, and Monckton Milnes. Hence her husband's bachelor evenings must have cost her little pain. Certainly she indicated her acceptance of the situation in a letter to her sister, dated March 20, 1840: "W. gets up early works hard all day and then I let him gad of an evening."[50] Thackeray, moreover, was grateful for the concession and paid tribute to it when he wrote in *Philip* that Charlotte encouraged her husband "to go abroad from time to time, and make merry with his friends."[51]

Yet loyal and uncomplaining as are Isabella's letters, one can read much between their lines. In January, 1840, she declined an invitation from her mother to come to Ireland for her *accouchement*. "My half [Thackeray] is miserable if he is away from me three days. What would he do if I left him at such a time as my confinement?"[52] Actually she is deceiving her mother to save her pride. During his Paris trip in 1838 William had chafed at each day of separation, but now he was fleeing from home at every opportunity. To be sure, Isabella had some evidence to back her statement: recently he had returned to her a few hours after starting for the country. His excuse was his fear that their roof, which was in a precarious state, might collapse in his absence. But the real motive for his return was his conscience and not the sort of tenderness that had suffused his letters from Paris, for less than a month later he was telling his mother how much better he would be away from home.[53]

Isabella's letters reveal no particular aversion to joining her mother at this time. Thackeray was instrumental in keeping them apart and in getting his grandmother, Mrs. Butler, to assume Mrs. Shawe's normal role of presiding over the confinement. Yet *la grandmère* was clearly as trying to Isabella as was Mrs. Shawe to Thack-

---

[49] The same, p. 447.
[50] The same, p. 432.
[51] *Works*, XVI, 562.
[52] *Letters*, I, 415.
[53] See above, pp. 82f.

eray,[54] though the latter with male obtuseness failed to perceive the fact. On the other hand, a senile touchiness enabled Mrs. Butler to see clearly that her own presence was unwelcome to the young wife.[55]

The grandmother, however, does not seem to have been responsible for finally pushing Mrs. Thackeray over the borderline of sanity. That distinction belonged to Mrs. Parker, a friend of the young couple, who had seen Mrs. Carmichael-Smyth on a recent visit to Paris. There the worthy traveler had received an earful of complaints about Isabella's neglect of duty. These she had brought back to London and poured into the ears of the child wife about a month before her confinement. "In the course of her depression" during Thackeray's absence in Belgium, "the poor thing . . . worked up these charges so as to fancy herself a perfect demon of wickedness," becoming so miserable that she "did her duty less than ever."[56] Moreover Isabella cherished a naïve but quite intense religious faith. Her duty to husband and children was linked in her mind with her obligations to the deity. The result of Mrs. Parker's disclosures was, as Thackeray wrote, to make her feel "God abandoned and the juice knows what." After she had been taken to Cork, Isabella used to sing Psalms with her sister Jane, weep a good deal, and deplore her faults and errors.[57]

The result of all this misery comes out in Isabella's last pathetic letter, written to her mother-in-law as the shadows were closing in. She apologized for the manifest incoherence of the letter, explaining that her spirits were low, her strength feeble, and her head flying away with her like a balloon. In the next breath she announces that William is off to Brussels. When she had begged him not to go, he had fobbed her off with "a round of old saws such as 'it is the tortoise and not the hare wins the race.'" Despondently she concludes: "il ne m'écoute pas and I must e'en let him make his fortune his own way." She tries not to interfere with him and speaks of fears—probably religious—which she hopes are cowardly and ex_

[54] *Letters*, I, 431, 464.

[55] See Thackeray's letter of 20-21 August, 1840, to his mother: "poor old Gran . . . has got a crotchet that Isabella dislikes her—indeed she doesn't, but old Gran is a sad pestering old body" (*Letters* I, 465).

[56] Thackeray's letter to Mrs. Carmichael-Smyth, written on September 1, 1840. *Letters*, I, 469.

[57] The same, pp. 476 and 478.

aggerated. Then comes the telling admission: "when people do not raise their expectations to too high a pitch they cannot be disappointed."[58]

This apparent irrelevancy should be compared with a suggestion made by Isabella to her own mother during the preceding January. Her sister Jane was in the process of refusing a suitor repeatedly.[59] Isabella observes that

there are so many things that even two or three years better acquaintance with men and manners have taught me to look at in less austere a light than I might have done at Jane's age . . . I might in conversations combat ideas and notions of perhaps *ideal perfection* which do not exist in this tainted world.[60]

These observations on "ideal perfection" contain in a nutshell Isabella's tragedy. Trained by her inadequate education, romantic notions, and enthusiastic bridegroom to regard marriage as a constant idyll between perfect mates, reality was too much. Her husband's relatives were harping on shortcomings of which her own religion had already made her too conscious. Moreover there was no longer any blinking at his imperfections—particularly his genius for rationalizing his absences when she most needed him at home. Isabella was seeking straws of comfort in the negative philosophy of not expecting perfection. The effort was too much and she was sinking.

The symptoms of the young wife's madness were in part the natural outcome of her immature temperament. She resorted to forms of childish disobedience.[61] These in turn resulted from her jealousy of Thackeray's attentions to his elder daughter. By emulating Annie's ways of gaining attention, Isabella was subconsciously striving to divert some of it to herself. Anny, in turn, was competing with her new-born sister by the same tactics.[62] Even Isabella's attempts at suicide on the steamer enroute to Ireland were hysterical bids for attention. Her accompanying symptoms of alternating lethargy and delusion were simply retreats from reality.

That Thackeray's continual departures from home had much to do with his wife's condition is clear. She broke into hysteria when

[58] The same, p. 461f.
[59] The same, p. 437.
[60] The same, p. 414.
[61] The same, pp. 483f.
[62] The same, p. 468.

he left her to go on the Belgian jaunt and did everything to hold him at her bedside when they were in Cork.[63] Most telling was her delusion that people who left the room would never come back.

Thackeray was leaning heavily on religion in this crisis and was attempting to build up his wife's religious faith as an aid to her cure. Once he attributed her madness to "want of trust in God."[64] Possibly he had held up to Isabella his mother's strong faith as a model to her in her hours of darkness, thereby only accentuating her feeling of inadequacy and stirring up her latent antagonism to her mother-in-law.

There is no doubt that the tug of war between Thackeray and Mrs. Shawe over Isabella—symbolized in his writings by the struggle over Rosy between Clive Newcome and Mrs. Mackenzie—was in reality more than that; it was a struggle between Mrs. Carmichael-Smyth, abetted by Mrs. Butler and Thackeray's cousin, Mary Graham, on the one hand; and the Shawe women on the other.[65] This quarrel between two groups of women subjected Thackeray, the man in the middle, to intense strain. His maleness revolted at finding himself in a vortex of conflicting female egos, while the feminine side of his nature exaggerated the strain to his sensibility.

To make things worse, Thackeray's tenderness and sympathy with Isabella's concerns in the early stages of his marriage had probably abetted the disaster rather than averted it. A more masculine husband would have made it clear from the start that women's sphere of activity was none of his business. This attitude would have made Isabella more self-reliant in the smaller concerns of daily life. Consequently when his maleness asserted itself in the exultant pose of doing the world's work and fighting the world's battles, she would not have felt so deserted during the absences which that pose justified. She had of course long found that her husband's Achilles heel was his fondness for remorse. Naturally she played on that weakness in her need of sympathy. He complained of the pitiful looks that she kept fixed on him[66] as he felt increasingly to blame

---

[63] The same, pp. 474f.

[64] The same, p. 480.

[65] Miss Graham had usurped Mrs. Shawe's function of attending Isabella's second confinement as Mrs. Butler did during the third. Apparently as a consequence there was hard feeling between the two women, which Isabella tried to smooth over (*Letters*, I, 369). Thackeray once pointed out that Jane was jealous of all his family (The same, p. 477).

[66] The same, p. 467.

for his continual desertions of the family fireside. He coupled his duty to accept more seriously his marital duties with Isabella's responsibility to do more about hers.

We have both of us avoided them as yet, and not met them honestly as we should. I must learn to love home more, and do my duty at the fire side as well as in my writing-room: and I do see how out of all this dreadful trial profit will come to us, if it shall please God to let us have the chance. Make me more humble, O God, and less selfish: and give me strength to resist the small temptations of life that I may be fitted for the greater trials.[67]

Typically, however, this insight arrived too late, for the damage was done and Isabella was never to recover. With the insight came the damning guilt which then and later drove Thackeray to forego his usual activities and torture himself trying to nurse his wife back to health. The experience was valuable to posterity, for it deepened his writings emotionally and provided an edifying example of heroism in adversity. Yet from the practical standpoint, the effort was a drain on his sensitive emotions. Moreover, it was eventually waste energy, since Isabella never recovered.

At Margate, prior to the Irish trip, when Thackeray gave up his first attempt to nurse his wife, he was not far wrong in saying that it would drive him mad to be much longer alone with her.[68] He was understating too when he wrote: "I am so unused to living alone keeping back perforce a great fund of animal spirits that want to break out in the shape of argument or jollification that the bottling of them in is annoying to me."[69] Again the ambivalence of Thackeray's strength and weakness is apparent; a weaker man would have run out of the situation at the beginning. A stronger man would have undertaken the nursing responsibility and rebuilt his personality and life around it. Thackeray first called heavily on God for strength, then on his mother, then surrendered the burden altogether.

Allowing Mrs. Carmichael-Smyth to provide money for himself and care for his children after the terrible weeks at Cork was, of course, a necessary step. During the dark days when her offer from Paris of help emphasized Mrs. Shawe's selfishness all the more,[70]

[67] The same, p. 478.
[68] The same, p. 473.
[69] The same, p. 467.
[70] See above, p. 72.

Thackeray even began to count on his mother for what it would have been folly for her to provide—custodial care for Isabella when her convalescence should begin: "When she is better, dearest Mother you must come to my aid as I am sure you will, and help in the hard task of guarding her body."[71] And the next day the plea is made again:

When my little woman gets well—as she will please God. It must be your task to *keep* her so: to put her mind into healthful train and make her able to perform the duties which she will be called on to fulfil.[72]

Here at last comes to light a fatal assumption on which Thackeray had founded his marriage—that his indolent and immature wife should revere and emulate her mother-in-law as an ideal housewife. Forgotten was the fact that he himself had once resented—and was again to resent—his mother's perfection and belief that others should be perfect as she. Unperceived as yet, though some day to be learned, was the element of jealousy in her nature. Yet apparently it had already begun to warp her dealings with her daughter-in-law. In time it would strain them intolerably. Thackeray was still prone to see people as principles of good and evil. He wrote the letters just quoted while under the roof and domination of Mrs. Shawe at the most painful stage of their feud. The hapless Irishwoman then appeared to him most devilish. By contrast, Mrs. Carmichael-Smyth's generosity cast an even more radiant aura about her. Her son felt toward her as he had on vacations from Charterhouse. Forgotten was his intelligent advice to her in the early stages of Isabella's illness that she "would do more harm than good here."[73]

Thackeray's return to his mother after Isabella's collapse was more than a mere physical migration or a financial submission; it was an emotional return to the embracing maternal bosom. Writing to FitzGerald, the novelist confessed:

Since my calamity, I have learned to love all these people a great deal more—my mother especially God bless her who has such a tender yearning big heart that I begin to cry when I think of her.[74]

71 *Letters*, I, 477.
72 The same, p. 478.
73 The same, p. 469.
74 *Letters*, II, 4. Written January 10, 1841.

The young author's most ambitious flight from the nest had ended with his return there to nurse a broken wing. He, his wife, and their two daughters seemed like four children to Mrs. Carmichael-Smyth. When Thackeray watched her embracing his daughters, he had "to walk off for the sight is too much" for him.[75] His mother's embraces of Anny and Minny awakened memories of long gone days when he had received such caresses. His sentimental side, so successfully covered up during the writings of the past four years, was disclosed again. In his first piece of writing after the calamity, *The Second Funeral of Napoleon*,[76] there is a description of an English family watching the ceremonies. As Thackeray admitted to FitzGerald, this was both a word picture of his own family[77]—with Anny and Minny disguised as boys—and a literary expression of the author's newly awakened tenderness. To justify this new sentimentality, he imputed it to sympathy with his mother's and grandmother's timidity. They feared lest the Anglophobia that reigned in Paris on that day might end with a massacre of all English in the city:

The two elder ladies had settled between them that there was going to be a general English slaughter that day, and had brought the children with them, so that they might all be murdered in company.
God bless you, O women, moist-eyed and tender-hearted! In those gentle, silly tears of yours, there is something touches one, be they never so foolish.[78]

The "melting mood" was further elaborated, as Thackeray commentators have observed,[79] in the later chapters of *Samuel Titmarsh and the Great Hoggarty Diamond*, which appeared in *Fraser's Magazine* from September to December, 1841. Here the death of his infant daughter two years earlier gave the pretext for a new emotional dimension in a novel written hitherto on the flat two-dimensional plane of the earlier Thackerayan satirical fiction. The novelist projected his emotions into Titmarsh's long-suffering wife, Mary. Then as he wrote of the dead child "in its wicker cradle, with its fixed smile on its face," he decided that "the angels in heaven must have been glad to welcome that pretty innocent smile."[80]

[75] The same, p. 4.
[76] *Works*, III, 424–426.
[77] *Letters*, II, p. 4.
[78] *The Second Funeral of Napoleon. Works*, III, 426.
[79] See Saintsbury's Introduction, *Works*, IV, xif.
[80] Chapter 12. *Works*, IV, 126.

Many years later, when re-reading *The Great Hoggarty Diamond*, Thackeray wrote of its power to reduce him to tears. He admitted that "it was written at a time of great affliction, when my heart was very soft and humble."[81] Furthermore, he recognizes that the archetypal heroine of his books was not Mrs. Brookfield or his mother,[82] "but that poor little wife."[83]

When she was first brought to Paris after her insanity, Isabella was taken to a sanitarium called Esquirol's *Maison de Santé*. On her husband's first visit there, she kissed him "very warmly and with tears in her eyes," then went away "as if she felt she was unworthy of having such a God of a husband."[84] Since the feeling of unworthiness had been an earlier symptom of her disease, Thackeray's surmise as to her thoughts at this time must have been correct. Yet he described it just as he was so often in later books to describe the deification by women of certain male characters with whom he identified himself. One recalls Amelia Sedley's idolatry of George Osborne, Helen Pendennis's adoration of her son Arthur, and Rachel Castlewood's famous prostration of herself before Henry Esmond as she exclaims: "Don't raise me . . . Let me kneel . . . and—worship you."[85] It was all-important that Thackeray, in the emotional turmoil of those dark days, should regard his wife's need of him as a form of worship; at the center of his being was the need of receiving women's worship to counterpoise his dependence upon them.

By April of 1841 Isabella was well enough to be taken home—and Thackeray tried again the experiment of nursing her himself. Six weeks of that drudgery was all he could bear this time, and by the beginning of June, although Isabella remained under his roof and supervision, he had engaged a woman to do the work.

The early summer of 1841 was the blackest time of Thackeray's whole career except perhaps the weeks in Cork during the year before. He confided only semi-jocosely to Mrs. Proctor that he was so misanthropic it was good news to hear of others' "misfortunes."[86]

---

[81] *Letters*, II, 440. Written on October 14, 1848.

[82] This alludes to a letter of the preceding June (*Letters*, II, 394) when Thackeray told Mrs. Brookfield that she was "only a piece of Amelia—My Mother is another half: my poor little wife *y est pour beaucoup*."

[83] *Letters*, II, 440.

[84] The same, p. 3.

[85] Book III, chapter 2. *Works*, XIII, 332.

[86] *Letters*, II, 22.

Finally, half-crazed with drudgery and the lack of stimulating society, he took flight in July to the North of England, gathering material for an article and visiting the family of Monckton Milnes at Fryston Hall in Yorkshire.

This breath of cultured aristocracy may have saved the novelist from spiritual asphyxiation, but on the way back to Paris, remorse struck him. To gird himself for the onerous duties ahead, he began a diary, which opened with a prayer attributing all his sorrows and disappointments to his own errors or weaknesses. He prayed for divine aid in combatting lust and sloth, in keeping his family "out of misfortunes which result from my fault," and in being "interested in their ways and amusements."[87] The day after his return home, he added: "O God, O God give me strength to do my duty."[88]

Never had Thackeray's profound intuitive sense gone deeper than it went in this final probing of his shortcomings as a husband and father. To be sure he was torturing himself unduly, for he had not by ordinary standards failed in any sense. But it must be remembered that the masculine side of his character constantly impelled him out into the stimulating world of men. There the male's need of competition found vent in the matching of intellect against intellect, and work was the order of the day. Yet participation in such congenial pleasures had largely disqualified Thackeray for the feminine world of home, where his emotional desire for self-esteem was nicely satisfied, while his competitive instincts rusted in boredom.

Boredom is one of the most insidious forms of self-indulgence, and Thackeray's self-indulgent temperament—as in the days at Taprell's—was protesting with outbursts of *ennui* at his demands. For that temperament hated above all else to stay in one place for long periods, especially when there was little money in the till wherewith to purchase amusements.

A chance for Thackeray to improve Isabella's health and, at the same time, relieve his own boredom temporarily, came with an excursion to Boppard-on-the-Rhine from August to October. The experiment failed in both objectives. The hydropathic cure there was of no benefit to the wife, and the husband only relapsed into an *ennui* so intense that even an escape tour he took to Heidelberg

[87] The same, pp. 30f.
[88] The same, p. 32.

from the original escape tour to Boppard drove him into worse "loneliness and low spirits."[89]

After Thackeray and Isabella had been back in Paris a while, the last year's idyllic feelings toward his mother had largely vanished. With the straitened circumstances of the whole group, the increased age and querulousness of the Carmichael-Smyths, the varying tastes which years of separate living had effected in basically different temperaments, not to mention Mrs. Carmichael-Smyth's ever-growing Evangelicalism, Thackeray's *ennui* grew more intense even than in the days at Larkbeare. He complained to FitzGerald: "I have no amusement at Paris, nobody to talk to, and home, I am very ashamed to confess bores me. There is that stupid old Governor of mine: we are always on the point of quarreling, though we never do."[90] History had reversed itself. Whereas, in Thackeray's days as a law student, London had been prison and Paris freedom, Paris was now the prison and London the haven of escape.

A final break was inevitable, in spite of Thackeray's good resolutions of the summer before. By May of 1842 he had re-occupied the house on which he still held the lease at 12 Great Coram Street, London, and had taken up residence there. His decision to leave his wife and children in Paris was to bear fruit in many a passage of sentimental writing.

Apparently Thackeray provided the rent of the Coram Street house, and his stepfather's brother, Charles Carmichael, paid the running expenses so that he might live there with his wife, the former Mary Graham. Ever since Mrs. Carmichael-Smyth had reared this orphaned niece, and especially during Thackeray's college days, Mary had played a younger sister's role to the novelist. She was in time to receive her reward by being made the original of Laure Bell in *Pendennis*. Subsequently, as we have noted,[91] she had nursed Isabella through her second confinement. Still more recently, in the summer of 1841, Mary had loaned her foster-brother £500 to relieve the financial distress into which he was plunged by Isabella's insanity.[92]

[89] The same, p. 37.
[90] The same, p. 38.
[91] See above, p. 87, n. 65.
[92] The loan has its fictional counterpart when Laura lends Arthur Pendennis the money to pay his college debts.

Once Thackeray was domiciled in London with the Carmichaels, all his old temperamental mechanisms came into play against poor Mary. This foster-sister, although affectionately reared by Mrs. Carmichael-Smyth, resented Thackeray's first place in his mother's love. She felt moreover what Thackeray himself would have been first to admit—that he made an inadequate return of that love. When therefore she achieved a good marriage and, at the same time, put the once-superior foster-brother heavily in financial debt to her, Mary Carmichael considered their relative positions somewhat reversed. Moreover, she had acquired "an inordinate sense of personal worth" because of the praise that her minor literary and musical talents "commanded in the provincial society frequented by the Carmichael-Smyths."[93] While today it is incredible that she should set those talents beside Thackeray's, she could still so delude herself when the days of his fame still lay ahead. In London Mary aspired to social position in her natural social sphere. This was the culturally pretentious upper middle class which Thackeray was later to ridicule so savagely in *Mrs. Perkins's Ball* (1847), *The Lion-Huntress of Belgravia* (1850), and Mrs. Hobson Newcome's soirée.[94] Not unnaturally Mary tried to turn their common home in Great Coram Street into a center for the very kind of social life that her more talented foster-brother found most stultifying.

The experiment in co-living quickly ran its natural course. By May of 1842 Thackeray was complaining to his mother that Mary "is excessively fond of domination and first-fiddle-playing."[95] Then as usual he tried to soften the harsh words with a conventional *douceur*: "I'm sure . . . her heart is in the right place." But a few lines later comes the confession that Mary is already jealous lest her unborn child receive less of Mrs. Carmichael-Smyth's love than his own daughters.

A month later there was another such explosion on Thackeray's part, more violent because the pressure was greater, though it too started with a perfunctory exculpation of the "she's one of my best friends, but—" variety:

bating jealousy on her part, which you told me of, and of which I have seen some curious instances—she is a good fellow; She is . . . jealous of your love for me, . . .

[93] This is Professor Ray's suggestion. See "Biographical Memoranda," *Letters*, I, cx.
[94] *The Newcomes*, chapter 8.
[95] *Letters*, II, 46.

is of a passionate temper, and fancies those explosions of love in which she indulged formerly rather creditable and indicative of immense sensibility—it was all temperament.[96]

Certainly Thackeray's extraordinary insight into women's temperaments lends weight to this diagnosis. Yet very probably—as in the case of Mrs. Shawe—he exaggerated Mary's shortcomings because he was so terrified by aggressive women. To correct his fear of being unjust, he characteristically set out to find the beam in his own eye before taking the mote from his foster-sister's. He recalled that he was heavily in Mary's debt and added "perhaps I'm trying to run her down myself because of the 500£."[97] Inevitably Isabella, who as a wife was as good as dead—though Thackeray still visited her faithfully—began to assume the aura of distance when compared with the presence of Mary in the house: "Ah! there was more nobleness and simplicity in that little woman . . . than I've seen in most people in this world."[98]

Thackeray's friction with Mary Carmichael inevitably created some disharmony between him and her husband. This he summed up with shrewd insight in a letter to his mother: "I wish I had his home-loving virtues . . . and shall always admire them and him: if he were as clever as he is simple and good and generous there would be no end to him."[99] But this was only a feeling akin to that which Thackeray felt for his stepfather. It stemmed from the craving for frank, simple associates who would contribute to his peace of mind. Yet his dilemma was that such men, like their simple, artless female counterparts, were unable to participate in the hilarity, the banter, the triumphs in wit play that satisfied his competitive instinct, banished his ever-recurring melancholy, and gave exercise to his swift and fertile fancy.

Thackeray may have decided to visit Ireland in the summer and early autumn of 1842 partly to satisfy the old instinct toward flight whenever home circumstances became unpleasant. Certainly life with the Carmichaels was far from ideal. Yet a more urgent reason for the trip was the presence of his family plate in the vaults of Chapman and Hall, the publishers. It had been pledged to them

---

[96] *Letters*, II, 52f.
[97] The same, p. 53.
[98] The same, p. 53
[99] The same, p. 72. Written on August 12, 1842.

against an advance royalty on the book which had not been written during the Cork visit two years before. Thackeray had found he could not nurse Isabella and write about Ireland at the same time.

The budding authority on Hibernian *mores* left England on July 4 for his second trip across the Irish Channel and returned on November 1, 1842. He chronicled his tour in *The Irish Sketch Book*, which appeared in May of 1843. It is both his longest piece of nonfiction and his most ambitious literary project up to that time. And being very autobiographic, it affords a wealth of neglected data on his ideas and development during a time when his letters are comparatively scanty. *The Irish Sketch Book* reveals its author as a man of talent who is at a loss for something to say. He is undecided on where his power lies and how he can fill two volumes with data about a country where he had spent less than four months and against which he held strong prejudices. The techniques he used to get himself out of this dilemma afford valuable biographic clues.

Thackeray's prejudices came into conflict with his sense of fairness, his oft-expressed unwillingness never "to hit an unfair blow." This attitude stemmed in turn from the evolving code of the British gentleman, as well as from Thackeray's growing dislike of unpleasantness, and from his old, morbid fear of retaliatory attack from an unexpected quarter.[100] So he went to Ireland, seemingly determined to measure his experiences there against the rod of his own judicial, urbane taste and his gentlemanly distrust of all excess. Thus the extremes of British landlordism and the more fanatical aspects of Home Rule both offended him, as did the opposed bigotries of Ulster Presbyterianism and South-of-Ireland Catholicism. He addressed himself to the cultivated circles of both countries in the hope that their emotions were not too deeply involved on one side or the other. In the case of the English his instinct was true, for Thackeray was appealing to the class of man with whom he was accustomed daily to associate. But from the cultivated, semi-Anglicized Irishmen of Lever's circle in Dublin, Thackeray had to learn almost the same lesson that Dickens was learning after the nearly simultaneous publication of *American Notes*. Even judicially-minded, urbane citizens of a country with a national sense of inferiority can not remain dispassionate when their homeland is castigated—albeit

[100] See above, pp. 11f.

in the kindliest way—by an author from a nation which regards itself as superior.

And the fact that Thackeray did regard England as superior to Ireland often peers through the lines, in spite of his disarming label of himself as a Cockney,[101] time and again throughout the book. The same brand of self-deprecation was later used in *The Book of Snobs* when Thackeray called himself "Mr. Snob," or during the attacks on worldliness in the later novels, when he posed as a tired old worldling. But such thin devices are mere straws before the angry retaliations of victims cut to the quick.

Yet the Cockney pose represents more than Thackeray's effort to disclaim any superiority to his readers. It was also adopted in the hope of persuading them that he was strictly city-bred. As such he was unfit to play a heroic role while traveling in a wild country replete with every physical discomfort. Thus, commenting on five yachtsmen who shared the coach with him at one stage of the journey, he burst into irony:

What a wonderful thing pleasure is! To be wet all day and night; to be scorched and blistered by the sun and rain; to beat in and out of little harbors and to exceed diurnally upon whiskey-punch—faith, London, and an armchair at the club, are more to the tastes of some men.[102]

Akin to this anti-romantic, almost timorous distrust of the traveler who courts discomfort and danger was Thackeray's feeling about wild scenic beauty. He was willing to admit the glory of Connemara of Westport Bay,[103] and even to write pretty verbal landscapes in such places. But usually he avoided these challenges, often petulantly, as when he wrote:

the best guide-book that ever was written cannot set the view before the mind's eye of the reader, and I won't attempt to pile up big words in place of these wild mountains, over which the clouds as they passed, or the sunshine as it went and came, cast every variety of tint, light, and shadow; nor can it be expected that long, level sentences, however smooth and shining, can be made to pass as representations of those calm lakes.[104]

---

[101] *Works*, V, pp. 29, 44, 49, 54, 57, 114, 116, 128, 137, 148, 217, 224, 231, 250, 263, 303, 325, 326, 332, 336, 340, 353.
[102] *Works*, V, 114.
[103] The same, pp. 208, 230f.
[104] The same, p. 208.

In effect, Thackeray was learning a lesson that he was to apply in writing his great novels: that verbal landscapes are a form of literary virtuosity which readers usually skip and which, therefore, the author might as well omit. As a former art student who had despairingly given up the task of trapping scenery with paint or pencil, he was even better able to see the hopelessness of portraying it in words. One solution to the dilemma was that which he used in describing the parks of Powerscourt, near Dublin. Here he burlesqued the pseudo-Biblical "grand style" of certain Romantic prose writers:

And we stood and looked: and said in our hearts it was beautiful, and bethought us how shall all this be set down in types and ink? (for our trade is to write books and sell the same—a chapter for a guinea, a line for a penny): and the waterfall roared in answer, 'For shame, O vain man! think not of thy books and of thy pence now ... It is enough that thou hast seen a great thing: is it needful that thou shouldst prate of all thou hast seen.[105]

If awe in the presence of natural beauty still seemed mawkish to Thackeray, he was by now quite acclimated to the tender domestic emotions. For example, his sojourn in Cork during the journey of 1842 was really a sentimental pilgrimage to the scene of his great ordeal two summers before. So deeply did he relive those earlier memories that into the narrative of what befell him in 1842, he even incorporated a sentimental event from the 1840 journey.

At that time the Thackerays had been occupying lodgings in an outlying district of Cork called Grattan's Hill. There, as the author sat writing to his mother, he could hear "Anny with her stout voice roaring above those of a half-dozen good-natured dirty little companions that she has found in the children ... of the lodging house."[106] The overwrought father was grateful to the humble Irish family for thus relieving him from the burden of watching his three-year-old child during those days of desperate anxiety. On his visit to Cork in 1842 he wrote to Mrs. Carmichael-Smyth:

I have had some weary work here, going about to the old haunts, where I was with the poor little woman ... I went to Grattan's Hill but could not find my dear little Nanny's friends Minny and the rest, they were out with their mother—what a sickness the place gave me! and this opposite door, where the mother used to live![107]

[105] The same, p. 256.
[106] *Letters*, I, 476.
[107] The same, II, 68f.

In spite of the failure to see his former landlord's family during this second visit to Cork, Thackeray made of this relationship a sentimental episode for *The Irish Sketch Book*. M. A. Titmarsh, the ostensible narrator, wanders out—seemingly by chance—to Grattan's Hill and notices a house, still inhabited but falling into ruins. It is occupied, Titmarsh naïvely tells us, by a friend, but he neglects to say that the friend is himself as he had been two years before. This man "lodged there with a sick wife and a couple of little children; one of whom was an infant in arms."[108] Sentimentality sweeps Thackeray off his feet at the thought of how Anny had been accepted by his landlord's family:

one and all ready to share their little pittance with her, and to give her a place in their simple friendly hearts. God almighty bless the widow and her mite, and all the kind souls under her roof!"[109]

This family, it is clear, had furthered greatly Thackeray's progress on the road to democratic sympathies:

How much goodness and generosity—how much purity, fine feeling, nay, happiness, may dwell amongst the poor whom we have just been looking at! Here, thank God, is an instance of this happy and cheerful poverty: and it is good to look, when one can, at the heart that beats under the threadbare coat, as well as the tattered old garment itself.[110]

While Thackeray was still in this mood, he had another sentimental experience that affected his opinion of Irish Catholicism: he visited a convent near Cork. Imbued from boyhood with the anti-Catholic bias of Evangelicalism, he had been reinforced in that prejudice by an insatiable reading of the Gothic romances. Yet his constant striving for fair-mindedness had nevertheless brought him to Ireland with "a strong predisposition in favor of the Catholics."[111] On arrival, however, first-hand experience with the Roman Church in Ireland had re-awakened the old prejudices and driven him to inveigh against what he termed its "slavish brutal superstition."[112]

More than Thackeray's abstract sense of propriety was roused here: the treatment of the young nuns at the Ursuline Convent had painfully reminded him of Isabella's captivity in the various sanitaria

[108] *Works*, V, 89.
[109] The same, p. 91.
[110] The same, p. 91.
[111] *Letters*, II, 78.
[112] The same, p. 78.

where she had passed the two preceding years. The young Ursuline nuns themselves seem to have stirred the tender sensuality which children constantly awakened in him and which lay behind much of Isabella's appeal to him. His mind teeming with recollections of *The Monk* and other anti-Catholic Gothic romances, Thackeray speculated over possible *oubliettes* below the floor of the convent. He found himself wondering as he looked at one nun whether her "poor little, weak, delicate body" was "scarred all over with scourgings, iron-collars, hair shirts."[113] The query was a comic exaggeration, of course, but it reveals both the rabid anti-Catholicism of Thackeray's conditioning and his revulsion to cruelty towards the helpless and tender. These feelings were closely linked with his neurotic absorption in whipping and with his later concern with ogres and other terrorizers of childhood like Bluebeard.[114]

An inspection of a nun's little treasure-chamber gave Thackeray "the same sort of soft wonder" as one feels "when a child takes you by the hand, and leads you solemnly to some little treasure of its own."[115] Finally the wicket where the nuns made their final vows proved altogether too much for him:

I felt a sort of shudder at looking at the place. There rest the girl's knees as she offers herself up, and forswears the sacred affections which God gave her; there she kneels and denies for ever the beautiful duties of her being—no tender maternal yearnings—no gentle attachments are to be had for her or from her,—there she kneels and commits suicide upon her heart.[116]

The image of Isabella accounted also for Thackeray's interest during the Irish tour in public institutions. During this period he was seeking what did not then exist in Great Britain—an insane asylum for his wife that was not utterly unspeakable. The search, combined with his lifelong interest in boys' schools, and the example of Dickens' constant investigations of public institutions, led Thackeray to feel that his writing too might develop in that direction. The descriptions of nearly all such institutions in *The Irish Sketch Book* are warped characteristically to fit one of his emotional biases, just as had been the case with the nunnery.

[113] *Works*, V, p. 74.
[114] See below, pp. 117f.
[115] *Works*, V, 76.
[116] The same, p. 77.

Thackeray's predilection for frank, manly young men who were physically attractive and not too intellectual came to light in his account of the robust, rollicking farmers' sons in the coach en route to study for the Catholic priesthood at Maynooth. The passage is a counterpart to the lamentations for the novice nun, except that its subjects are male:

The poor freshman . . . has but twelve hours more of hearty, natural, human life. To-morrow they will begin their work upon him; cramping his mind, and biting his tongue, and firing and cutting at his heart,—breaking him to pull the Church chariot. Ah! why didn't he stop at home, and dig potatoes and get children?[117]

At his cousin Elias Thackeray's school for very young children at Dundalk, Ireland, the sound of children singing a hymn about heaven set off an inevitable chain reaction of tears as the novelist recalled his own dead infant:

It was a hymn about heaven, with a chorus of 'Will not that be joyful, joyful?' and one of the verses beginning 'Little children, too, are there' . . . it brought tears to my eyes, though it is ill to parade such kind of sentiment in print. But I think I will never . . . forget that little chorus, nor would any man who has ever loved a child or lost one.[118]

The Irish Sketch Book constantly shifts from passages of this sort to describing the conviviality and camaraderie of life in Ireland. Thereby it attests to the polarization of Thackeray's temperament at this middle stage of his career between sentimentality and Bohemianism. He took a Pickwickian joy in casual encounters with random boon companions at inns and on stage coaches. The dinners with Lever and his circle in Dublin were only the climax to many casual social gatherings in the provincial districts of Ireland. Furthermore, the novelist's barely suppressed grief for Isabella had clearly not anesthetized his sexuality. The Thackeray of 1842 was far more *entgegenkommend* with women than had been the young Cambridge undergraduate of 1830, whose "buckish" manner had concealed a deep shyness. *The Sketch Book* abounds in raptures over the beauty of Irish women, and Thackeray never failed to comment on the presence of a beautiful chambermaid. At that time the inns of Ireland apparently specialized in such types. Thackeray described to Fitz-

117 The same, p. 250.
118 The same, p. 286.

Gerald one such maiden at a Welsh inn where he stopped en route
to Ireland as "the most sumptuous creature ever seen—yellow haired
brown eyed dazzling fair with a neck like a marble pillar, and a
busk o heavens!"[119] At a humble inn in the remote Ulster village of
Limavaddy, he was so overcome by the stockingless barmaid that he
spilled his ale on his pantaloons. After his recovery, he immortalized
the girl in a poem called *Peg of Limavaddy*:

> This I do declare,
>   Happy is the laddy
> Who the heart can share
>   Of Peg of Limavaddy;
> Married if she were,
>   Blest would be the daddy
> Of the children fair
>   Of Peg of Limavaddy;
> Beauty is not rare
>   In the land of Paddy,
> Fair beyond compare
>   Is Peg of Limavaddy.[120]

Nor can one easily forget the tale of Thackeray's adventure on
the stage to Killarney in the company of the yachtsmen. The whole
party gave a ride to five "pretty, gay, frolicsome, lively, kind-hearted,
innocent women . . . and for the rest of the journey there was no
end of laughing and shouting and singing and hugging." Soon more
interesting things happened: "a very pretty woman fell off, and
showed a pair of never-mind-what-colored garters, and an interesting
English traveller fell off too."[121] The latter, it is clear, was Thackeray
himself; in fact the frontispiece to the book shows how the accident
occurred—at the moment before it, he was sitting on the back step
of the carriage holding the lady affectionately around the waist.
Plainly a more assured Thackeray was emerging from the shell of
the confused young man who had tacked and veered indecisively
through his 20's. From this more resolute author great things were
forthcoming.

[119] *Letters*, II, 62.
[120] *Works*, V, 338.
[121] The same, p. 115.

CHAPTER IV

The Rise to Fame

THACKERAY'S way of life between his return from Ireland in November, 1842, and the re-establishment of his family life in September, 1846, can be described in terms of goals. His long range objective was to acquire a house in London where his daughters could be with him. There he hoped that Isabella too would preside after she had recovered her wits. The achievement of such a home was a matter of finance. In 1842 Thackeray's income from writing merely paid his own and his family's daily living expenses, now much augmented by the fact that the four Thackerays were living under three roofs. Even to make the Irish tour he had been forced to encroach on a nest egg previously set aside for his daughters. Now this sum must be repaid, together with the loan from Mary Carmichael,[1] as well as one of the debts from *The Constitutional* held by a man named Hickman.[2] To go on paying daily living expenses, plus the repayment of debts, plus the finding of enough money to support the still more expensive household which he hoped to establish—all this required a stepping up of income.

Yet in 1843 Thackeray was writing quantitatively as much as any man's time and energy could have permitted. His pen was pouring manuscript incessantly into publishers' offices: the chapters of *The Irish Sketch Book* found their way into Chapman and Hall's to appear as a book in March; reviews of contemporary French and German literature were appearing from time to time in *The Foreign Quarterly Review*; and nearly every month saw a piece of fiction by Thackeray in *Fraser's Magazine*. Truly it could be said that his narrative genius was incubated within the covers of that famous periodical.

The trivialities of *The Great Hoggarty Diamond's* early chapters had turned to pathos, as we have seen,[3] in the later chapters when the author's personal tragedy had possessed his imagination. Then,

[1] See above, p. 93.
[2] *Letters*, II, 49 and *passim*.
[3] See above, p. 90.

as if he were afraid of having shown himself in too sentimental a light, Thackeray decided to trample aggressively on his own past. This task he performed in creating George Fitz-Boodle. Proud now of the hardness and drive with which he was conducting his life, he made this new hero partially a caricature of the younger Thackeray of 1830. Fitz-Boodle is proud of an impressive pedigree, which includes a general who fought with Marlborough.[4] Thackeray too had been proud of his descent from the semi-legendary Roaldus de Richmond, though he later ridiculed this connection.[5] He continued to be proud all his life of his kinship with Marlborough's brother officer and antagonist, General John Richmond Webb.[6] Fitz-Boodle had gone to a Charterhouse, which was very thinly veiled as Slaughter House, and had carried away from there his creator's dislike of the school's useless curriculum.[7] Fitz-Boodle had gone up to the University a *gauche* youth who "could no more dance nor prattle to a young girl than a young bear could."[8] At the university he drank in moderation, studied little, and left without a degree.[9] Like Thackeray, George was dismayed when he came to London about competition offered in the professions by young men with less gentility and more industry.[10] He was lonely in chambers, and found relief in gambling and in convivial meetings around a table where "claret-bottles circulated a great deal too often." A French card shark Monsieur Lalouette, won from him "two-and-thirty nights in the course of a couple of score of nights' play."[11] He loved small children and pined for them in his loneliness.[12]

Finally Fitz-Boodle escaped to the continent. There he repeated Thackeray's experience of taking lessons in Paris from the famous dancing-teacher, Coulon, and laughing so hard at the master that he was asked not to return to the class.[13] More important, George enacted, on a comic plane in the little German court of Kalbsbraten-Pumpernickel, many of Thackeray's experiences at Weimar.

[4] *Works*, IV, 239.
[5] *Letters*, I, 325.
[6] Webb is held up to honor at Marlborough's expense in *Henry Esmond* (book 2, chapter 15.)
[7] *Works*, IV, 283. See above, pp. 22f.
[8] *Works*, IV, 283.
[9] The same, p. 205.
[10] The same, p. 229. See above, p. 53.
[11] The same, p. 201.
[12] The same, p. 209.
[13] *Letters*, I, 85. *Works*, IV, 284.

So Thackeray ridiculed his own past by weaving many of its incidents into the life of a rather fatuous young-man-about-town. He was adding a few brush strokes to the portrait of himself as a buffoon which he assiduously if spasmodically cultivated.[14] This self-portrait had both personal and professional value, for by placing certain feelings of unworthiness in a mask-like portrait of a being like himself but not himself, he was in a way exorcising them. Professionally this action entertained the public and enhanced the author's income.

But as Fitz-Boodle's adventures are unrolled before our eyes, the mask constantly grows thinner and more of the author's real features peer forth. The device of using Fitz-Boodle as a mouthpiece for many of his own pet ideas and prejudices—particularly many of his phobias about snobbery—caused Thackeray to turn him into something of an autobiographical hero, an entity somewhat different from a mere comic mask.

It was necessary for Thackeray to contribute something almost every month to *Fraser's Magazine* to maintain his surest source of bread-and-butter during the early 1840's. Hence he found himself seeking a new set of characters to write about when he finished off Fitz-Boodle in the spring of 1843. It is symptomatic of the basic duality of his life—the contrast between himself and the world of women—that he should turn from the narcissistic self-contemplation of Fitz-Boodle to the multiform diversities of womanhood: *Men's Wives* ran in *Fraser's Magazine* from March through November of 1843. It lays bare, in four stories, four types of womanhood which were to be basic in the large mass of Thackeray's later fiction.

Mr. and Mrs. Frank Berry[15] typifies the henpecking shrew with insatiable social ambitions. The choicest specimens of her ilk in the later books are Lady Susan Scraper in *The Book of Snobs*,[16] Mrs. Bute Crawley in *Vanity Fair*, Mrs. Hobson Newcome in *The Newcomes*, Lady Miles Warrington of *The Virginians*, Mrs. Talbot Twysden of *Philip*, and Lady Kicklebury, who figures in sundry lesser satires.[17]

[14] See below, pp. 201f.

[15] *Works*, IV, 317-341.

[16] Chapter 6. *Works*, IX, 287f.

[17] Most notably in *The Kickleburys on the Rhine* (*Works*, X, 213ff.) and *The Wolves and the Lamb* (the same, XVII, 1ff.), from which she emerges reincarnated as Lady Baker of *Lovel the Widower* (the same, pp. 57ff.).

The Ravenswing[18] takes its title from the stage name of a constant wife married to a cad who, of course, subjects her to every sort of indignity. The basic situation suggests that of Barry Lyndon and his Countess, not to mention Amelia Sedley Osborne and her husband, George. The locale of the story in the world that lies below respectability, however, relates it to earlier books such as *Catherine* and *A Shabby Genteel Story*, written before Isabella's collapse.

Dennis Haggarty's Wife[19] is an even closer literary expression of Thackeray's hatred for Mrs. Shawe than is the later and more famous portrait of "the Campaigner" in *The Newcomes*.[20] *The ———'s Wife*[21] depicts, in a medieval setting, the rearing of a motherless daughter by a licentious father without moral scruples.[22]

Thackeray had written *Men's Wives* under the *nom de plume* of George Fitz-Boodle, and it was therefore automatic for him to continue its use in his next serialized publication for *Fraser's Magazine*, "The Luck of Barry Lyndon, a Romance of the Last Century. By Fitz-Boodle."[23] Those circumstances suggest that the book merely continued the perpetual series of Thackerayana which filled a certain slot in *Fraser's*. Yet the facts are otherwise. Thackeray had long meditated this *réchauffée* of the eighteenth-century picaresque novel. It was to be fiction of a higher order than he had yet written, something that would get him out of the journalistic rut which seemed never to secure him much more than bread-and-butter. The story of Stoney-Bowes, the Irish adventurer who had married and then made miserable the widowed Countess of Strathmore, had been recounted to Thackeray by his friend John Bowes Bowes, descendant of the unhappy countess, when the novelist had visited the north of England in the summer of 1841. He had then written to James Fraser his intention of using the material for a story,[24] although that purpose was to lie in abeyance for two years. Thackeray's plan, as expressed in 1841, was to make the Stoney-Bowes story the basis of a literary attack. One avowed purpose of *Catherine* had been to heap scorn on the sentimentalized crime fiction of

---

[18] *Works*, IV, 342ff.
[19] The same, pp. 463ff.
[20] See above, p. 73.
[21] *Works*, IV, 483ff.
[22] See below, p. 120.
[23] *Works*, IV, 3ff.
[24] *Letters*, I, xci.

Ainsworth and Dickens; now *Barry Lyndon* was to emulate, somewhat ironically, Charles Lever's swashbuckling braggart hero, Harry Lorrequer.[25] Thackeray's Irish tour had supplied him with much local color for the background, once the decision was made to lay his scene in Ireland.[26]

Thackeray's failure to stir the public fancy with *Catherine* had left unsatisfied his old ambition to depict moral callousness ironically and unsentimentally, as Fielding had handled it in Jonathan Wild. But only Saintsbury among the commentators on the book has pointed out[27] that Barry is not, like Jonathan Wild, without moral feeling from the start. His career is a study of the disintegration that comes to a man brought up under a false and obsolete code of honor. More specifically, Barry is what Thackeray felt he himself might have become had he been the only child, not of Mrs. Carmichael-Smyth, but of the mother whom fate gave to Barry. That lady was a former Dublin belle with a set of values both eighteenth-century, Hibernian, and hedonistic—essentially those qualities which Lever held up to praise in his novels. Although Barry's mother acquired, with the onset of middle age, some Evangelical traits—making more obvious her relationship with Mrs. Carmichael-Smyth—she never outgrew certain of her more archaic notions, especially her approval of dueling. After the affair in which her sixteen-year-old son erroneously believed he had killed an English captain, she heard the account of his action with "pride and exultation.[28]"

Barry Lyndon is, in fact, a continuous glorification of fraud and violence. Its violence partly stems from an aggressive streak in the Irish character which had constantly frightened Thackeray during his Irish journey. But the more important sin which the book ironically exposes is that ruling vice of the Thackerayan canon—self-delusion. Redmond Barry—or Barry Lyndon as he becomes after

[25] Thackeray's letter to Fraser states: "I have in my trip to the country, found materials (rather a character) for a story, that I'm sure must be amusing. I want to write and illustrate it, and as you see how Harry Lorrequer succeeds ... why should not my story of BARRY-LYNN ... answer ... as well" (*Letters*, II, 29. Written on July 24, 1841).

[26] George Saintsbury observed, a little inaccurately, of *Barry Lyndon* (*Works*, VI, ix) that the "Irish tour ... of course suggested it."

[27] "The far from ungenerous scapegrace of the early chapters, and the not altogether hateful *picaro* of the middle, *might* grow into the unmitigated and even cowardly scoundrel of the end" (*Works*, VI, xi).

[28] Chapter 2. *Works*, VI, 47.

his marriage—possesses the form of that vice which Thackeray also bestowed on a whole line of Irish characters, including Major Gahagan, the Mulligan of *Mrs. Perkins' Ball*, and Captain Costigan in *Pendennis*. All these men had a grandiose conception of themselves as knightly, heroic, and of kingly lineage, coupled with a blindness toward the sordid reality of their true living conditions.

Yet, if Barry is the antithesis of his creator, there is some self-identification between author and character, especially during the latter's boyhood. Not only does one notice the curious inter-relationship of the two mothers, so like and so unlike; there are other parallels: in his adolescence Barry, like Thackeray, has a serious illness, during which he grows many inches,[29] and both young men are "pigeoned" by knaves during their first fling at metropolitan life.[30] More curious yet, Barry has an experience that recalls the flattening of Thackeray's nose in his schoolboy fight with Venables.[31] Only Barry does not undergo the disfigurement; he inflicts it on his English enemy, Captain Quin, later to be his adversary in the duel: "I had the satisfaction of seeing the captain's nose was bleeding, as mine was—*his* was cut across the bridge, and his beauty spoiled for ever".[32]

Thus the Barry of the earlier chapters is a sort of obverse image of Thackeray's self-portrait. It is similar to it in many details, yet it is the reverse in other respects wherein Thackeray regarded himself as weak and inferior. Barry during his days as the Chevalier de Balibari, the continental gambler, possesses extraordinary *sangfroid*. Though his testimony on this score is unverified, the trait was indispensable to his occupation, and his account must be substantially accurate. With the Barry of the later chapters Thackeray had no sympathy and therefore no self-identification; he was tired of the book and tired of the man. Hence he had no compunctions in representing his erstwhile hero-villain as a sodden domestic tyrant, given to ungovernable fits of rage. When Barry's son died, the father gave vent to a bawling tantrum of sorrow such as Thackeray would expect of an Irishman.[33] Barry shows none of the "manly,"

[29] Chapter 1. The same, p. 28.
[30] Chapter 3. The same, pp. 51–61.
[31] See above, p. 24.
[32] Chapter 2. *Works*, VI, 37.
[33] Chapter 19, the same, p. 284.

sentimental grief which his creator felt at his own daughter's death.

Thackeray was weary of *Barry Lyndon* long before the writing of the later chapters.[34] And to this weariness one may attribute much of what Saintsbury calls Thackeray's failure to maintain "steadily his own attitude towards the story."[35] Not only is Barry the wrong person to moralize upon the evils of the Seven Years War; he even allowed himself in his old age a nostalgic reverie on the tender emotions of youth in a manner like that of *The Roundabout Papers* during Thackeray's closing years.

Shall we go on in this strain, and discourse through this entire chapter upon the nature and peculiarities of love, and its influences upon the youthful bosom? No, no! such things had best be thought about, not spoken of. Let any man who has a mind to do so, fall back in his chair, dropping the book out of his hand—fall back into his chair, and call back the sleeping sweet reminiscences of his early love-days, long before he ever saw Mrs. Jones. She, good woman, has sent down half a dozen times already to say that tea is waiting. Never mind; sit still, Jones, and dream on. Call back again that early, brilliant, immortal first love. What matters what the object of it was? Perhaps a butcher's daughter down the village; perhaps a great, skinny, ogling French governess; perhaps a fat, meek, fair-haired clergyman's daughter, that was ten years older than yourself.[36]

In the great novels to come, Thackeray licensed himself thus to address his readers whenever the mood struck him. He was either his own narrator, as in *Vanity Fair* and *Pendennis*, or was using as mouthpiece a character whose attitudes were so like his own that the digressions are not incongruous. Such is the case with Henry Esmond, with the George Warrington who narrates the later chapters of *The Virginians*, and with Arthur Pendennis as the spokesman in *The Newcomes* and *Philip*. But despite the strange parallels between the youthful Barry Lyndon and his creator, that hero's basic attitudes are poles apart from his creator's. Hence Thackeray realized the artistic incongruity of his nostalgic digression and omitted it after the first version of *Barry Lyndon*. Regarded biographically rather than critically, however, the passage shows how early Thack-

[34] See his diary for January 17–18, 1844. "wrote Barry, beginning however to flag. In these days got through the fag end of Chap. IV of Barry Lyndon with a great deal of dullness unwillingness and labor" (*Letters*, II, 141); for August, 1844, "B.L. lying like a night-mare on my mind" (the same, p. 149); for November 1–3, 1844, "wrote Barry—but slowly and with great difficulty . . . wrote Barry, with no more success than yesterday . . . finished Barry after great throes late at night" (the same, p. 156).

[35] *Works*, VI, xi.

[36] Chapter 1. The same, pp. 2of.

eray's premature middle age really began. He was only thirty-two when he wrote it, yet here already he is assuming the world-weary post of the nostalgic arm chair philosopher.

This world-weariness can be imputed in part to the tensions under which Thackeray was working at this period. Added to the strain of writing a book like *Barry Lyndon*—in which he lost interest very quickly—there was his separation from his family to brood over, his anxiety about Isabella's chances of recovery, and the demands of the hack work which he was performing for various publications, including that lusty fledgling magazine, *Punch*. Yet in spite of this voluminous literary output, Thackeray still deluded himself with the old legend of his indolence. Thus on one occasion, after toiling until five in the evening at *Barry Lyndon*, he reproached himself for being so tired that he had to go to bed at nine-thirty, adding: "I have been so idle all my life that continued labour annoys and excites me too much."[37]

Early bed-going was not, however, Thackeray's usual end to a hard day's work. A few weeks before the nine-thirty bed hour, he had written of being so "weary with writing" that "the evenings amusement did not cure."[38] He had by now given up the Coram Street house and was living in lodgings, from which escape during the evenings was necessary to avoid fits of black depression.[39] Thackeray was always subject to attacks of melancholy, but its immediate causes differed with each stage of life. In the early 1840's his depressions stemmed chiefly from loneliness and overwork. Convivial evenings served a double purpose: they relieved the loneliness and provided literary local color which he was too busy to seek out during the daytime. Hence the important role which evening parties play in his writings.

Sometimes Thackeray attended convivial stag gatherings, and these he usually enjoyed to the utmost, although they were often followed by "blue devils" on the mornings after. At other times, he went to mixed gatherings, where he seems to have been happiest during the parting of the sexes after dinner. It was then that the

[37] *Letters*, II, 143.

[38] The same, p. 140. Written on January 11, 1844.

[39] The name "atra Cura" or "black care" was commonly applied to melancholy by public school men, who knew their Horace, in reference to one of the most frequently quoted tags from that poet: "post equidem sedet atra Cura" (Odes, III, i, 40).

men settled down to their claret. Seemingly such occasions gradually outnumbered the stag parties as more and more of his friends married. In March of 1843, he confessed to his mother that "the dinner-parties pour in rather too plentifully. I had 5 invitations for last Saturday; and a dinner every day in the week, the same this week."[40]

Not until 1847 did Thackeray get "taken up" by the "great world" and become a "literary lion." Hence during the early 1840's he dined out at the homes of men who were either former school or college friends, acquaintances from the world of art and letters, publishing connections, or relatives on either his or Isabella's side of the family. Inevitably this entertaining had a bourgeois flavor which repelled him; he hankered for the wit play of stag Bohemian gatherings or of a few literary households like the Procters.' At the duller parties he was doubtless liberal in helping himself from the after-dinner decanter so useful as anaesthesia for his boredom. The resentment occasioned by this *ennui* accounts for the long-standing animus in Thackeray's fiction at the pretentious snobbery of bourgeois evening parties.

During all this time Thackeray was developing a consciousness of his own human limitations. Thus he wrote to Isabella from London in March of 1844: "my disposition is such that when I am in one place I long invariably for another, and I think now about the little room in the Champs Elysées as the most delightful little retreat in the world."[41] Now that London was again his residence and Paris his asylum of escape, Thackeray burned the candle more freely at both ends in the French capital than was his wont at home. A diary kept intermittently in 1844 tells the story of one of those flights. On July 3 he dined "with Fraser, and passed a great deal too jovial a night." On the eighth he "spent the evening at Stevens's, too much drink." The fifteenth witnessed "a costly dinner" with "a merry party" where Thackeray was "the soberest of the set for a wonder." The Stevens's repeated their prior hospitality with a roaring party on February 10.[42]

After his return to England in March, Thackeray apparently settled down again. On his birthday, July 18, he "formed a world of

[40] *Letters*, II, 97.
[41] The same, p. 166.
[42] The same, pp. 139, 140, 141.

good resolves, as my custom is upon this day. Pray God I could keep them or some of them And do my duty by myself and my children!"[43] The journal for the following months testifies to no such constant revelry as had marked the holiday season in Paris. On August 9 there is mention after a dinner of the "usual feverish symptoms in the morning" with the comment, "Cant I for Heaven's sake be moderate?"[44] But Thackeray's more habitual mode of life was that described to his mother on March 28, 1845: "I go out as usual 6 times a week to dinner: but am pretty moderate and have adhered firmly to my resolution against brandy and water."[45]

Thackeray's decision to place his daughters under Mrs. Carmichael-Smyth's care had meant giving her hostages for his own morality. Inevitably she developed renewed faith in her right to supervise his conduct, and one finds him defending it in almost the same words he had used before Isabella's collapse.[46] "I could not go on with this unless I had the fun in the evening, and the quantum of wine:—it is very brutal and unworthy but so it is."[47] His periods of virtue are stressed. "They say the town is very gay; but I have almost left off going to Operas and Theatres, and come home early . . . and so go quietly to bed."[48] As far back as 1842 Thackeray had been forced into some ingenious fence-straddling to tone down the facts without prevarication.

Please to make yourself easy about the drink. I am very moderate, drinking sherry and water after dinner and can't-abiding whiskey. I don't know what the young people have frightened you about with my London doings.[49]

A month later, when he left on the Irish tour, Thackeray had to rebut an insinuation by his mother that the money for his traveling expenses, which was drawn from a special reserve for his daughters' benefit, would be spent in riot.

With regard to my own delinquencies, I know I spend more than other people, but not in the proportion you suppose . . . please God the money never shall be

[43] The same, p. 144.
[44] The same, p. 148.
[45] The same, p. 190.
[46] See above, pp. 83f.
[47] *Letters*, II, 101. Written in March, 1843.
[48] The same, p. 109. Written in May, 1843.
[49] The same, p. 70. Written on July 29, 1842.

spent as you prophecy, and the portion I have drawn out shall be refunded ... By the way, I have kept clear of the whiskey, which I found very unwholesome and not very pleasant.[50]

This letter was indubitably truthful. From the time about 1841 when he re-established his publishing connections, until 1846, when he set up a home for his daughters, Thackeray was single-mindedly bent on re-establishing his family life. At first he had pictured a recovered Isabella presiding at his table, then as that hope waned, he had counted on his mother to manage the household. Whenever he had a spare day in London, it seemed as if he went hunting for a house suitably large and comfortable, yet within his means. The fact that this dwelling remained a will o' the wisp for so long led him further and further into literary schemes of a more and more ambitious sort. Only thus could he bridge the gap between his means and his needs. *Barry Lyndon* and the 'Novel Without a Hero,' as *Vanity Fair* was at first called, were the most ambitious of those schemes. The correspondence of these house-hunting, Bohemian years from 1842 to 1846 never mentions our novelist's old desire to write more ambitious books merely so that he might emulate Bulwer or Dickens.

In 1845 when 'the railway mania' offered a quicker way of getting the eagerly-desired home, Thackeray, like several thousand of his countrymen, speculated in shares and lost. This reverse piled another debt on top of what he already owed to Mary Carmichael. Then there was the sum needed to reimburse his parents for his daughters' keep, plus some unforgiven remnants of his stepfather's old debts which Thackeray felt morally obligated to pay. Inevitably he was under pressure to step up his earnings.

In October of 1845, Thackeray settled the problem of maintaining Isabella where he could see her more often. She was brought to England and placed under the care of a family in Camberwell. There she received frequent visits from her husband until, by June, 1847, she lost interest in seeing him and he had to look at her out of the window of a cab.[51] Thenceforth it is quite possible that Thackeray never again set eyes on Isabella. Nowhere in the *Letters* does he allude to a meeting. On the other hand, he constantly refers to

[50] The same, pp. 74f.
[51] The same, p. 306.

letters from her guardians reporting on her condition,[52] a device to which he would hardly have resorted had he been visiting her. She became completely indifferent to anything "but her dinner and her glass of porter,"[53] and he obviously loved only the memory of what she had been, accepting her in her present state as a mere charge on his pocketbook which he bore manfully and without repining.

The replacement of Isabella in Thackeray's affections by Anny and Minny was a process which may have begun before her insanity.[54] At any event, it was well under way by 1842, when he wrote of hearing the absent Anny's "voice a dozen times a day" and of "blubbering"[55] when he wrote to her. It was the thought of her and Minny as much as of their dead sister that reduced him to tears at the sound of the singing children in Dundalk[56] and that drove him to the Foundlings Church in London to hear the young voices that inspired the scene in *Vanity Fair*, where Amelia Osborne weeps at sight of the boy whom she has recently surrendered.[57] In all four instances, the death of the little Jane Thackeray, the singing at the orphanage, the episode in *Vanity Fair*, and Thackeray's own present situation, the tears came from his inability "to think of children parted from their parents ... without a tendency to blubbering."[58] Now he is aware that the wrenches between his boyhood vacations and his returns to school are still affecting his adult emotional life. He recalls his painful returns to school from holidays when, like any schoolboy, he had fought to conceal his tears. Yet they had smeared the pages of his first epistle to his mother. He is no more self-indulgent now about his weeping on the sheets of his letters to Anny. Thackeray doubts whether there is any "sort of sentiment ... more useless and foolish in the world," but confesses himself "as weak to this day upon the point" as he had been at school.[59]

Even while he was blubbering as he wrote to the absent Anny, Thackeray had been looking forward to having her and Minny as

[52] The same, p. 545; III, 69; III, 388; IV, 62.
[53] The same, II, p. 440. See also III, 419.
[54] See above, pp. 8of.
[55] *Letters*, II, 53.
[56] See above, p. 101. Also *Letters*, II, 84.
[57] Chapter 50. *Works*, XI, 630–633.
[58] *Letters*, II, 197.
[59] The same, pp. 172 and 197.

house-companions. Subconsciously he hoped that his deepest needs would be solved when they should grow to womanhood reared according to his wishes—docile, devoted, and without aggressive desires. By 1848, when Anny was only eleven, her father was able to see this design unfolding: "In 3 years she will be a charming companion to me: and fill up a part of a great vacuum which exists inside me."[60] And by 1855 the scheme was so well fulfilled that he could compare his family circle with what to him was the perfect household arrangement, that of the Turks: "I have 2 little wives not jealous of each other; and am at last most comfortable in my *harem.*"[61]

But that Elysium was far ahead. In 1846 when Thackeray gained the objective of his own household in Young Street, Kensington, the new arrangement marked a turning point in his life. For one thing his attention was turned toward problems of household management. The reorientation soon became so apparent in his writings that he was able in time to qualify as the most highly versed of all male authors in domestic details.

To take one example, Thackeray was always prone to see social questions, not in the abstract, but as they infringed on his personal life. This tendency deflected his concern over the problem of social justice to the minor area of relationships between employers and domestic servants. This limitation of scope can be explained partly by Thackeray's unwillingness to write passionately—as did Dickens and Kingsley—about social injustice in the larger areas of national life. Some of it too can be explained by that pathological terror lest any resentment be directed toward him by anyone in his immediate presence, a fear which goes back to his schooldays.[62]

Thackeray's distrust of hostile servants is more subtly revealed by his constant harping on the criticism of its employers by "the awful kitchen inquisition which sits in judgment in every house."[63] The idea that one's servants were judging and, by implication, finding one wanting was to him horrible. Yet on the other hand it was

---

[60] The same, p. 382.

[61] The same, III, 415.

[62] See above, pp. 11f.

[63] *Vanity Fair*, chapter 44 (*Works*, XI, 561). Compare *Pendennis*, chapter 60 (*Works*, XII, 783); *Henry Esmond*, book 1, chapter 12 (*Works*, XIII, 135); *The Newcomes*, chapter 14 (*Works*, XIV, 186); *Philip*, chapter 21 (*Works*, XVI, 315).

sheer bliss to dwell on certain acts of devotion from servants in the past. There was Brodie the Scotch maid who had nursed his daughters on the tragic voyage to Cork in 1840.[64] Of her he had written:

She was sick almost every ¼ of an hour, but up again immediately staggering after the little ones feeding one and fondling another. Indeed a woman's heart is the most beautiful thing that God has created and I feel I can't tell you what respect for her.[65]

Quite naturally Thackeray made every effort to be as friendly with servants as was permitted by his natural diffidence and sense of caste. Thus in September, 1852, when everyone was out of London but the novelist and his cook, he thought of mitigating their common loneliness by joining her in the kitchen. Then of course he thought better of it:

How dismal it must be for poor Eliza who has no friends to go to: who must stop in the kitchen all day ... I feel a mind to ... sit in the kitchen with Eliza but I daresay I shouldn't amuse her much and after she had told me about the cat and how her father was we should have nothing more to say to one another.[66]

And writing on a topic which became a favorite of his, the butlers' and footmen's clubs which met in the back parlor of public houses, Thackeray observed that,

with the best wishes, it is impossible for the present writer to join either the Plate Club or the Uniform Club (as these *réunions* are designated), for one could not shake hands with a friend who was standing behind your chair—or nod a how-d'ye-do to the butler who was pouring you out a glass of wine.[67]

Some of Thackeray's interest in servants can be attributed to the Nineteenth Century's regard for the quantity and quality of one's domestics as the first criterion of status. Certainly to him a person's

[64] See above, p. 85.

[65] *Letters*, I, 476.

[66] The same, III, 75f.

[67] *Our Street* (*Works*, X, 100). Thackeray developed this idea further in *The Newcomes* when Colonel Newcome says, à propos of his son's friendship for the painter J. J. Ridley, son of Lord Todmorden's butler: "a young man whose father may have had to wait behind me at dinner should not be brought into my company" (Chapter 19. *Works*, XIV, 241). Ridley's right, in view of his father's occupation, to associate with gentlemen is also discussed in *Philip* (Chapters 4 and 6. *Works*, XVI, 43 and 73). Thackeray's sympathies of course lay with Ridley. Other menservants' clubs are found in *The Irish Sketch Book* (Chapter 9. *Works*, V, 111); *Pendennis* (Chapters 60 and 67, *passim*); *The Virginians* (Chapter 46. *Works*, XV, 475).

social prestige was of all topics in the world the most interesting. He had always studied with a connoisseur's eye the number of any host's servants, together with the excellence of their accoutrements and deportment. And none of his unmaskings of false fronts gave him more joy than exposing the innocuous little sham of calling in the local greengrocer or some other convenient tradesman and disguising him as the butler or footman at a dinner.[68]

Not the least cause of Thackeray's skill in writing of things domestic was his sybaritic attachment to the minor comforts of life; as a consequence he had long been interested in the machinery which secured those little comforts for men. Furthermore, Isabella's ineptitude as housewife during her four years of married life had imposed on him more household management than usually falls to the lot of husbands. So, despite the drastic change in living habits brought about by his shift from bachelor Bohemianism to bourgeois domesticity, Thackeray was better equipped by temperament and training than most men to make the change.

But over and above Thackeray's new concern after 1846 with domestic management, there looms the question of his greater interest in the world of childhood. He had attempted to invade the area of juvenile fiction in 1843 when he had wanted to prepare for Chapman and Hall a book to be called *Fairy Ballads by W. Thackeray*.[69] Nothing had come of it. But during all these years he had increased his mastery over the written burlesque of imaginative fiction. Such writing is, of course, closely related to children's literature. The inspiration for these burlesques came from Thackeray's subordination of his youthful romanticism at the outset of his literary career to the grim demands of satire. In the satirical fantasy he could still have his romanticism by simply inverting it for the purpose of ridiculing contemporary manners. The parody of an *Arabian Nights* story in *Sultan Stork* (1842),[70] the pseudo-Oriental lampoon on the writer John Abraham Heraud entitled *The Legend of Jewbrahim-Heraudee* (1843),[71] the modernized sequel to the Bluebeard legend

---

[68] *The Second Funeral of Napoleon* (*Works*, III, 398); *The Book of Snobs*, "Dining-Out Snobs" (*Works*, IX, 368); *Mrs. Perkins's Ball* (*Works*, X, 13); *Vanity Fair* (Chapter 318. *Works*, XI, 466); *Pendennis* (Chapter 34. *Works*, XII, 436); *Mr. Brown's Letters to his Nephew*, "Great and Little Dinners" (*Works*, VIII, 319).

[69] *Letters*, II, 92.

[70] *Works*, IV, 181ff.

[71] *Works*, VII, 239ff.

called *Bluebeard's Ghost* (1843),[72] and the burlesque of Dumas's *Othon l'Archer* entitled *A Legend of the Rhine* (1845),[73] all have the Thackerayan quality of ridiculing the grotesque and unreal by giving a contemporary flavor to its incidents.

In *Sultan Stork* the disguised King of Persia sounds like a London clubman as he compliments his august contemporary, the King of Hindostan on that dignitary's elegant way of life: "Hindostan, my old buck . . . what a deuced comfortable sofa this is; and, egad, what a neat turn-out of a barge."[74] In *The Legend of Jewbrahim-Heraudee*, published in 1842 when Sir Robert Peel imposed his famous income-tax, King Poof-Allee threatens in a moment of anger to "levy an income-tax to-morrow upon all Armenia."[75] *Bluebeard's Ghost* is, except for the names of the principal characters, virtually a Thackerayan novelette of contemporary upper-middle-class manners and snobberies. Though *A Legend of the Rhine* is laid in a medieval setting, one finds such deliberate anachronisms as an otherwise correctly armed knight carrying an umbrella and carpet-bag.[76]

This mixture of the old and unfamiliar with the contemporary and prosaic also predominates in the burlesque, *Miss Tickletoby's Lectures on English History* (1842).[77] Here Richard the Lion Hearted discloses to the minstrel Blondell, his presence in the Austrian dungeon by playing on the piano *God Save the King* and *Home, Sweet Home*, which he had learned from Madame Vestris. To these Blondell reciprocates with *Rule Britannia*.[78] The same effect is similarly employed in certain of his ballads such as *King Canute* (1842), where the worthy eleventh-century monarch is surrounded—like Wellington or Marlborough—with aides-de-camp;[79] or *The King of Brentford's Testament* (1841), where a vaguely Hanoverian sovereign becomes a socially ambitious city merchant;[80] or *The Legend of St. Sophie of Kioff* (1839), where the historic Russian city is stormed by

[72] *Works*, VI, 342ff.
[73] *Works*, IX, 3ff.
[74] *Works*, IV, 196.
[75] *Works*, VII, 244.
[76] *Works*, IX, 5 f.
[77] *Works*, VII, 251ff.
[78] The same, p. 294.
[79] The same, p. 132.

Cossacks as numerous as hairs in the beard of Count d'Orsay, the famous contemporary dandy.[81]

This technique produces a satiric effect upon adults by destroying the subject's pretensions to genuine antiquity and romantic interest. At the same time it holds up to ridicule the contemporary reference by placing it in an incongruous setting. To children who lost the point of the satire, such books still possess the charm that comes with the unexpected recognition of the familiar among the unfamiliar.

Thackeray was to continue this type of writing in *Proposals for a Continuation of Ivanhoe* (1846)[82] and *Rebecca and Rowena* (1850)[83] and to culminate it in *The Rose and The Ring* (1855).[84] Meantime, the better to qualify himself for leading children into the world of fantasy, he embarked on a program of reading juvenile books—thriftily converting this domestic need into financial gain by reviewing a batch of them in *Fraser's Magazine* for April 1846.[85] At the beginning of 1847, he was rhapsodizing over the discovery of Hans Christian Andersen[86] and complaining that a gift of *Aunt Carry's Ballads for Children* had been sent to him just too late to be reviewed in "A Grumble about the Christmas Books," which he had written for *Fraser's Magazine* of January, 1847.[87]

If Thackeray felt himself responsible for his children's imaginative development, he was no less responsible for their religious education. In the first place, even left to himself he was not the man to have slighted this task, and moreover Mrs. Carmichael-Smyth would never have let it be slighted. Her reluctance to surrender Anny and Minny to him was due partly, of course, to her deep attachment to them; yet she also feared for their morals if they were reared in the aura of Bohemian bachelorhood. But the plan that she should live with them in London had been ended by her husband's refusal to leave Paris,[88] and she had to bow to their father's superior claim

[80] The same, pp. 16ff.
[81] The same, p. 86.
[82] The same, X, 463ff.
[83] The same, pp. 495ff.
[84] The same, pp. 307ff.
[85] "On Some Illustrated Children's Books," *Works*, VI, 567ff.
[86] *Letters*, II, 263.
[87] *Works*, VI, 581ff
[88] *Letters*, II, 238.

upon his daughters. She saw, however, that by this arrangement
her son was giving her hostages for his own moral improvement,
and her hopes seemed well-founded when, a few weeks after the
girls' arrival in Young Street, he wrote:

God Almighty grant I may be a father to my children. Continual thoughts of them
chase I don't know how many wickednesses out of my mind: Their society makes
many of my old amusements seem trivial and shameful.[89]

The change in Thackeray's ways was not really hard to effect.
We have seen his increasing discontent with bachelorhood, and at
least twice he wrote of a licentious widower rearing a daughter, in
both cases with evil results. Though Thackeray was no libertine,
he was so prone to guilt and remorse that he may well have been
dreaming up a Freudian fantasy about himself when in 1843 he included in his series of tales, *Men's Wives*, the story called "The
————'s Wife." It deals with a soldier-of-fortune from Renaissance Germany who drove his wife insane and then reared his orphaned daughter in an atmosphere of license until she became utterly
corrupt.[90] Furthermore, sometime between 1844 and the beginning
of 1847[91] Thackeray penned the second chapter of *Vanity Fair*, which
describes how Becky Sharp acquired her Bohemian standards of
life in the studio of her widowed artist father.

So Thackeray found no particular strain in becoming a church-
goer[92] and even reported he liked it. In fact, as we shall see,[93] he had
been for a time coming under the religious sway of William Brookfield and was about ready for this change of heart. It was probably
the chief cause of his gradual capitulation to the *mores* of Victorian-
ism. Moreover, he had never forfeited his essential faith; he had
merely been for some time unsympathetic toward established forms
of worship. Naturally he and Mrs. Carmichael-Smyth had had their
differences over this question.

In December of 1839, when Thackeray was most strongly under
Carlyle's influence, he had written his mother attacking the notion
that Hell and pain were inherent in the divine plan because of God's

[89] The same, pp. 255f.
[90] *Works*, IV, 486ff. See above, p. 106.
[91] See below, p. 137, n. 5.
[92] *Letters*, II, 262.
[93] See below, pp. 130f.

need to secure the moral improvement of man. Thackeray, probably following Carlyle, tried to argue that Good was eternal and non-material and that evil was inherent in matter and would end "when our bodies crawl away into worms or bud into daisys [sic] and buttercups, or explode into gas," at which point "our souls if they live cannot but be happy."[94]

Thereafter Thackeray seems to have avoided theological discussions with his mother until, in 1845, he made her his confidante over the problem of including in *Notes of a Journey from Cornhill to Grand Cairo* certain passages describing Jerusalem:

I am gravelled with Jerusalem, not wishing to offend the public by a needless exhibition of heterodoxy: nor daring to be a hypocrite. I have been reading lots of books—Old Testament: Church Histories: Travels and . . . find there was a sect in the early Church who denounced the Old Testament: and get into such a rage myself when reading all that murder and crime which the name of the Almighty is blasphemously made to Sanction: that I don't dare to trust myself to write.[95]

This blast roused in Mrs. Carmichael-Smyth the fear that her son was about "to preach heterodoxy." He answered her letter with a statement of his religious position as of that date:

Why do I love the Saviour? (I love and adore the Blessed Character so much that I don't like to speak of it) . . . But the Great Intelligence shines far far above all mothers and all sons—the Truth Absolute is God.[96]

But, on the other hand, his independent spirit—associating orthodoxy with all the oppressive schoolmasters and college dons of his unhappy younger days—could not stomach it.

I cant be hypocritical . . . which surely is a . . . sin against God. We don't know what orthodoxy is indeed. Your orthodoxy is not your neighbour's—Your opinion is personal to you as much as your eyes or your nose or the tone of your voice.[97]

A sort of simplified nature worship lay at the heart of the personalized religion which Thackeray had by this time developed, partly in protest at his mother's Evangelical asceticism. His religion seems to have been an amalgam of Wordsworthian pantheism, Coleridgean mysticism, Carlylese adaptations of German metaphysics, and the

[94] *Letters*, I, 403.
[95] *Letters*, II, 204. Written on July 26, 1845.
[96] *Letters*, II, 206. Written on August 2, 1845.
[97] The same, p. 205.

new Higher Criticism of the Bible. Thackeray's faith held as one of its articles that whatever was pleasant and beautiful was meant by God to be enjoyed. Writing to Mrs. Brookfield in 1848 about "the multiplied phenomena of nature," he inquired rhetorically: "Who is to say that we are to ignore all these or not value them and love them because there is another unknown world yet to come?"[98]

The application of such a religious philosophy to Thackeray's pleasure-loving way of life is clear, but it would hardly convince his mother that he was fit to rear his daughters. Hence his letters to her of the 1846–1857 period are sprinkled with superficial pieties and such semi-jocose interjections as the following: "I get painfully moral every day."[99] And when Mrs. Carmichael-Smyth began to get interested in *Vanity Fair* as its monthly numbers appeared during 1847, she apparently expressed some doubts as to the value for teaching religious principles of a book full of selfish characters. Thackeray, who certainly had an ethical but hardly any pious motive when he started the book, was ingeniously able to convince his mother that his great novel was a religious work. After discussing the godlessness of nearly all the characters,[100] he bursts into a prayer: "Save me, save me too O my God and Father, cleanse my heart and teach me my duty."[101]

Thackeray's writings had taught him to use his own moods, without actual insincerity, to control the reactions of his readers. It was a lesson he had undoubtedly learned from the women who had controlled his life and whose control he so resented—his mother not least among them. So just as he assumed a not insincere religious pose to convince her of his conversion, he was able to answer, with a flood of the deepest pathos, the heart-rending sorrow which she seems to have manifested at giving up Anny and Minny—possibly with the hope that she could get them back. Mrs. Carmichael-Smyth, it would appear, worked deliberately but indirectly on Thackeray's sympathies: she confided her grief in a letter to Anny, which the child of course read to her father, and to which he replied:

You know how it pains me to think of my dearest mother being unhappy; Anny read me your letter the other day: it brought back all sorts of early early times, and

[98] The same, p. 474.
[99] The same, p. 234. Written in March, 1846.
[100] See below, p. 137.
[101] *Letters*, II, 309. Written July 2, 1847.

induced an irresistible burst of tears on my part at which the Child looked as-
tonished. Her eyes were quite dry. They don't care: not even for you. They'll
have to complain some day of the same indifference in your Grand-grandchildren.[102]

Thackeray is skillfully deflecting Mrs. Carmichael-Smyth's aggression away from himself to Anny by weeping with his mother and
emphasizing the child's callous indifference. He is now ready to
carry out his true mission—an assertion of his mastery in his own
household:

But it is best that they should be away from you:—at least that they should be
away either from you or me. There can't be two first principles in a house. We
should secretly be jealous of one another: or I should resign the parental place altogether to you and be a bachelor still.[103]

Mrs. Carmichael-Smyth was thereafter reduced to a sort of guer-
rilla warfare, conducted by mail from Paris over minor issues. Thackeray had magnanimously granted her complete authority over his
daughters while they were under her roof, even when she was having
them treated by a homeopathic doctor in whom he had no faith.
He had only written: "As long as they stay with you, you must
tend them as you think best."[104] Yet in February of 1848, after the
girls had been under his charge for a year-and-a-half, he was—
ironically—telling his absent mother that he must follow his convictions, not hers in the choice of a doctor for Anny.[105]

Then there was the question of Mrs. Gloyne, an attendant of
Isabella's who had been transferred to the Young Street household
as a companion to old Mrs. Butler. That lady had been taken from
her daughter's care and given a home by her grandson, apparently
to compensate his mother for the loss of Anny and Minny by also
relieving her of a troublesome charge.[106] Now for reasons unknown,
mother and son both agreed that Mrs. Gloyne must go, but Thackeray insisted that she have the right to come in by the day to call
on Mrs. Butler, while Mrs. Carmichael-Smyth was for even refusing
her that satisfaction.

The major struggle between mother and son, however, was the
great teapot-tempest of the governess. The decision to have his

102 The same, p. 255.
103 The same, p. 255.
104 The same, p. 81. Written in September, 1842.
105 The same, p. 349.
106 The same, p. 288.

daughters reared in this manner had made possible the bringing of the girls to England without their grandmother. Seemingly Mrs. Carmichael-Smyth felt that by keeping a governess of her own selection in her son's household, she would have a deputy there to impose a certain measure of her control. Yet she was unwillingly blundering into the most serious domestic trouble faced by Thackeray between Isabella's insanity and the climax of the Brookfield affair. The author frankly admitted that a pretty governess would arouse his amorous instincts;[107] yet the sequence of plain women who held the position nearly all offended his instincts in one way or another: they were too vulgar, or too ignorant, or unable to cope with the high-spirited Anny. And the worst of all was the original holder of the position, Mrs. Carmichael-Smyth's nominee, Bess Hamerton, a woman from her own circle in Paris. Bess committed two unforgivable offences in Thackeray's eyes: she was both vulgar and Irish:

She's not an English lady—that's the fact. I sit entirely dumb and stupefied before her . . . The commonplaces in that enormous brogue kill me: and she falls to worrying Nanny as soon as I go out.[108]

After the novelist had discharged Miss Hamerton by what he doubtless considered a "frank, manly letter," made painfully tactful by his unwillingness to inflict pain, Mrs. Carmichael-Smyth's expostulations broke loose. Her letter is lost, but its tenor may be guessed from her son's reply:

Poor dear Bess used to raise my gorge with her coarseness, and rebukes of the children for being vulgar . . . I never said or did a rude thing to her; although you all give it against me. I persist that the proper thing in life is to call a poker a poker—Good God what was I to do when of her own accord she offered to stop the rest of the year with me?[109]

In the summer of 1847, however, Thackeray unwisely joined his household with his mother's in Boulogne for a vacation. Whether Miss Drury, with whom he was still satisfied, went too is unknown, but by October 21 a disagreement had broken out between Mrs. Carmichael-Smyth and her son which was serious enough to be

[107] The same, pp. 233, 288, 289, 306, 318.
[108] The same, p. 286. Written on March 16, 1847.
[109] The same, p. 288.

termed by him "the first difference . . . between me and my dearest Mother."[110] Writing to his brother-in-law on November 15, Thackeray reported that "the children are still with my mother at Paris, between whom and me still goes on the first dispute we ever had in our lives—about the governess question: on which I intend to have my own way."[111] Since this was two weeks after he had written his mother that he had already engaged a Miss Alexander as governess,[112] it would appear that she was nursing her grudge over the appointment, although in his first letter to Mrs. Carmichael-Smyth about the quarrel he had encouraged her to help him find a woman:

How to find a Governess is now the puzzle—if Charlotte Ritchie [a cousin living in Paris] would but come over for a little while . . . As for a Governess—I dont intend her to go into society and to appear among my friends only as little as possible—I'll wrap her up in precautions. I'll keep myself safe and clear in conscience regarding her.[113]

The inference is that Miss Drury had gone with the Thackerays to Boulogne and that Mrs. Carmichael-Smyth had resented her as her son's appointee in succession to Bess Hamerton. Therefore the had quarreled with Miss Drury and driven her away. Thackeray had naturally taken the younger woman's part, thus precipitating the quarrel with his mother. Significantly he twice uses the trick of building a backfire from his own grief to mollify Mrs. Carmichael-Smyth, a device which may be an extension into manhood of a boyhood trick: certainly he had often averted punishment by arousing her compassion for his suffering. Now he opened the subject in his October 21 letter by saying: "God forgive me if I have wronged you my dearest old Mother: the wrong has made two of us very miserable."[114] And in the following letter he addresses her as "my dearest old Mother—whom I have caused to suffer of late. God help us—which has had . . . the greater pain of the 2? This business has made me feel ten years older—and you dearest old Soul?"[115] Further to win over his mother's approval of Miss Alexander he pointed out the worthiness and need of her family and the fact that the mother

[110] The same, p. 318.
[111] The same, p. 324.
[112] The same, p. 321.
[113] The same, p. 318.
[114] The same, p. 317.
[115] The same, p. 322.

was "a tender grey-haired long-suffering looking woman, with something that reminds me of my dearest old Mother."[116]

Although Thackeray doesn't accuse Mrs. Carmichael-Smyth to her face of being jealous of any governess he might engage, the thought was clearly in his mind and had been there since he had contemplated engaging one before the renting of the Young Street house. For in the opening chapters of *Vanity Fair*, almost certainly written in the winter of 1845–1846,[117] Thackeray's interest in governesses is shown by his making Becky Sharp start her career as one. And his concern over his mother's jealousy over the governess he might engage is reflected in Mrs. Sedley's fears that Becky might ensnare her son Joseph. When her husband points out this danger to Mrs. Sedley, her first thought is to pack Becky off, and she is only dissuaded because,

though nothing is more keen, nor more common, nor more justifiable, than maternal jealousy, yet she could not bring herself to suppose that the little, humble, grateful, gentle governess, would dare to look up to such a magnificent person as the collector of Boggley Wollah.[118]

Yet on more than one occasion Thackeray had confided to his mother his fear of falling in love with a governess. Hence he was not at all averse to subtly rousing her jealousy, just as he had flagrantly raised it as a young man when he had written her of his infatuations for actresses. Unfortunately, however, circumstances caused this new jealousy to flame high in Mrs. Carmichael-Smyth's bosom.

Charlotte Bronte's *Jane Eyre* was published in October of 1847, the same month in which Thackeray reported the breach with his mother over Miss Drury. By December its phenomenal success was focussing public attention on its central situation of a governess who is nearly seduced by her employer. Yet he is unable to marry her because he is concealing a mad wife. The vague similarity between Rochester's situation and Thackeray's helped start the preposterous rumor that the latter had seduced his daughters' governess. Two other circumstances helped fan the flames of gossip. One was the general interest in Becky Sharp, a governess of doubtful morals, who

[116] The same, p. 322.
[117] See below, p. 137, n. 5.
[118] Chapter 4. *Works*, XI, 37.

was more than half through her career in the monthly numbers of the now popular *Vanity Fair*. Another was the fulsome dedication to Thackeray which Miss Brontë rather unwisely affixed to the Second edition of *Jane Eyre* in January, 1848.[119]

In 1856 Thackeray was to describe in a letter to Mrs. Sartoris the circumstances of this rumor:

> my relations some 7 or 8 years ago accused me too (no didn't accuse, only insinuated) that I had cast unlawful eyes on a Governess—the story of Jane Eyre, seduction, surreptitious family in the Regent's Park, and ... all grew out of this confounded tradition—and as I never spoke 3 words to the lady and had no more love for my Governess than for my grandmother, and as the calumny has been the cause of a never-quite-mended quarrel and of the cruelest torture and annoyance to me, whenever I hear of poor gentlemen and poor governesses accused of this easy charge, I become wild.[120]

That Mrs. Carmichael-Smyth gave some belief to this rumor will be seen in the next chapter, when we consider the conduct of Helen Pendennis in regard to her son's flirtation with Fanny Bolton.[121]

During the years 1846–1850 all the currents of Thackeray's life and work changed their course. The new household in Young Street and the readjusted relationship with his mother each played its share in the change. Equally important are a shift in his attitude toward the public which evolved during the writing of *The Book of Snobs*, a religious conversion of sorts, the success of *Vanity Fair*, and the affair with Mrs. Brookfield. All these events combined to effect the metamorphosis of Thackeray from a slashing satirist to a sentimental novelist.

Of course the seeds of sentimentality had been planted in him during childhood, and they had made a lusty growth after Isabella's collapse. Then they had lain fallow except when they had sent up such occasional green shoots as the description of the children's singing at Dundalk,[122] or the subsequently excised bit of nostalgia in *Barry Lyndon*.[123] The morality, too, was implicit in the satire, for Thackeray was always consciously placing himself in the great English satirical tradition that went back through Fielding to the

[119] *Letters*, II, 340f. n.

[120] Quoted by Gordon N. Ray, "New Light on Thackeray," *The Sunday Times* (London, May 29, 1949).

[121] See below, pp. 159f.

[122] See above, p. 101.

[123] See above, p. 109.

Elizabethans. This tradition had constantly avowed the moral function of satire. But most Victorians regarded satirists as godless men and knew little or nothing of that tradition. The idea of satire as morality was foreign to them, for they regarded morality with approval only if preached from a pulpit or by an avowedly religious author like Dickens. Hence the implicit morality in Thackeray's work before 1846 carried little weight with the public.

Hitherto Thackeray's satire had reached a relatively small group of discriminating readers; in fact he had known the dangers of addressing satire to the semi-educated, respectable women of England as early as 1841. That year, in *The Second Funeral of Napoleon*, he had accused his imaginary correspondent, a Miss Smith of London, of pouting on reading the book and exclaiming: "I will read no more of this Mr. Titmarsh; there is no subject, however solemn, but he treats it with flippant irreverence."[124] *The Second Funeral* had had such a miserable sale, however, that Thackeray had resorted to canvassing his friends to encourage its sale.[125] Consequently the fear that his satire would be badly received by women readers was, at that time, largely academic save that it reveals the presence, then as always, of his congenital fear of displeasing women.

With the success of *The Book of Snobs*, however, the problem became very real. The pretty little note which is reproduced verbatim in one of the papers called "Snobbium Gatherum,"[126] was probably an authentic letter to Thackeray under his pseudonym of Mr. Snob; certainly its style is that of a well-bred young Englishwoman of the day. Thackeray could hardly have imitated its flatness. The reputed authors were "three sisters from seventeen to twenty-two," worried lest he account them snobs. The basis of their fears was their having an earl as grandfather, keeping a coachman, owning plate, wearing crinoline, and possessing other symbols of snobbery in the Thackerayan canon. With charming gallantry he put to rest the young ladies' fears:

You Snobs, dear young ladies! I will pull any man's nose who says so. There is no harm in being of a good family. You can't help it, poor dears. What's in a name? What is in a handle to it?[127]

[124] *Works*, III, 421.
[125] *Letters*, II, 7.
[126] Chapter 39 in the original series, Chapter 32 in the revised series. *Works*, IX, 426f.
[127] The same, p. 428.

He concludes with the familiar defense, implied in the pen name "Mr. Snob," of his own snobbery: "I confess openly that I should not object to being a Duke myself; and between ourselves, you might see a worse leg for a garter."[128]

This *riposte*, jaunty and gallant as it is, discloses the fundamental weakness in Thackeray's satirical position. With his dislike of giving offense, he was not sure enough of the purity of his own motives or the exact identity of his goals to maintain always his satirical pressure. In this warfare on snobbery, for example, his underlying feeling of inadequacy—as we have seen—[129] was responsible for his dispassionate fairness. The fairness, in turn, drove Thackeray to examine his motive and wonder "am I a snob too?" Then he communicated this doubt to his readers with that insinuating sort of "I'm no better than you" which was really a means of warding off counterattack in advance. It was a way of saying, "I'm going to hit you, but I don't really mean it, so don't hit me back." Such attitudes are inevitably confusing. When one sees Thackeray screaming time and again to abolish peerages, court guides, and words like "aristocracy" from the language, yet insinuating that he too is bitten with the virus of snobbery, one's confidence in his attack is shaken.

Thackeray would defend himself if so taxed by citing his hatred of hypocrisy. Yet certain elementary precautions are not hypocrisy if they are taken by a man in the leading position which should properly be the satirist's. It would be fatal in a company commander to examine the state of his courage in the presence of his troops before a battle. It is certainly injudicious for a college teacher to protest to his class the ignorance of his subject which he feels, or for a priest to interpolate into his sermon a confession of his own sins. The fact that this habit was becoming a mannerism with Thackeray in *The Book of Snobs*, written just prior to the beginning of *Vanity Fair*, is significant. Apparently there were cracks in his satirical

[128] Compare the more familiar passage in "The Influence of the Aristocracy on Snobs" (Chapter 3. *Works*, IX, 273f.): "How can we help cringing to Lords? Flesh and blood can't do otherwise. What man can withstand this prodigious temptation? . . . There are only a few . . . philosophers who can behold the state of society . . . and mark the phenomenon calmly. And of these calm moralists, is there one, I wonder, whose heart would not throb with pleasure if he could be seen walking arm-in-arm with a couple of Dukes down Pall Mall?"

[129] See above, p. 96.

armor even before he undertook the great novel on which his reputation as a satirist largely depends.

It should not be forgotten that Thackeray's personal life, as well as his relationship to his public, was driving him into a style more calculated than his former satire to win readers. One must consider at this time the domestic reorientation of his life. It came, as we have seen, from having his daughters with him and from ingratiating himself with his mother to compensate for taking the children from her.[130] And finally there is William Brookfield's influence to consider.

Thackeray had in 1842 resumed an earlier acquaintance with this former member of the Apostles set from Cambridge. Brookfield had by now become curate of St. James's, Piccadilly, and of the District Church of St. Luke's in London. In spite of his eloquent sermons and genuine sympathy for the poor, Brookfield was not famed for his sanctity. But he was so cherished by his contemporaries as a wit that Dr. William Hepworth Thompson, master of his and Thackeray's old college, called him "by far the most amusing man I ever met, or ever shall meet."[131] It was undoubtedly this quality in Brookfield that appealed to Thackeray, although one suspects that the novelist may also have stayed in the curate's good graces partly to have an excuse for frequently seeing his wife. Brookfield was the sort of churchman who falls under the suspicion of his fellows for "levity and looseness of talk." At any rate the saintly John Allen, with whom Thackeray had wept over his own religious doubts at Cambridge long before,[132] made such accusations against Brookfield when Thackeray tried to enlist his aid in gaining for his friend a position as School Inspector. Thackeray's reply to Allen, although full of loyal indignation, is a masterpiece of sophistry. He interprets the so-called "levity" as "humourous, generous affectionate frankness."[133] Yet anyone who knows that Allen lived his religion twenty-four hours a day can see from Brookfield's letters to his wife and friends that the latter was full of levity in Allen's sense. On one occasion in 1840, he performed a burlesque of his former rector at Southampton before a group that included the erstwhile "Apostle," Richard

[130] See above, p. 122.
[131] Charles and Frances Brookfield, edd., *Mrs. Brookfield and Her Circle* (New York, 1905), I, 238.
[132] See above, p. 46.
[133] *Letters*, II, 280.

Chenevix Trench, who was in time to become Archbishop of Dublin. Trench laughed but thought the performance indecorous.[134] And in 1845 when Mrs. Brookfield wrote her husband of how she and her youthful Hallam cousins nearly exploded with laughter at some fatuity in a sermon by a country parson, Brookfield wrote back that he thought the scene a good substitute for Haymarket Theatre.[135]

Brookfield was a predecessor of the twentieth century clergyman to whom religion is a business. It is something to be conducted at high pressure during working hours and completely put out of mind during times of relaxation. Even to his wife his letters breathe no word of religious feeling; they are an endless chronicle of bustle— countless chores done, sermons written, other churchmen seen— usually for political purposes. But these letters also show that Brookfield only achieved real happiness in the hours when his church work was done and when he was relaxing with Thackeray and other boon companions. More significantly they never mention any serious talk during these times.

Therefore the reader stares hard at the text when Thackeray tells Allen how his "multiplied conversations" with Brookfield have done him such good that he thanks God "for his friendship as one of the greatest benefits ever awarded to me."[136] The novelist points out that this friendship with a leading author of the godless magazine *Punch* could well bring Brookfield under the suspicion of fellow churchmen.[137] Then Thackeray makes the amazing statement: "it is not Punch that has perverted Brookfield; but Brookfield has converted Punch!"[138] Thackeray explains that the cleric's influence on him has encouraged him to bring pressure on the magazine and make it abate its famous Anti-clerical campaign, which had been spearheaded by Douglas Jerrold.

In all of this, the pros and cons of Brookfield's true character are

[134] *The Cambridge "Apostles,"* ed. Frances M. Brookfield (New York, 1906), p. 32.

[135] *Mrs. Brookfield and Her Circle*, I, 168.

[136] *Letters*, II, 274.

[137] It speaks well for Brookfield's independence that his letters contain no hint of safe-guarding his career in the choice of friends. His wife showed more concern in this respect than he. On one occasion she quashed a scheme for them to share a house with the Duff Gordons, fearing that churchmen calling on Sunday might detect them engaged in buffoonery with their housemates, not to mention "Mrs. Norton, Mr. Thackeray, and Mr. and Mrs. Wigan" (*Mrs. Brookfield and Her Circle*, I, 253 f.).

[138] *Letters*, II, 274.

irrelevant. Seemingly he was a man doing the best he could in a profession which he never should have entered. The important thing is that a witty, worldly man like himself had effected a partial religious conversion in Thackeray when saintly people like Allen and Mrs. Carmichael-Smyth had failed. The answer is not paradoxical either. Even those Thackeray respected, like Allen, or loved like his mother, were identified with the sort of religious asceticism that was suspect to him as being alien to his temperament. Brookfield, on the other hand, was a man temperamentally akin to the novelist. Moreover, his religion stressed kindness and good works, made no strenuous demands, and did not insult Thackeray's intelligence.

This partial conversion is thus an important factor in starting Thackeray's long retreat from writing slashing satire to becoming the sentimental moralist of *The Roundabout Papers*. And thanks to the correspondence with Allen and others on the subject of Brookfield's levity, one can mark a spot in Thackeray's writing which reveals the turn insofar as important events, which inevitably take place gradually, can be marked in time.

With the success of *The Book of Snobs* and the consequent need of enlarging its scope to include snobs in all classes of society, it was clear that "Clerical Snobs" would have to be included. Yet when Thackeray came to this group, he spent more time praising the clergy than ridiculing it. He made such comments as:

Punch would not set up his show in a cathedral, out of respect for the solemn service celebrated within. There are some places where he acknowledges himself not privileged to make a noise, and puts away his show, and silences his drum, and takes off his hat, and holds his peace.[139]

The writer then turned and denounced the thousand newspapers who pilloried the clergy for every wrong it committed, hinting that the authors of such attacks did not often go to church. This was a sneer at Jerrold, with whom Thackeray was often on touchy terms. Almost immediately, there came an unmistakable allusion to Brookfield in a glorification of "the town clergyman threading the dirty stairs of noxious alleys upon his sacred business."[140] Then after a

[139] Chapter 11. *Works*, IX, 308. Published in May, 1846.
[140] The same, p. 309.

feeble jibe at the wealth of certain Irish bishops and a comment on the real poverty of most country vicars, Thackeray concluded:

But what is this? Instead of 'showing up' the parsons, are we indulging in maudlin praises of that monstrous black-coated race? O saintly Francis, lying at rest under the turf! O Jimmy, and Johnny, and Willy, friends of my youth! O noble and dear old Elias! how should he who knows you, not respect you and your calling? May this pen never write a pennyworth again if it ever cast ridicule upon either![141]

Nine months after the publications of this tribute to Brookfield and to Thackeray's other friends and relatives in the ministry, Allen's accusation of levity against his clerical friend put Thackeray on guard. Seemingly Brookfield's future was imperilled by the danger of his missing out on a valuable appointment at a time when his finances were low indeed. And the cause of the danger was Brookfield's supposed "levity," another name for the quality that in Thackeray could be termed "satire." Allen's stricture roused the novelist's anxieties lest his own literary future be imperilled by a set of humorous, scoffing values which was cherished both by him and Brookfield but was distrusted by many of their contemporaries. Now, added to this anxiety, was the stringent prospect that both his friend and that friend's wife—as beloved to him as to Brookfield—could be made acutely miserable by their upholding of those values.

Thackeray felt that the words of his recantation in *Punch* nine months before must be brought urgently to the attention of Allen and of others, both by letters and, if necessary, by some new and pointed allusion in *Punch*. So the statement in the first letter to Allen that Brookfield had converted *Punch* was reinforced by explicit reference to Thackeray's tribute to the church:

Two years ago I used only to make a passive opposition agst [sic] the Anti-church and Bishop sneers—last year I made an active one (Jerrold and I had a sort of war and I came off conqueror) and it was through his influence—It's something to stop half a million of people from jeering at the Church every week . . . It's William Brookfield who stopped it, and you may tell the Bench so and I wish you would— by his kindness, his tenderness, his honest pious life.[142]

[141] The same, p. 310. Francis was an uncle of Thackeray's and Elias the cousin in Dundalk (see above, p. 101). Jimmy was James White, Johnny was Allen, and Willy was Brookfield (*Letters*, II, 274n.).
[142] *Letters*, II, 274 f.

Four days later, Thackeray in alarm sent Allen some further arguments in Brookfield's favor, at the same time writing to Henry Reeve, a friend on the Privy Council, and begging his influence in countering Allen's charges. Furthermore, as luck would have it, a Reverend Alexander John Scott, who was both a Presbyterian minister and writer for the *North British Review*, chose this moment to write Thackeray a flattering invitation of some sort. In accepting, Thackeray saw a chance to ingratiate himself with a man who was both a churchman and a reviewer. So he assumed the role of the moralist jester, pointing out that "the business of grinning" grows "every day graver and graver." Then he calls Scott's attention to *The Book of Snobs* peroration in that day's *Punch* and suggests its tone is "rather fulsome" coming from "worldly men" like himself "stained with all sorts of dissoluteness." At the end he apologizes for thus making a father confessor of a comparative stranger: "I dont know why I preach this sermon to you, only that the matter is lying on my mind, and I am touched by your good opinion."[143]

Finally since Thackeray was, at the same time, penning the last chapter of *The Book of Snobs*, he gave new evidence of his change of heart in the oft-quoted peroration to that series:

To laugh at such is *Mr. Punch's* business. May he laugh honestly, hit no foul blow, and tell the truth when at his very broadest grin—never forgetting that if Fun is good, Truth is still better, and Love best of all.[144]

Then Thackeray became frightened lest he had gone so far in appeasing the righteous as to offend his unregenerate associates. He dashed off an explanation of his conduct to Mark Lemon, the editor of *Punch*, explaining that he hoped the peroration wouldn't "be construed in any unpleasant way by any other laborer on the paper." More specifically, he hoped that Jerrold wouldn't "fancy that I reflect on him now as he did in the Parson-Snob Controversy. I think his opinions are wrong on many points, but I'm sure he believes them honestly, and I don't think that he or any man *has* hit a foul blow in Punch."[145]

Thackeray then went on to explain his newly conceived role of Satirical-Moralist, the same role he was to assume five months later

---

[143] The same, p. 283.
[144] *Works*, IX, 493.
[145] *Letters*, II, 281f. Written on February 24, 1847.

when he convinced his mother that *Vanity Fair* was a moral book.[146]
He explains to Lemon that *The Book of Snobs* peroration applies to
"all of us who set up as Satirical-Moralists" and have "a vast multitude of readers whom we not only amuse but teach." He confesses
that "a few years ago I should have sneered at the idea of setting
up as a teacher at all, and perhaps at this pompous and pious way
of talking about a few papers of jokes in Punch—but I have got to
believe in the business, and in many other things since then."[147]

Technically speaking, Truth, in the sense of whole truth, has little
place in great satirical writing, for such writing must be selective;
it must emphasize the unfavorable aspects of the object under attack. And the code of the English gentleman and sportsmen who
hits "no foul blow" is far easier to apply to prize fighting than to
satire. Granted that such extremes as foul or sacrilegious epithets,
or references to personal misfortunes or calamities should not be
applied to one's adversary, it is hard to apply Thackeray's rule
without enormously weakening the primary function of satire—
to make ridiculous the values of which the satirist disapproves. So
with the words "Truth is best," Thackeray has prepared his way for
a retreat along the path that leads away from hard-hitting satire.
The retrogression was to be less apparent in *The Book of Snobs*, however, than in the great novel whose first monthly number appeared
before the lesser work had run its course in *Punch*. *Vanity Fair* is
the first manifestation of Thackeray's new concept of what a Satirical-Moralist should write.

[146] See below, p. 137.
[147] *Letters*, II, 282.

CHAPTER V

At the Summit

IN THE letter to Mark Lemon wherein Thackeray justified his new concept of the Satirical-Moralist[1] he avowed that

a solemn prayer to God Almighty was in my thoughts that we may never forget truth and Justice and kindness as the great ends of our profession. There's something of the same strain in Vanity Fair.[2]

Professor Ray has located the passage in *Vanity Fair* of which the novelist was speaking. If Thackeray's usual rule of barely meeting his deadlines holds good here, he would have written chapter 8 of *Vanity Fair* in the last week of February, 1847. And the letter to Lemon was written on February 24 of that year. In the aforesaid eighth chapter Thackeray begs from his readers the right not only to introduce his characters, but

to step down from the platform, and talk about them: if they are good and kindly, to love them and shake them by the hand; if they are silly, to laugh at them confidentially in the reader's sleeve: if they are wicked and heartless, to abuse them in the strongest terms which politeness admits of.[3]

It is clear that Thackeray was trying here to divide his characters into three groups: the good, typified by Amelia, who were to be loved, and Dobbin, who was to be shaken by the hand; the silly, typified by Jos Sedley, who were to be laughed at; and the wicked and heartless, represented by old Sir Pitt Crawley, and later General Tufto or the Marquis of Steyne. The first and last correspond to the white-and-black divisions into which readers expected to find characters divided, the third to the class of fools which Thackeray, consciously writing in the old tradition of English satire, claimed the right to pillory.

Unfortunately, however, the division of characters into three groups in no way explains all the persons of the book; the title sug-

[1] See above, p. 134.
[2] *Letters*, II, 282.
[3] *Works*, XI, 96.

gests that all—or nearly all—should be enslaved to vanity in one way or another, and the sub-title "A Novel Without a Hero" further suggests that none of the male characters will qualify as thoroughly admirable. A number of lesser persons like Mrs. Sedley fall into none of the three categories. And five months after attempting his threefold division, Thackeray told his mother that he wanted "to make a set of people living without God in the world . . . greedy pompous mean perfectly self-satisfied for the most part and at ease about their superior virtue."[4] Of all his characters, he conceded humility only to Dobbin and Briggs, though Amelia's was to come "when her scoundrel of a husband is well dead with a ball in his odious bowels; when she has had sufferings, a child, and a religion." Also Amelia has "LOVE—by which she shall be saved."

Here is an entirely unexpected conception by their creator of the characters in *Vanity Fair*, based not on a threefold division into good, bad, and foolish types, but on a twofold division into a proud majority and humble minority.

The answer is that neither Thackeray's explanation to the public nor the later letter to Mrs. Carmichael-Smyth really provides any overriding philosophy for *Vanity Fair*. Beyond what is implied in each of the three titles: "Vanity Fair," "A Novel Without a Hero," and "Pen and Pencil Sketches of English Society," plus the concept of himself as puppet-master, Thackeray had no such philosophy. His general plan for the book, whatever it was, had evolved at an undetermined date in the past, probably during the opening months of 1845, shortly before he had requested Colburn to send back to him "the commencement of a novel which I gave into your hands."[5] Thereafter *Vanity Fair* had grown organically like all of his novels as the characters began to live their own lives, refusing to be molded by their creator.[6]

[4] *Letters*, II, 309. Written July 2, 1847.

[5] The same, p. 198n. The letter is dated May 8, 1845. Thackeray had probably written the manuscript since the beginning of January, 1845, for bibliographical evidence suggests that much of it may coincide with the earlier chapters of the John Pierpont Morgan Library ms. of *Vanity Fair* (chapters 1–6, 8–13). Page 20 of this ms. contains in that earlier portion, which is probably the work recovered by Thackeray from Colburn, the probable reference to *Mrs. Caudle's Curtain Lectures* which survived in chapter IV of the finished book (*Works*, XI, 36). Since Mrs. Caudle only began running in *Punch* with the first number of January, 1845, Thackeray could hardly have referred to it before then.

[6] As Thackeray once explained to some friends: "The characters once created *lead me*, and I follow where they direct" (*Letters*, III, 438n.).

But any talk about Thackeray's characters is useless without a redefinition of his method of creating them, for a vast deal of misunderstanding has grown up on that score. The general truth has long been established that he drew from single living models many minor characters like Wenham in *Vanity Fair*, who is a portrait of Croker, or even an occasional intermediate figure like Foker in *Pendennis*, notoriously sketched from Andrew Arcedeckne.[7] More often, however, the intermediate characters are composites of more than one person. In fact Thackeray himself described how he developed them in talking about Captain Costigan in *Pendennis*, who is invented "out of scraps, heel-taps, odds and ends of characters."[8]

However, the sources from which he derived such scraps are so various as to deserve some consideration. Save in burlesques of fellow authors, Thackeray was notoriously not a borrower of characters from the books of others, though he often used historical figures like George Washington or General Webb. Inevitably such creatures—for example, Richard Steele and George Washington—although substantially like their originals, have a good deal of Thackeray himself in their make-ups. Other less well-known historical beings like Stoney Bowes[9] and one of the Marquises of Hereford[10]—it is uncertain which—serve as the nucleus of such re-named Thackerayan creations as Barry Lyndon and the Marquis of Steyne. The overwhelming majority of Thackeray's characters are drawn, however, not from people he read about but from people he knew.

This huge body of originals subdivides in turn into persons he merely knew and persons of his immediate circle—that is to say, his family and intimate friends like the Brookfields. Many of the characters have appearances, mannerisms, and speech habits drawn from people he merely knew, but their emotions and conduct in crises are those of their counterparts in his immediate circle. The reason for the distinction is clear: Thackeray did not know the persons whose externals he was copying well enough to picture how they might act at such times, but he could predict the feelings and

---

[7] Lewis Melville, *Some Aspects of Thackeray* (Boston, 1911), pp. 159–160; 168–170.

[8] "De Finibus." *Works*, XVII, 597.

[9] See above, p. 106.

[10] Melville, *Some Aspects of Thackeray*, pp. 154–159. Yet even in this case Thackeray knew a contemporary enough like Steyne so that he was able to write, of a dinner at Sir William Molesworth's, that he had sat opposite "the Marquess of Steyne" (*Letters*, II, 397).

conduct in those circumstances of people like the Brookfields, his family circle, or himself.

In fact, Thackeray, like any good writer of fiction, is his own best model, since any one of his deeply studied characters—even some of the female ones—draw at least some of their substance from aspects of his own character. Inasmuch, moreover, as he was a notably subjective writer, this dictum applies more to him perhaps than to any English writer of fiction before his day save perhaps Sterne. The subjectivity explains much about Thackeray's row of partly autobiographical heroes, and sheds interesting light on certain moments in the lives of women characters, such as Amelia's tears in the Foundling Church,[11] and Becky Sharp's hurling of the dictionary out of the coach window.[12]

The fact that Thackeray's major characters derive their emotions and conduct in major situations from the way he or some member of his intimate circle would feel or perform in such situations leads to another axiom. The interplay of these characters is pivotal in the sense that the action of the novels revolves about them. Many of these are mother-and-son dualisms based on that between Thackeray and Mrs. Carmichael-Smyth. This appears with little disguise in the interaction of Pen and his mother in *Pendennis;* it shows itself with more disguise in the tension between Mme. Esmond Warrington and her twin sons in *The Virginians*, or in that between Redmond Barry and his mother in *Barry Lyndon*. In *Vanity Fair* the emotional interaction between Thackeray and Mrs. Carmichael-Smyth provided a peripheral relationship between a major character, Amelia, and a secondary character, her son Georgy.

Since *Vanity Fair* has two parallel plots, each would necessarily have its pivotal relationship. To make more striking the parallelism, both are triangles: The immoral Becky passes up the love of a by-now relatively moral husband, Rawdon Crawley, for that of a profligate admirer, Steyne. Amelia passes up the love of a worthy admirer, Dobbin, for the memory of a worthless husband, George Osborne.

The first triangle is exceptional in being the only major relationship from the great novels of Thackeray's maturity which is not

[11] See above, p. 114.
[12] See below, pp. 141f.

based on personal experience. Neither he nor any member of his immediate circle appears to have been a Becky, or a Rawdon, or a Steyne, though Mrs. Butler may have furnished hints for Rawdon's aunt, Miss Crawley.[13] Only now at the peak of his inventive power could he have organized such a group revolving around his most memorable character, Becky Sharp. She could hardly have been any woman he knew intimately.

The vividness of Rawdon and Becky's *milieu* can be traced to Thackeray's long steeping of himself in the traditions of the fashionable Regency world, both from books, oral tradition, and boyhood memory. Moreover when he wrote the chapters in question he was newly admitted to the Blessington-D'Orsay circle, which preserved that world, with appropriate changes, in an early Victorian setting. Many of the fashionable beings in this "great world" were developed by Thackeray from background characters in his earlier fiction. Others were people whom he had written about in non-fictional works like *Mrs. Perkins' Ball*, *Our Street*, and *The Book of Snobs*, which are essentially portrait galleries. General Tufto is lifted bodily from *The Book of Snobs*,[14] to play his part as Rawdon's commanding officer. And Rawdon himself in his early, unregenerate phase is largely an evolution from Captain Legg in *The Book of Snobs*. For example:

There is many a young fellow of the middle classes who must know Legg to be a rogue and a cheat; and yet, from his desire to be in the fashion, and his admiration of tip-top swells, and from his ambition to air himself by the side of a Lord's son, will let Legg make an income out of him; content to pay, so long as he can enjoy that society. Many a worthy father of a family, when he hears that his son is riding about with Captain Legg, Lord Levant's son, is rather pleased that young Hopeful should be in such good company.[15]

What is stated passively in the case of Captain Legg is worked out in terms of action in *Vanity Fair*. George Osborne was born "of the middle classes"; he had every reason to know that Rawdon was, if not "a rogue and a cheat," at least a man who supported himself by gambling; George would "go to the deuce to be seen with a lord";[16]

---

[13] See above, p. 65.

[14] Chapter 9. *Works*, IX, 302f. A Lord Tufto who holds military command is mentioned in *Fitz-Boodle's Confessions* (*Works*, IV, 213).

[15] Chapter 23. *Works*, IX, 387f.

[16] Chapter 14. *Works*, XI, 169.

and his father wanted him to "mix with the young nobility."[17]

The odds and ends that went to make up the miraculous creation
of Becky Sharp are too numerous to be traced down in detail.[18] She
is made to start her life as the illegitimate[19] daughter of a Soho
artist and a French opera dancer so that she will be linked with
four social groups of dubious respectability. She is illegitimate, she
is half-French,[20] her mother was in the opera chorus, and her father
was an artist.[21] In the Bohemia of her childhood Becky learned
something far more dangerous than loose talk and loose morals. She
learned mimicry,[22] a talent which, in Thackeray's case as in her own,
led to those worse evils—levity and satire. Then like Thackeray
she was sent to a school which was the female counterpart of Dr.
Turner's at Chiswick, where he had been unhappy as a boy.[23] At that
school Becky picked up a veneer of artlessness, performing "the
part of the *ingénue*,"[24] just as the timid Thackeray had been an
unaggressive schoolboy. But, like Thackeray, Becky had acquired
a deep and lifelong resentment of pompous, pious, respectable, snobbish authority, particularly when it was symbolized by the female
tyrant, Barbara Pinkerton. And when she drove away from the
school for the last time, Becky signified her rebellion against that
authority, not only by throwing away that pedantic symbol, Dr.

[17] Chapter 13. The same, p. 155.

[18] One of Becky's historical forbears from the Regency period was Lady Morgan, whose
career has striking parallels to that of Thackeray's heroine. These have been traced by Mr.
Greig (*Thackeray: a Reconsideration*, p. 103).

[19] The fact that Thackeray had originally intended to make Becky illegitimate is shown
by a cancelled passage on page 8 in the *Vanity Fair* ms. in the Morgan Library. After citing
Becky's fictitious noble ancestry from the Entrechats of Gascony, the ms. reads: "Ill natured
persons however say that Rebecca was born before the lawful celebration of her excellent
parents' union." The cancellation was undoubtedly due to fear of Victorian prudery, though
Thackeray hints at the fact later when Mrs. Bute Crawley discovers how Becky's father had
not married Becky's mother "till a short time before her death." This circumstance would
imply that the child was at least conceived, and probably born before the marriage (Chapter
19. *Works*, XI, 230).

[20] Professor Ray has pointed out (*Thackeray and France*, p. 278) the overtones of Becky's
French parentage.

[21] Chapter 2. *Works*, XI, 15f.

[22] Chapters 2 and 17. The same, pp. 17 and 230.

[23] See above, p.7. The fact that Thackeray has his own boyhood in mind when he wrote
of Becky's rebellion on leaving Miss Pinkerton's is borne out by his sudden digression on the
beloved subject of the persistence into maturity of dreams about being whipped by schoolmasters (See above, pp. 8f.).

[24] Chapter 2. *Works*, XI, 17.

Johnson's *Dictionary*,[25] but by exploding verbally to Amelia in a declaration of freedom. It reminds one of those tirades against female domination to which Thackeray's autobiographical heroes were to become addicted.[26] The culmination of Becky's tirade: "*Vive la France! Vive l'Empereur! Vive Bonaparte!*"[27] proclaims her preference for French to English standards, both in morality and political freedom. The pious, English, bourgeois Amelia is properly shocked.

But the spirit of rebellion cannot normally explode outright. More often in fellow-rebels like Thackerays and Beckys it works through the spirit of mimicry and satire. So Becky has already shown her resentment of Miss Pinkerton by caricaturing her to the artist Sharp and his Bohemian friends.[28]

Three more times during the course of *Vanity Fair* Becky entertains ungodly persons by mimicking the pious, or the respectable, or the pompous. On one occasion she charms the wicked General Tufto with a sermon such as Rawdon might preach if she could carry out a mock threat of getting him a living.[29] And so she delights the equally wicked Lord Steyne with a burlesque of Lady Southdown's sermon when that redoubtable woman had simultaneously dosed Becky with tracts and physic in a bedroom at Queen's Crawley.[30] Finally our heroine mimics Jos Sedley to her two German student admirers after Jos has called on her at the Elephant Hotel in Pumpernickel.[31]

Not only was Becky's satirical propensity a reflection of Thackeray's own love for ridiculing pompous, respectable hypocrites; when he fancied himself under attack as a satirist he actually made of Becky a shield behind which to take refuge. At the same time as he was disclaiming any malicious satirical intent in the peroration of *The Book of Snobs*, he was striking the same chord in *Vanity Fair:*

[25] Significantly, Thackeray was never an admirer of Johnson. The descriptions of him in *The Virginians* (Chapters 26 and 32. *Works*, XV, 268 and 330) and *Philip* (Chapter 6. *Works*, XVI, 78) emphasize his boorishness and gluttony. The Roundabout Paper, "Small-Beer Chronicle," accuses him of snobbery (*Works*, XVII, 512).

[26] See above, pp. 73f.

[27] Chapter 2. *Works*, XI, 14.

[28] The same, p. 17.

[29] Chapter 30. The same, p. 365f.

[30] Chapter 41. The same, p. 528.

[31] Chapter 65. The same, p. 835.

Otherwise [he states] you might fancy it was I who was sneering at the practice of devotion, which Miss Sharp finds so ridiculous; that it was I who laughed good-humouredly at the reeling old Silenus of a baronet—whereas the laughter comes from one who has no reverence except for prosperity, and no eye for anything beyond success. Such people there are living and flourishing in the world—Faithless, Hopeless, Charityless: let us have at them, dear friends, with might and main. Some there are, and very successful too, mere quacks and fools: and it was to combat and expose such as those, no doubt, that Laughter was made.[32]

It is largely because Becky and Thackeray have so much in common that he grew fond of her despite himself. Then too he sympathized with her courage in facing the world with no original assets save her wits. Better still, she had fought her way to conspicuous social eminence, only to be driven thence by the powers of respectability. Thackeray too had begun his literary career with no capital but his wit and a few connections. He too had forced his way to eminence. Now having arrived there, he was worried lest his literary success be endangered by the forces of entrenched respectability. Nowhere is that fear more apparent than in the famous digression out of chapter 64 of *Vanity Fair*. There he lashes at Mrs. Grundy for not letting him tell the facts of Becky's career on the continent after her fall, when she was being snubbed by Lady Partlet, Lady Slingstone, and their ilk:

a polite public will no more bear to read an authentic description of vice than a truly-refined English or American female will permit the word 'breeches' to be pronounced in her chaste hearing. And yet, madam, both are walking the world before our faces every day, without much shocking us . . . It is only when their naughty names are called out that your modesty has any occasion to show . . . sense of outrage, and it has been the wish of the present writer, all through this story . . . only to hint at the existence of wickedness in a light, easy, and agreeable manner, so that nobody's fine feelings may be offended.[33]

Certainly Thackeray is identifying here Becky's respectable oppressors with his own. Yet there is an ambivalence in his feelings toward Becky, for she was both aggressive and artful. These were the two qualities that he distrusted in all mortals, and particularly in women. Becky's artfulness or guile, moreover, is the type that Thackeray especially dreaded, for it is a mask over the unquestioned

[32] Chapter 8. The same, p. 96.
[33] The same, p. 812.

sexual charm that is the real secret of her power. Much of the early part of *Vanity Fair* was written in the early months of 1846,[34] and in March of that year Thackeray wrote his mother about the governess question, which would have to be settled before his daughters could live with him that summer: "Unless I liked a Governess I couldn't live with her and if I did—O fie. The flesh is very weak, le coeur sent toujours le besoin d'aimer."[35] As we have noted before,[36] Thackeray seems to have been thinking about his own mother's suspicions of the governess he might engage when he depicted Mrs. Sedley's sudden jealousy at the thought of Becky's ensnaring Jos. Since in Thackeray's unflattering self-portraits of himself he constantly depicts himself as lazy, gluttonous, and physically unattractive, he partly conceives himself in the role of Jos when Becky sets out to trap that luckless gentleman.[37] And the episode is a working out of his fears that some enticing governess might use the advantage she would gain—should Thackeray succumb to her charms—to become his mistress and thereafter dominate his life. Perhaps it is significant that he breaks into French in describing those fears to his mother as if she were thinking of a Frenchwoman. Later, when the time approached, he thought of obtaining a German governess. Then flinching at that prospect,[38] he settled on a succession of British women with whom his troubles, though numerous, had nothing to do with the non-existent physical charms of the ladies in question. As long as they were under their father's roof, Anny and Minny never had a French governess.

In addition to his experience of French *grisettes*,[39] Thackeray had

[34] Stevenson, *The Showman of Vanity Fair*, pp. 143f.

[35] *Letters*, II, 233.

[36] See above, p. 126.

[37] This statement in no way rules out the possibility that Thackeray may have taken, as the chief prototype for Jos Sedley, some outsider such as his cousin, George Trant Shakespear. See Gordon N. Ray, "New Light on Thackeray," *The Sunday Times* (London, May 29, 1949). Professor Ray points out that new documents have permitted him "to identify Sedley as George Trant Shakespear." The apparent inconsistency between this identification and my parallel between Jos and the novelist himself is explained by the statement made above that the appearance, speech, and mannerisms of a character might be copied from those of an outsider, while he might behave in a crisis as Thackeray would fancy himself behaving if he were that outsider.

[38] See the letter to Mrs. Carlyle of July 25, 1846: "For God's sake stop Mme. Bolte. I have governidges calling at all hours with High Dutch accents ... And I don't want a Ger-woman." (*Letters*, II, 242f).

[39] See above, p. 68.

of course observed Englishwomen who resembled Becky in one way
or another, the most notable being one Theresa Reviss, a dependent
of the Buller family.[40] Yet here the resemblance derives from parallel
circumstances of life, or appearance, or personal mannerisms and
habits of speech. The inner Becky, as I have said, is not motivated
by emotional drives copied from those of any woman in Thackeray's
immediate circle. She is nevertheless an exceptionally vivid character
because she is compounded so largely of rebellion and guile. Thackeray understood the rebel's psychology because he was himself a secret rebel; he knew the trickster's because he dreaded it.

Like the Crawley circle, the Sedleys, Osbornes, and Dobbins had
counterparts among Thackeray's acquaintance. One recalls at once
the widely-known identification of Dobbin and John Allen.[41] Yet
many of these characters are to some extent developed from hints in
Thackeray's earlier work. In *The Great Hoggarty Diamond*, for example, the snob Milly Roundhead boasts of her acquaintance with
"Alderman Dobbin's gals."[42] In *A Shabby Genteel Story* Osborne and
Amelia's situation is foreshadowed in the elopement of a young officer
and his sweetheart. His regiment is ordered to Belgium, she follows,
and he is killed at Waterloo, leaving her to bear his child in a Brussels rooming house. A foolish English civilian, Gann, who happens,
like Jos Sedley, to be on hand, lives ever afterward in the false
glory of being a Waterloo veteran.[43] Curiously enough Gann in later
life behaves less like Jos than he does like Jos's father after the old
Sedley's business collapses and he fecklessly loses what is left in
shady and unsuccessful get-rich-quick schemes.[44]

But this is all relatively unimportant compared to the curious
parallels between Amelia, George Osborne, and Dobbin on the one
hand, and between Thackeray, his womenfolk and the Brookfields
on the other. The novelist once wrote to Mrs. Brookfield: "You
know you are only a piece of Amelia—My Mother is another half:
my poor little wife *y est pour beaucoup*."[45] Clearly, when Thackeray
caused Amelia to grieve over the loss of Georgy, he was thinking of

---

[40] *Letters*, I, clvii–clx.
[41] See Mudge and Sears, *A Thackeray Dictionary*, p. 301.
[42] Chapter 4. *Works*, IV, 40.
[43] Chapter 1. *Works*, III, 281ff.
[44] The same, pp. 286 f.
[45] *Letters*, II, 394. Written in June, 1848.

the sorrow his mother had felt at each separation from him and, more specifically, at losing Anny and Minny.[46]

Amelia's resemblance to Isabella is most pronounced during the Waterloo chapters. Thackeray's description of her agony at that time is clearly based on recollections of his wife's insanity, with its alternations between stupor and mania. Amelia "who for many hours had been plunged into stupor, raved and ran hither and thither in hysteric insanity—a piteous sight."[47] He momentarily identifies himself with Jos and puts that character into his place when, years before in Paris, he had been unable to continue the nursing duty and had turned it over to a woman: "Jos could not bear the sight of her pain. He left his sister in charge of her stouter female companion."

Mrs. Brookfield gives every appearance of having known from the outset the dubious honor Thackeray paid her in making her a prototype for Amelia. Only such knowledge could explain the great antipathy she had conceived for that hapless heroine. A woman of her charm and intelligence would inevitably resent any man's identifying her with such a weak creature. If she had not been told of the identification or guessed it, Mrs. Brookfield would hardly have taken the pains she went to in professing her dislike of poor Miss Sedley. In July of 1847 she confided to her husband that she wished Thackeray "would give Amelia a few more brains."[48] In October of 1847 she confided to Harry Hallam:

Mr. Thackeray has now got a 2nd Amelia, Lady Jane Sheepshanks. I wish he had made Amelia more exciting especially as the remark is he has thought of me in her character. And on the plan of 2 negatives making one affirmative, I suppose I may take the 2 dull ones of the book to make one Mrs. B. You know he told William that though Amelia was not a copy of me he should not have conceived the character if he had not known me—and though she has the right amount of antiphlegm and affectionateness she is really an uncommonly dull and a selfish character.[49]

On congratulating Thackeray when he ended the book, she pronounced it "altogether delightful except Amelia herself who provokes

[46] See above, p. 122.
[47] Chapter 32. *Works*, XI, 397.
[48] *Mrs. Brookfield and Her Circle*, I, 224.
[49] The same, pp. 247f.

one to a degree which makes one rejoice with real malice at her child's being preferred to her at last."[50]

In fact, though Thackeray had probably kept Mrs. Brookfield in mind as a prototype for Amelia from quite an early stage in the book, the resemblance grew as his affection for his friend's wife increased. When Amelia is in the first flush of her married love for George, she "had rather a mean opinion of her husband's friend, Captain Dobbin. He lisped—he was very plain and homely-looking: and exceedingly awkward and ungainly. She liked him for his attachment to her husband . . . and she thought George was most generous and kind in extending his friendship to his brother officer."[51] This was written in the summer of 1847, and one is struck by the similarities between Amelia's feelings toward Dobbin and Mrs. Brookfield's attitude toward Thackeray at that time. His devotion to her husband was at its height, but with her he was not yet very intimate. As Professor Ray expresses it: "deeply as he admired Mrs. Brookfield, he found little favor in her eyes. She was accustomed to admiration, and there was nothing as yet to center her attention on Thackeray's burly person. During these years he remained to her William's friend."[52]

It is chiefly in the later chapters of *Vanity Fair*, after Dobbin had returned from India, that one senses how certain biographical forces are at work. Thackeray's resentment over Mrs. Brookfield's coolness toward him was reflected in Dobbin's growing anger over Amelia's flaccid acceptance of his devotion. It is more than coincidental that the very same chapter wherein Thackeray absent-mindedly gave Amelia's maid the name of Mrs. Brookfield's maid, Payne,[53] is the one where Dobbin finally rebels at Amelia's petticoat tyranny. The passage is in the tradition of those where the autobiographic heroes emancipate themselves from dominating women:[54]

No, you are not worthy of the love which I have devoted to you. I knew all along that the prize I had set my life on was not worth the winning; that I was a fool, with fond fancies, too, bartering away my all of truth and ardour against your

[50] *Letters*, II, 395.
[51] Chapter 25. *Works*, XI, 293.
[52] *Letters*, I, xcvii.
[53] The same, p. 394. Chapter 66. *Works*, XI, 845.
[54] See above, pp. 73f.

little feeble remnant of love. I will bargain no more: I withdraw. I find no fault with you. You are very good-natured and have done your best; but you couldn't—you couldn't reach up to the height of the attachment which I bore you, and which a loftier soul than yours might have been proud to share. Good-bye, Amelia! I have watched your struggle. Let it end. We are both weary of it.[55]

The artistic flaw is comprehensible, however, when one recognizes that Thackeray is disgorging his resentment at Mrs. Brookfield's arms'-length treatment of his admiration. Only after the break-up of the affair three years later did he ever again speak of it in this manner.[56]

A similar resentment, pent up in this case for four years, came to light when Thackeray caused George Osborne to fall on the field of Waterloo with a bullet through his heart. I agree with Professor Stevenson's inference that the act was a symbolic killing of Brookfield,[57] the result of a subconscious jealousy which psychologically was in no way incompatible with the novelist's fondness for the cleric. Certainly there are parallels with Brookfield in Osborne's middle-class origin, his pride in associating with aristocrats, his vanity about his good looks, his bland acceptance of his wife's devotion, and his tendency to neglect her. Curiously, however, no surviving written opinion of Thackeray's betrayed any conscious resentment of these traits in Brookfield until long after *Vanity Fair* was finished. In fact the novelist reflected his own admiration of Brookfield when he depicted the homely, awkward Dobbin's devotion to Osborne, espcially when he caused Dobbin to say that in his youth he was "flattered beyond measure" by Osborne's preference for him and "was more pleased to be seen in his company than in that of the commander-in-chief."[58] This is curiously like a quotation from Lady Ritchie: "I have heard my father say that in his early days at Cambridge it was considered a distinction by the young men to be seen out walking with Mr. Brookfield."[59]

When Dobbin expostulates with his sisters for tearing other women to pieces with their gossip,[60] he is a mouthpiece for his creator, who was constantly harping on that topic. And Dobbin has a dry sense

[55] Chapter 46. *Works*, XI, 853.
[56] See below, pp. 171f.
[57] *The Showman of Vanity Fair*, p. 174.
[58] Chapter 61. *Works*, XI, 774.
[59] *Letters*, I, xcv n.
[60] Chapter 18. *Works*, XI, 218f.

of comedy which approximates Thackeray's satire. A vain, stupid officer described Dobbin as "a dry fellow . . . that took the shine out of a man in the talking line."[61] Finally, Dobbin's guffaws of ill-concealed mirth at Mrs. O'Dowd's boasts about the glories of her homeland[62] are, in thinly disguised form, Thackeray's constant ridicule of Irish snobbery.

Somehow the specific parallels in *minutiae* between Dobbin and Thackeray seem less important than the fact that Dobbin's rise is in ways like Thackeray's. I don't mean that there is likeness in the outward symbols of respect which both attained; Dobbin's winning command of a regiment was in no way parallel to Thackeray's financial success. But Dobbin's victory in transcending his ugly duckling beginnings to become the most respected man in his circle parallels the spiritual victory which Thackeray won over circumstances when he forced the world to recognize his merit.

Of course no one knowing Thackeray would expect him to glory much in his new fame. Anyone with his melancholy temperament would quickly locate the drawbacks which are inherent in greatness. Yet a trace of exultation sparkles through a letter he wrote to Isabella's rather unimportant brother: "The great people I know would make your eyes wink."[63] Addressing his mother, he characteristically denies any personal satisfaction in this new acquaintance, but he admits that he tells his grandmother of the lords he meets because "it delights the old lady hugely."[64] Here surely is the biographical basis of the Baroness Bernstein's joy when Harry Warrington is taken up socially by the nobility.[65]

Although Thackeray had no illusions that the friendship of such grandees as the Duke of Devonshire or Lord and Lady Ashburton would effect any miraculous change in his existence, he was pleased by his fine new connections. They satisfied long-starved fibres of his being. Appeased at last was his romantic love of titles, which he had been too honest to deny when he had written the famous passage in *The Book of Snobs* about the joys of walking with two dukes.[66] After getting to know a duke, Thackeray was to put the same

---

[61] Chapter 60. The same, p. 767.
[62] Chapters 28 and 32. The same, pp. 343 and 399.
[63] *Letters*, II, 305. Written on June 21, 1847.
[64] The same, p. 309.
[65] *The Virginians*, chapter 28. *Works*, XV, 288.
[66] See above, p. 129, n. 128.

thought as Mr. Snob had expressed into the mouth of his Mr. Brown in 1849: "I own that to walk with a lord, and to be seen with him is a pleasant thing. Every man of the middle class likes to know persons of rank. If he says he don't—don't believe him."[67]

Furthermore, a suspicion was quickly confirmed that the conversation of the nobility can be as insipid as table-talk at Osborne Senior's dinners or the persiflage at Mrs. Perkins's ball. Yet Thackeray knew that, on the other hand, he could often find in the great world the stimulating talk between men and women that he had previously found only in a few houses like the Procters'. So our author, speaking through Mr. Brown, observed that "there is no more dangerous or stupefying position for a man in life than to be a cock of small society." Brown sets "it down as a maxim that it is good for a man to live where he can meet his betters intellectual and social."[68]

Thackeray was more inclined to accept *entrée* into the great houses because he wanted to compensate for the old feeling that losing his patrimony had pushed him out of his class. The feeling was in fact partly illusory, since he had never in his worst poverty severed friendship with men like Milnes or the Bullers. Yet he seems to have feared that the fashionable world, on hailing *Vanity Fair*, would regard its author as a man whom they might "take up," like Carlyle or Dickens, on the score of his genius and in spite of plebeian origin. Thackeray wanted to make clear that such were not his circumstances and that he had a right to be accepted into great houses on the basis of his birth as much as of his talent. Hence at this period his mother's patrician bearing was a great asset. On beginning a very promising correspondence with Lady Castlereagh, who was desirous of "taking him up" socially, Thackeray writes that he would "be proud to show her ladyship" his mother and "ask whether among all the Duchesses and Empresses of this life there are many much finer ladies."[69] He complimented Mrs. Carmichael-Smyth herself on the testimony she and her husband provided to his aristocratic lineage. Although "the great people" seemed surprised "that I am a gentle-

---

[67] *Works*, VIII, 284.
[68] The same.
[69] *Letters*, II, 459. Written on November 28, 1848.

man—they dont know who I had for my father and mother ... I have never seen finer gentlefolks than you two—or prouder."[70]

Yet for him to take up the new connections meant, as Thackeray well knew, countless charges of snobbery by old friends who had admired him as the castigator of snobs. This whole situation was given tangible form when he went with Leech, Lemon, and other *Punch* associates to Drury Lane to see an exhibit of horsemanship. A party containing Count Dorsay, Lord Chesterfield, and Lord Granville invited Thackeray "very good humouredly" into their stage box and he went, only to torture himself by thinking that Leech and Lemon were probably saying, "That d—— lickspittle Thackeray." Yet he pointed out in his diary that he "didn't kiss anybody's tails at all."[71] Without knowing all the circumstances, one suspects that Thackeray mismanaged the affair.

In the first place, his success in avoiding outward marks of sycophancy is beside the point. In the second place, he was snobbish in accepting an invitation that did not include his companions, and he was really conscious of that fact. Yet he developed an ingenious excuse for himself. In fact, one can see here in mature form one of Thackeray's boyhood patterns of behavior, that of wanting something, feeling he shouldn't have it, but electing to have it anyway with the comforting prospect of atonement by the device of appropriate penance. In this case the penance was the exquisite pain of thinking that Leech and Lemon were engaged in sinister talk about him behind his back. Conceivably they thought nothing of the matter.

So the course of Thackeray's correspondence from some time in 1847 until well on in 1849 is an endless business of steeling himself against the pain of being thought a snob so that he could enjoy the fruits of success. Whether or not he really was one is a question over which gallons of ink have been shed—unnecessarily it seems to me— since the issue inevitably depends upon the critic's definition of the almost indefinable word "snob." Certainly Thackeray was not a tuft-hunter of the egregious kind that he had done so much to bring into disrepute. The important question is, what effect did the whole

[70] The same, p. 334.
[71] The same, pp. 359-360. Written on March 10, 1848.

complex of association grouped around the question of social distinctions have upon him?

Here the testimony of Thackeray's letters should be taken only after considering his feeling toward the correspondent to whom he is writing. For example, Edward FitzGerald, the man who was still officially, if not in fact, his dearest friend, had renounced snobbery and all its ways. Now Fitz was in danger of believing Carlyle's reports that Thackeray had become a tuft-hunter. Hence it was necessary for the novelist to register with FitzGerald forthright denial of snobbish traits. "All that about being a Lion is nonsense! I cant eat more dinners than I used last year and dine at home with my dear little women three times a week: but 2 or 3 great people ask me to their houses: and Vanity Fair does everything but pay."[72]

On the other hand, Mrs. Carmichael-Smyth would not see the problem as one of class "turn-coatism" so much as one of morality and religion. Since she regarded the aristocracy as worldly and corrupt and was afraid her son would too easily conform to its ways, he bombarded her with protestations that he was unchanged. Though he lived "with all sorts of great people . . . their flattery has not turned" his head.[73] Later he assures her: "I don't care a straw for the great people I find: only knowing them makes me a little more impatient of the airs of the small great."[74] For he has "many serious thoughts and will try and not be vain of praise."[75] In the combined exhaustion and exhilaration of finishing *Vanity Fair*, he clings closer to his mother as his moral and religious support:

May God Almighty keep me honest and keep pride and vanity down. In spite of himself a man gets worldly and ambitious in this great place: with every body courting and flattering. I am frightened at it and my own infernal pride and arrogance . . . all of a sudden I am a great man. I am ashamed of it: but yet I cant help seeing it—being elated by it trying to keep it down . . . I'll go and take a ride and think about my mother and my dear little women.[76]

Thackeray also kept in mind the need of reassuring Mrs. Carmichael-Smyth that his social triumphs were not making him neglect

[72] The same, p. 365. Written in March, 1848.
[73] The same, p. 351. Written on February 5, 1848.
[74] The same, p. 374. Written on April 14, 1848.
[75] The same, p. 383. Written on June 5, 1848.
[76] The same, p. 401. Written on July 18, 1848.

Anny and Minny. He was proud of having "refused Lord Holland himself on Sunday to dine with them."[77] The delicate equilibrium of authority between the novelist and his mother, which had shifted in Thackeray's favor after the battle of Boulogne,[78] continued so favorable to him that in October, 1848, he risked the experiment of having her and Major Carmichael-Smyth move into his house. The pendulum had swung, and he confessed to Mrs. Procter: "my mother is coming soon, thank Heaven, to take the command over me."[79] Having tasted for more than two years the joys of ruling a household, he was tired of the vexatious problems involved and welcomed turning them over to his mother, even though it involved also turning back some of the precious sovereignty he had wrested from her.

Significantly Thackeray did not attempt the dangerous experiment of keeping a governess in the same house with his mother; in fact he turned away a woman who had been about to take the position.[80] Apparently Mrs. Carmichael-Smyth herself carried on the education of her granddaughters until the end of March, 1850, when she and her husband faded back across the channel and Miss Trulock, most satisfactory of the Thackeray governesses, took over.[81]

That Mrs. Carmichael-Smyth kept thoroughly in her place during this sojourn in her son's house is indicated by circumstantial evidence. He never breathed to Mrs. Brookfield, to whom he was then in the habit of pouring out every detail of his life, any criticism

[77] The same, p. 335. Written on January 7, 1848.

[78] See above, pp. 124f.

[79] *Letters*, II, 428.

[80] The same, p. 439.

[81] The circumstances of this shift are hard to determine, since little is said about it in *Letters*. Mrs. Carmichael-Smyth was very ill with rheumatism at Young Street in November, 1849 (the same, II, 609). It is impossible to say whether she left London immediately after this illness as Professor Ray suggests (the same, I, lx), but nothing is said of her departure until Thackeray wrote from Paris on March 19, 1850, regarding prophecies of a revolution there, "I shall be across the water before that event: and my old Folks will be here instead" (the same, II, 653). On his return a week later Thackeray wrote Mrs. Brookfield: "my mother will come and see you to day," as if she were making her farewell calls. Nothing more is said of her presence in London until she came over in 1851 to hear the *English Humourist* lectures. By May of 1850 Miss Trulock is mentioned for the first time, but she was already an accepted member of the Thackeray family circle and was thinking of accepting a more lucrative offer (the same, p. 668). Probably Mrs. Carmichael-Smyth left London at the end of March and Miss Trulock took up her duties about that time.

of his mother for attempting to dominate him or interfere with his command of his daughters. On the other hand, he confessed to Mrs. Brookfield that Mrs. Carmichael-Smyth "is awfully afraid" of him.[82] His constant complaint is her gloominess, so deep that he "would die rather than make a joke to her."[83]

In fact, by May, 1849, after seven months of joint living, Thackeray was so bored with his mother's doleful ways that he was actually encouraging her to take the children to Paris, a thought which delighted her. He confided to Mrs. Brookfield that "the present state of home society has become intolerable to me from no fault of anybody's but my own sort of oversensitiveness and impatience with people who have no sense of humour—and though I shall grumble and *poser* myself in a pathetic attitude selon mon ordinaire, I shant be very unhappy."[84]

Though characteristically Thackeray took most of the blame himself, it is clear that the restored living arrangement could not long endure. It was solved temporarily by giving the girls to Mrs. Carmichael-Smyth in July. She was to take them for their vacation trip—not to Paris but to Wales. They were brought back from there hastily by Thackeray's nearly mortal illness in October. After that his long convalescence in Brighton kept him and his mother at arm's length until November, when he returned and she came down with rheumatism.

On Christmas evening, after a day which Thackeray would obviously have passed in the bosom of his family, he sat down to write his stint of *Pendennis* and suddenly exploded. The next day Mrs. Brookfield read the results of the explosion, a defense of his own middle-of-the-road brand of Christianity.[85] He blasts characteristically at excesses of fanaticism in both "high and low Church." One passage in particular points to exasperation against the need for daily tolerating his mother's piety, especially on Christmas Day when she would have been twice to church. The following is in part a quotation from her:

How good my [God] has been to me in sending me a back-ache—how good in taking it away: how blessed the spiritual gift which enabled me to receive the sermon

[82] *Letters*, II, 744.
[83] The same, p. 525.
[84] The same, p. 531.
[85] See above, pp. 121f.

this morning—how trying my dryness at this afternoons discourse etc.—I say it is awful and blasphemous to be calling upon Heaven to interfere about the 1000 trivialities of a man's life—that [God] has ordered me something indigestible for dinner (which may account for my dryness in the afternoon's discourse.) To say that it is Providence that sends a draught of air behind me which gives me a cold in the head, or superintends personally the action of the James's powder which makes me well.[86]

His mother's assumption of intimate and constant communication with the Deity rankled Thackeray so continuously that he wove it into the character of Mme. Esmond Warrington, the least attractive of Mrs. Carmichael-Smyth's literary antitypes, at the beginning of *The Virginians* (1857):

To be for ever taking Heaven into your confidence about your private affairs, and passionately calling for its interference in your family quarrels and difficulties . . . to know precisely its intentions regarding . . . others who differ from your infallible opinion—this was the schooling which our simple widow had received.[87]

Clearly the time was at hand when Mrs. Carmichael-Smyth would do well to return to Paris, as she of course must have perceived as well as her son. Since his victory in the Battle of Boulogne long before had stopped her from active interference in his life, she could only look sad in mute protest at his heterodox creed, his worldly pursuits, and the obvious fact that Mrs. Brookfield, and not she, was the emotional center of his life. It was hard then that her sad looks should irritate him, even if they did flatter his ego at the same time by reassuring him of her love. When she had come to make her home with Thackeray in the autumn of the year before, he had confided to Mrs. Brookfield:

I look at her character, and go down on my knees as it were with wonder and pity. It is Mater Dolorosa, with a heart bleeding with love.[88]

By the following April he was using the same term with a note of irony when he complains that he can never joke at home before the old people: "I think the dear old Mater Dolorosa gloomifies me more than the old gentleman."[89]

In the winter of 1851, when Mrs. Carmichael-Smyth was again

[86] *Letters*, II, 615.
[87] Chapter 5. *Works*, XV, 51f.
[88] *Letters*, IV, 419.
[89] The same, II, p. 525.

living in Paris and Thackeray was visiting her with his daughters, she is still called "Mater Dolorosa" with the same overtone of affectionate annoyance. On that occasion she looked so particularly sad that Thackeray tried to atone for his fancied neglect by a display of filial affection. Suddenly a fiddler appeared and the old lady brightened instantly. Her son concluded "that women with those melancholy eyes and sad sad looks are not always so melancholy as they seem . . . they have consolations, amusements, fiddlers." With one of those flashes of insight into his own weaknesses that grew moreo cmmon with age, Thackeray decided that such sad women "are not perpetually thinking of their children."[90]

Pendennis, Thackeray's next major novel after *Vanity Fair*, centers its action on the mutual love between Helen Pendennis and her son, Arthur.[91] That Helen Pendennis's character was modeled on that of his mother was so well known that Thackeray alludes to it in his letters casually as an accepted fact,[92] though Mrs. Carmichael-Smyth—defensively—professed to dislike the identification, just as Mrs. Brookfield had resented the earlier identification of herself with Amelia. We have seen also that Arthur is one of Thackeray's autobiographic heroes, though there are obvious differences between himself and his creator.[93] The second most important pivotal action of *Pendennis* comes from the struggle between Helen Pendennis and her brother-in-law, the Major, for the soul of the young man. Should he become a saint, as his mother desires, or a worldling, as his uncle wishes? Now even Major Pendennis, curiously, possesses a few incidental autobiographic traits. As his maker confided to Mrs. Brookfield, "my vanity would be to go through life as a gentleman—as a Major Pendennis."[94]

Arthur Pendennis, the young man, is a part-portrait of the Thackeray of twenty years before. But Arthur Pendennis, the groping soul struggling to choose between two ways of life, is clearly the Thackeray of 1848, beset with the temptations that came upon him with the fame of *Vanity Fair*.[95] His mother's influence during this

[90] The same, p. 747.
[91] See above, p. 5.
[92] *Letters*, II, 457; III, 13.
[93] See above, p. 38.
[94] *Letters*, II, 511. Written in March, 1849.
[95] See above, p. 152.

struggle clearly parallels Helen Pendennis's influence on her son. And Major Pendennis is at heart the Thackeray who would have confronted society in another twenty years had he allowed the easygoing, worldly side of his character to go unchecked.[96]

This aspect of *Pendennis* presents no striking novelty to the student of Thackeray's life and work. But so far as I know, no one has observed the parallel between the dates of the composition of that book and the dates of Mrs. Carmichael-Smyth's sojourn in her son's house. The first three chapters of *Pendennis* were written between August and October of 1848. During that time Thackeray eagerly awaited his mother's coming to Young Street and, at the end of it, he received her under his roof. During the remainder of the autumn, while she was domiciled with him, he deified her as Mater Dolorosa and the angel interceding for him in heaven. By his own confession the original Mater Dolorosa passage[97] was a *réchauffé* of something already inserted into *Pendennis*. It is easily identifiable as the statement that "almost every man" knows at least a few "women in whose angelical natures there is something awful, as well as beautiful, to contemplate; at whose feet the wildest and fiercest of us must fall down and humble ourselves, in admiration of that adorable purity which never seems to do or to think wrong."[98]

A little later, Thackeray came to relive those most sacred moments of his life—his homecomings from boarding school[99]—at the time when he depicted them in the life of Arthur Pendennis. As he wrote, his emotion was doubly surcharged, for he had just relived that homecoming experience when he witnessed the reunion of his mother with Anny and Minny under his roof in Young Street.

What passed between that lady and the boy is not of import. A veil should be thrown over those sacred emotions of love and grief. The maternal passion is a sacred mystery to me. What one sees symbolized in the Roman churches in the image of the Virgin Mother with a bosom bleeding with love, I think one may witness (and admire the Almighty bounty for) every day.[100]

[96] Here, as in the case of Jos Sedley, there is no inconsistency between Major Pendennis's reflecting inwardly certain tendencies in Thackeray himself, while outwardly he was drawn from a real-life prototype. Cf. Ray, *New Light on Thackeray*.

[97] See above, p. 155.

[98] Chapter 2. *Works*, XII, 18.

[99] See above, p. 16.

[100] Chapter 2. *Works*, XII, 25.

Helen Pendennis, also, testifies to the ambivalent nature of Thackeray's worship of his mother at such times as she didn't bore him with gloom or nag him with jealousy. He expected her to worship him in return. Because of this expectation, he saw to it in his book that Helen "worshipped . . . [Arthur] with an ardour which the young scapegrace accepted almost as coolly as the statue of the saint in St. Peter's receives the rapturous osculations which the faithful deliver on his toe."[101] The pretense of jocosity here, the passing of the blame onto the boy for receiving the idolatry, does not hide one fact. Thackeray harps too often on that note through his middle life to convince anyone that he was immune to the joys of idolatry from women. There is an undercurrent of seriousness in his jocosity when he teases his mother for regarding him as a "prodigy of a son."[102] Before too many years he was to let her, in the role of Rachel Castlewood, fall on her knees before him, in the role of Henry Esmond, and say, "Let me . . . worship you."[103]

But resemblances between what Thackeray wrote in letters about his mother and what he wrote at the same time in *Pendennis* about his hero's mother go beyond the mere deification of the two women. Helen, like Mrs. Carmichael-Smyth, conveniently exemplifies the beloved doctrine that a woman sufficiently dear to Thackeray and possessed of enough social grace, could be as much a lady as any peeress. The wording of the letter which he was to send Lady Castlereagh during the following month praising his mother[104] is followed almost verbatim in a passage from *Pendennis*. It occurs when John Pendennis steps into the county assembly with his wife on his arm "as much as to say, 'Look at that; my lord, can any of you show me a woman like *that?*' "[105]

As that novel progresses and Helen Pendennis is depicted in an increasingly unfavorable light, one can not help remembering one's chronology. The story was being written as Mrs. Carmichael-Smyth became constantly less welcome in her son's house, and she was becoming ever more jealous of her son's devotion to Mrs. Brookfield. The second sequence of chapters in which Helen plays a dom-

---

[101] The same, p. 19.
[102] *Letters*, II, 288.
[103] Book III, chapter 2. *Works*, XIII, 332.
[104] See above, pp. 150f.
[105] Chapter 2. *Works*, XII, 18.

inant part is that of the period between her son's disgrace at Oxbridge and his leaving home to make his fortune in London.[106] During that time she is like a saint to Pen except when he flirts with
Blanche Amory. Then the slight jealousy which she displays is an
excusable trait, as Thackeray feels, in view of the young lady's unworthiness.[107] However, Helen is cruel to Laura Bell when that
heroine quite properly refuses Pen's condescending offer of marriage.[108] The proposal was instigated by Helen herself and did not
represent a conquest over her jealousy; rather it was an effort to
hold on to her son by lashing him to a bride whom she had reared
as a virtual extension of her own personality.

Helen appears in her worst colors in the Bolton affair, when she
jumps to the conclusion that the porter's daughter who nurses Pen
in his illness is his mistress. She not only treats Fanny with relent-
less cruelty but intercepts her letter to Pen. The sickness is a reflection of Thackeray's nearly mortal illness in the autumn of 1849
when his mother, like Helen, rushed to her son's sickbed. Thackeray,
however, unlike Pen had no tender hands like Fanny's to nurse him
pending his mother's arrival: that role was performed by his servants
and Harry Hallam. Mrs. Brookfield, a formidable respecter of the
proprieties, only dared once to peek through the open door of the
sickroom. Possibly his development of Fanny into a nurse for Pen
in his solitary fever was a subtle rebuke to that lady for not filling
the same role for him: he later twitted her delicately on that score
and on her coy refusal to let him visit her when she was ill.[109]

Now in *Pendennis* Laura Bell seconds Helen in her jealousy of
Fanny. Quite possibly that attitude reflects a suspicion by Thackeray
that Mrs. Brookfield would present a solid front of jealousy with
Mrs. Carmichael-Smyth if he should take a mistress. Such a possibility was in his mind at this time to the extent that he could twit
Mrs. Brookfield before attending a ball in Paris, where he expected
to "meet all the pretty actresses of Paris." As he put the situation:
"Let us give a loose to pleasure. If it's wrong to attach oneself to
honest women: let us go & live with outlaws."[110] Fanny Bolton is

[106] Chapters 21–27. The same, pp. 248–348. Written in April and May, 1849.
[107] Chapter 24. The same, p. 298.
[108] Chapter 27. The same, p. 348.
[109] *Letters*, II, 658. Written on March 29, 1850.
[110] The same, p. 749. Written in February, 1851.

a symbol of such a hypothetical mistress, although Helen's jealousy of her was largely inspired by Mrs. Carmichael-Smyth's conduct in the teapot-tempest of the governess.[111]

The Bolton affair and the following incident of *Pendennis*, where Pen hastens his mother's death by denouncing her jealousy, were written in May and June of 1859, when Mrs. Carmichael-Smyth had moved back to Paris. In the extremely emotional chapter describing Helen's death, one senses a vicarious working out in fiction of all the tensions between Thackeray and his mother over the past few years. His recent resentment at her Mater Dolorosa looks is reflected in the moment when Helen first sees Pen before the fatal quarrel:

The spectacle of her misery only added somehow, to the wrath and testiness of the young man. He scarcely returned the kiss which the suffering lady gave him: and the countenance with which he met the appeal of her look was hard and cruel. 'She persecutes me,' he thought within himself, 'and she comes to me with the air of a martyr.'[112]

But Pen's denunciation of poor Helen, which takes place immediately afterward, belongs to the tradition wherein Thackeray's heroes proclaim their independence of feminine domination.[113] Yet it has special reference to the quarrel with his mother in Boulogne during the summer of 1846.[114] Then he had, in all probability, defended the governess just as Pen defends Fanny from his mother's jealousy:

It is you that are cruel, who attribute all this pain to me: it is you who are cruel with your wicked reproaches, your wicked doubts of me, your wicked persecutions of those who love me,—yes, those who love me, and who brave everything for me, and whom you despise and trample upon because they are of lower degree than you.[115]

Finally it seems as if Thackeray were denouncing his mother for the jealousy which he suspected her of harboring toward Mrs. Brookfield. Immediately afterward comes the tender reconciliation scene between Helen and her son, and it expresses Thackeray's remorse

[111] See above, p. 124. For these suggestions I am indebted to Professor Ray's "The 'Unwritten Part' of 'Pendennis' and 'Henry Esmond,'" *The Listener*, London, August 4, 1949, p. 197.

[112] Chapter 57. *Works*, XII, 730.

[113] See above, pp. 73f.

[114] See above, p. 124.

[115] Chapter 57. *Works*, XII, 730f.

for any pain he fancied himself to have inflicted on his mother. Finally, her death, which follows hard upon the reconciliation, is in the best vein of the maternal apotheoses:

Ever after, ever after, the tender accents of that voice faltering sweetly at his ear— the look of the sacred eyes beaming with an affection unutterable—the quiver of the fond lips smiling mournfully—were remembered by the young man. And at his best moments, and at his hours of trial and grief, and at his times of success or well-doing, the mother's face looked down upon him, and blessed him with its gaze of pity and purity, as he saw it in that night when she yet lingered with him; and when she seemed, ere she quite left him, an angel, transfigured and glorified with love—for which love, as for the greatest of the bounties and wonders of God's provision for us, let us kneel and thank Our Father.[116]

Here, I suspect, Thackeray is atoning for his mother's departure earlier that year from his roof to her own.[117]

The kinship between Laura Bell and Mary Carmichael should also come into any discussion of Helen Pendennis. The identity of the two women during Mrs. Carmichael's earlier and more ingenuous stage of life is beyond doubt. And Laura's payment of Pen's college debts corresponds, we have noted,[118] to Mary's financial rescue of Thackeray after Isabella's insanity. But curiously Thackeray had been seeing a good deal, during a visit to Paris in February, 1849, of the later and less attractive Mary Carmichael. Two or three months after that visit when he drew the picture of Laura as an almost ideal heroine, he gave her some of the traits that, as he complained to Mrs. Brookfield, offended him in the older woman. Possibly, as Professor Greig observes, "the meeting with Mary Carmichael in Paris . . . ruined the character of Laura."[119] Laura still loves Pen deeply, but she is not averse to poisoning Helen's mind subtly about him after the Fotheringay affair,[120] just as Thackeray had accused Mary of trying to supplant him in his mother's affections.[121] Laura is addicted to lavish displays of emotion toward Helen,[122] a quality which Thackeray had found objectionable in his

[116] Chapter 57. *Works*, XII, 735.
[117] See above, p. 160.
[118] See above, p. 93.
[119] *Thackeray: a Reconsideration*, p. 124.
[120] Chapter 21. *Works*, XII, 251.
[121] *Letters*, II, 506.
[122] Chapter 21. *Works*, XII, 252.

cousin.[123] And the verbal sparring during the proposal scene between Laura and Pen as to their own relative worth in respect to each other,[124] is a theme which is clearly in the back of Thackeray's mind whenever he alludes to the later Mary Carmichael.

The beginning of the relationship between Mrs. Carmichael-Smyth and Mrs. Brookfield reminds one of Thackeray's adolescent enthusiasms for actresses. He wrote to his mother about it in the same manner: "I don't think I have fallen in love with any body of late, except pretty Mrs. Brookfield."[125] In March, 1846, shortly before he set up the Young Street household, Thackeray's confidence sounds a little more serious:

Mrs. Brookfield is my beau-ideal. I have been in love with her these four years—not so as to endanger peace or appetite but she always seems to me to speak and do and think as a woman should.[126]

But one suspects that by April, 1848, when the novelist was entering on the last stages of *Vanity Fair* and was deeply involved with Mrs. Brookfield, he is sparing his mother all the facts. Thus he writes: "I am in love with my old flames: but there's no danger with any of them. Poor Mrs. Brookfield is ill on a sofa repeatedly: and I have no less than 3 others."[127] A month later the true state of his feelings is clearer; he admits having fears that his beloved is going into a decline from which she will never recover, then concludes bitterly:

Amen. It will be better for her—She never says a word but I know the cause of a great part of her malady. . .a husband whom she has loved with a most fanatical fondness. . .who is my friend too. . .upright generous kind to all the world except her.[128]

When Mrs. Carmichael-Smyth moved to London in October, 1848, Thackeray naturally introduced her to Mrs. Brookfield. Then he reported to the latter that his mother loved her and had talked about her at length with him.[129] Any hope that the two women might be-

[123] *Letters*, II, 496.
[124] Chapter 27. *Works*, XII, 343.
[125] *Letters*, II, 110. Written in May, 1843.
[126] The same, p. 231.
[127] The same, p. 374.
[128] The same, p. 380.
[129] The same, p. 453. Written in November, 1848.

come dear to one another, which may have been Thackeray's attitude at the end of that year, was again a victory of hope over
experience. Yet in one of his most impassioned letters to Mrs.
Brookfield he appointed her and his mother his advocates to intercede for him in Heaven should they precede him thither.[130] Yet such
heavy joint responsibility implies a sisterly feeling toward one
another which the two ladies could hardly ever achieve. In Thackeray's defense it must be said that the letter was written when he
had newly canonized his mother as Mater Dolorosa,[131] and when
Mrs. Brookfield had for some time enjoyed a certain sanctity as a
sort of angel or Madonna addressed as "my lady."[132]

It is necessary to examine Mrs. Brookfield's motivations and attitudes to understand her feelings toward Mrs. Carmichael-Smyth.
At this point one recalls that "my lady" suffered from a latent but
pronounced sense of insecurity. She was reared as the daughter of
an early nineteenth century family with all the circumstances which
that rearing implies of limited education and rigid emphasis on the
proprieties. Moreover, her intelligence seems to have been only
slightly above average. She would of course have learned early the
value of her extraordinary beauty in winning the favor of men.
Married at the age of twenty to a brilliant man twelve years older,
young Jane Octavia had to make difficult adjustments. In the first
place, she had to pick up by osmosis the education she had not
acquired. Then, since her husband was one of the first wits in a circle
of the wittiest men in England, she would have to strain constantly—
as her letters attest—to be witty too. She would have to compensate
for her feelings of inadequacy by continuing to use her beauty in
drawing men to her, particularly since her husband's frustrations
were also perversely satisfied by that process. Incidentally, such use
of her charms enhanced his professional prospects.[133] Yet she could

---

[130] The same, p. 470.

[131] See above, p. 155.

[132] See below, p. 169.

[133] Brookfield often joked with his wife on this subject during the earlier, happier days of
their marriage. He writes in May, 1852: "There was Spring Rice (one of . . . [your] lovers—
but their name is legion)" (Mrs. Brookfield and Her Circle, I, 152). He proudly tells her the
various compliments he has received about her, including one from Thackeray (the same,
p. 174. Written in August, 1845). In July, 1846, he tells her that Moxon and Alfred Tennyson
are among her "seven hundred and ninety-nine lovers" (the same, p. 191). After the break-
up in September, 1851, Thackeray confided to Kate Perry: "a part of poor Brookfield's pride
of possession was that we should envy him and admire her" (Letters, IV, 431).

not utilize this power in any way that might attract gossip. Her girl-hood conditioning in the proprieties, and her husband's position as a churchman both called for circumspection. Moreover since he himself had an inadequate sense of the conduct befitting his cloth,[134] she was constantly forced to caution him.[135]

Mrs. Brookfield was really torn between two codes. On one side were the proprieties—part-social, part-moral—in which she had been reared. These in turn were enforced by the smart society into which she and her husband were penetrating. On the other side were the part-moral, part-religious proprieties of the ruling ecclesiastical powers, against whom her husband was in covert rebellion. Moreover she was forced, in spite of having been reared in wealth, to manage a household and keep up a social front on a very small income. Naturally Mrs. Brookfield leaned heavily in all her perplexities on the husband with whom she was deeply in love. But he continued increasingly to neglect her and to take her devotion for granted. One does not need Thackeray's testimony after the climax in 1851[136] to establish that fact. It is clear from the tone of Brookfield's letters to her—egotistical as they are—reflecting the breathless bustle of his life, cloaking under persiflage an uneasiness in his dealings with her, never taking a moment for a word of tenderness.

With all these demands at war in her timid, uncertain little mind, Mrs. Brookfield was forced to equip herself for the evasive handling of difficult situations. It is no wonder that, in the affair with Thackeray, she "walked the precarious tightrope on which she found herself with great adroitness."[137] Tormented by her husband's neglect, she can hardly be blamed for not closing her front door to the almost daily calls of one of the wittiest of London's lions, particularly when he supplemented those calls with superbly written letters, breathing rhapsodic devotion. It is hard for me to find, with Professor Ray, "a rather repellent element of calculation in her character."[138]

Thus it is easy to understand why Mrs. Brookfield would evade any close relationship with Mrs. Carmichael-Smyth. Only under extreme pressure had she admitted Thackeray himself into her inti-

[134] See above, p. 130.
[135] See *Mrs. Brookfield and Her Circle*, I, 169, 253f.
[136] *Letters*, IV, 431. Also see above, p. 162.
[137] *Letters*, I, xcviii.
[138] The same.

mate life. Then she had opened the door readily to Anny and Minny since she had as yet no children herself. But it was rather overdoing it to ask her to take in the novelist's mother, who was not her sort to begin with. Moreover intuition would tell her at once that here was a mother of the possessive, jealous type. Hence Mrs. Brookfield was afraid of Mrs. Carmichael-Smyth.

During the convalescence from his nearly fatal illness in the autumn of 1849, Thackeray seems to have wondered why Mrs. Brookfield had not called more often. He inquired: "What makes you so frightened of my mother? It is only her figure-head which is awful; her guns are never shotted."[139] And when Mrs. Brookfield wrote Mrs. Carmichael-Smyth in April, 1849, Thackeray said of the letter: "O Mam how frightened you were when you wrote it—and what for were you in a fright? You have much more brains imagination wit than she—how conceited it is to be afraid then."[140]

Now since Mrs. Carmichael-Smyth had apparently ceased remonstrating openly with her son, he could not directly accuse her of jealousy. Nor did he want to stir up troubled waters by telling Mrs. Brookfield that his mother was jealous of her. Yet the fact appears between the lines of the letters. By the summer of 1849 he had already confided to his "dear lady" that he was bored with his mother's presence in his house. Mrs. Carmichael-Smyth had taken Anny and Minny to Wales,[141] while he fled to Brighton, and Inspector Brookfield descended on him at that resort. Writing Mrs. Carmichael-Smyth about the visit he carefully warns her: "Don't be alarmed Mrs. Inspectress isn't here."[142] Assuring his mother of his well-being, he protests he is "not minded in the least to break my heart. I was much worse this time last year." In fact, although Thackeray did not say so, the Brookfield affair was not waning; it was only more placid and stabilized.

Thereafter Mrs. Carmichael-Smyth and Mrs. Brookfield seem to have stayed at arm's length. They preserved the amenities and exchanged calls,[143] but Thackeray's letters to his mother significantly refrain from mentioning the woman who was then the emotional

[139] The same, IV, 422.
[140] The same, II, p. 525.
[141] See above, p. 154.
[142] *Letters*, II, 567.
[143] See above, p. 154, n. 81.

center of his life. The break with the Brookfields in September, 1851, which Mrs. Carmichael-Smyth could not escape knowing something about, is an event which Thackeray is significantly curt in discussing with the latter:

The Brookfield party is finally off for Madeira and we met at the Grange and parted not friends, but not enemies—and so there's an end of it.[144]

Furthermore, he was diplomatic but firm in warding off his mother's solicitude about his own unhappiness at this time:

these are blue devils that I can't show to my mamma; as you could not tell me your secrets about GP—so the griefs of my elderly heart cant be talked about to you: and I must get them over as comfortably as I best may. As a man's leg hurts just as much after it's off they say: so you suffer after certain amputations.[145]

This attitude is a far cry from that of the youthful Thackeray in 1830, confiding his inmost thoughts in the diary-letter to his mother. Yet he still needed a confidante, as we shall see,[146] and the fact that Mrs. Carmichael-Smyth failed to qualify points to Thackeray's fear of jealousy of Mrs. Brookfield.

The temperature chart of Thackeray's passion for Mrs. Brookfield is marked by two points of high fever, one during the winter of 1848–49 and one when the relationship was severed by Brookfield in September, 1851. Between those two dates, as Professor Ray has pointed out, both Thackeray and Mrs. Brookfield felt that "theirs was a permanent relationship about which they might build their lives."[147] The shock to this feeling of stability when the friendship ended naturally hurt Thackeray to the quick.

The main circumstances of the Brookfield affair are too well-established to be dwelled upon here, particularly the fact that apparently it was never marked by any physical token of feeling beyond a handclasp.[148] Its importance to Thackeray's emotional biography is more relevant, for it marks his emotional coming of age. Retarded by his unhappy schooling, by his strong attachment to his mother, and by his feelings of unworthiness, he was never in

144 *Letters*, II, 809.
145 The same, p. 813.
146 See below, pp. 178f.
147 *Letters*, I, xcix.
148 "Mrs. Brookfield seems never to have permitted [him] so much as an embrace or a kiss" (*Letters*, I, xcviii).

love until he met Isabella when he was twenty-five. That love, deep and sincere as it was, was the devotion of an emotional adolescent to an emotional child. After Isabella's insanity Thackeray appears to have progressed through a stage of trivial love interests,[149] with his emotional tenderness centered decreasingly on Isabella and increasingly on his daughters, so far as children could absorb the needs of a man's love. But from his first meeting with Mrs. Brookfield he began to experience new emotions. Since she was—by her own admission—vain,[150] since her husband's pride of possession was flattered by seeing a circle of admirers around her, and Thackeray himself was only one of those admirers, his admiration was not taken too seriously. In fact the lady herself does not seem to have been much attracted by this not-too-handsome admirer.[151]

The first complication in the harmonious relationship between Thackeray and the Brookfields occurred in February, 1847, during the commotion over *The Book of Snobs* when Thackeray professed himself so strongly under Brookfield's influence.[152] While visiting that gentleman and his wife at Southampton, the novelist had breathed some of the new drug, ether, as a parlor amusement. Under its influence he had proclaimed his enthusiasm for Mrs. Brookfield in such strong language that her husband felt compelled to remonstrate. Thackeray explained—perhaps lamely—that he was already deifying that lady in such a way that Brookfield could have no reason to feel jealous. Mrs. Brookfield—the novelist explains—is one of a class of objects which includes "children, landscapes, harmonies of colour, music," and Thackeray's daughter Minny. All of them have a beauty which effects the novelist with "a spiritual sensuality," and his "love for one is as pure as [his]. . .love for the other."[153] If such were not the case, the letter goes on, he would long before have cut the Brookfields.

This confession more or less establishes the strange *modus vivendi* which Thackeray maintained with his fried and friend's wife for over four years. As he masked his irritations with his mother by

[149] See above, pp. 101f.
[150] "How foolishly, blindly fond *I* am of being liked and admired(?). If I had not the restraint of very deep affection for you [Brookfield], and some restraint of conscience, I should be. . .still on the look out for conquest" (*Mrs. Brookfield and Her Circle*, I, 163).
[151] See above, p. 147.
[152] See above, pp. 130f.
[153] *Letters*, II, 272.

periodically deifying her or compelling her to deify him, he deified Mrs. Brookfield in order to mask the intense sensuality which he felt for her. Yet that quality is easy to perceive. The lady's refusal to permit him to enter her bedroom during her first lying-in[154] was based in part on her modesty, but also no doubt on her intuitive perception that he took an extraordinary interest in that bedroom.

In *Vanity Fair* it is interesting to note that the literary parody at the start of Chapter 6 features an imaginary burglar who "carries off Amelia in her night-dress."[155] Dobbin, too, reflects this interest on the part of his creator when, on the eve of Waterloo, he yearns to witness Amelia's farewell to George in the sanctity of their room.[156] A few pages later, the author, speaking *propria persona*, adds: "We too have forborne to enter into that sad chamber. How long had that poor girl been on her knees! what hours of speechless prayer and bitter prostration had she passed there!"[157] Thackeray was to adore drawing pictures—verbal or graphic—of Mrs. Brookfield on her knees at prayer, in part because that attitude displayed the sanctity which he loved to attribute to her, in part because the rite went on while she was in her nightgown by the side of her bed. Thus he writes her: "as I went up to bed I thought about this time she's" and instead of finishing the sentence draws a picture of a woman saying her prayers.[158] So Dobbin in Pumpernickel watches for Amelia's light to go out.[159]

At other times when Thackeray felt that this desire was not entirely sacred, he identified himself with Iachimo in *Cymbeline* stealing into the chamber of Imogen.[160] Reading the letters to Mrs. Brookfield cursorily, one is struck with the way her bed-going weaved itself like a refrain into them: "I have got a box of preserved apricots . . . and two shall be put under my lady's pillow every night."[161] A stupid dinner at Spa was all over by nine-thirty, "an hour before Payne came to fetch you to bed."[162] Describing the quarters which

---

[154] The same, p. 650.
[155] *Works*, XI, 61.
[156] Chapter 30. The same, p. 370.
[157] Chapter 31. The same, p. 381.
[158] *Letters*, II, 469. Written December 18, 1848.
[159] Chapter 63. *Works*, XI, 810.
[160] Chapter 12. The same, p. 139.
[161] *Letters*, II, 323. Written in November, 1847.
[162] The same, p. 416. Written in August, 1848.

had been given him on a visit to an Oxford college, he complains that the bed was so hard he couldn't sleep and adds "but I hope you did well after that long journey."[163] In December, 1848, during the time of his most passionate avowals, he writes: "it is just $10\frac{1}{2}$ o'clock. I wonder what you are doing?" Then follow about twenty words, apparently so intimate that Mrs. Brookfield overscored them beyond recovery.[164] On a trip to Paris he likes "to say Good night . . . just before jumping into the comfortable French bed. May you sleep in yours."[165] Inquiring about her health on a trip to the country, he asks whether she had "clothes enough to" her bed.[166] So the tale could go on to the end of the Brookfield correspondence.

Thackeray's desperate efforts to find a socially acceptable basis for his affair with Mrs. Brookfield, drove him to clothe it in the trappings of a medieval courtly love drama. The most prominent aspect of this drama was his way of apotheosizing his inamorate. She is, as we have seen, "his lady" who is like an angel for whom his love is pure. Moreover, we have seen how she is to act with his mother as intercessor to secure his admission to heaven. On a trip to Paris he feasts his senses at the Louvre on the Venus de Milo and some Titians, but is careful to assure Mrs. Brookfield that she wouldn't like them. On the other hand, he wants to copy a Virgin and Child and present it to her.[167]

Had circumstances ever made it possible for them to marry, Thackeray might have eventually expected of his "dear lady" a devotion such as he exacted of his mother. As it was he contented himself with the obverse side of the coin: prostrating himself before her. Yet here his old sense of unworthiness made him feel, as always, that though his greatest frustrated ambition was to enact the handsome lover, he must instead play a comic role. That role, furthermore, was a useful disguise for the true nature of his emotions. He calls himself "the buffoon your humble Servant"[168]—another way of making himself medievally into her privileged court jester. He was addicted in his correspondence with other ladies to knighting

163 The same, p. 446. Written on November 1, 1848.
164 The same, p. 473.
165 The same, p. 495. Written in February, 1845.
166 The same, p. 494. n.d.
167 The same, 504. Written in February, 1849.
168 The same, p. 475. Written in December, 1848.

his favorite *nom de plume* and calling himself the Chevalier de Titmarsh,[169] or more amusingly "ce scélérat de Titmarsh."[170]

Another protective device for justifying his love for Mrs. Brookfield was Thackeray's establishment of himself as her honorary
brother. This plan was stumbled upon after they had made some
intimate disclosures to one another at Clevedon Court, her father's
estate, in November of 1848.[171] Assuming too much from her confidence, he tried by passionate avowals to put their friendship on a
more emotional basis. She adroitly repelled these tactics by telling
him: "if you do not write in more commonplace style to me I shall
be quite unable to answer you at all."[172] At about that time Jane's
uncle, Henry Hallam, protested at the warmth of Thackeray's
affection for his niece.[173] So the "dear sister" letters began and con
tinued while the volcano of the novelist's passion lay dormant for
nearly three years. Sometimes he intensified the greeting to "my
dear, dear sister,"[174] or—if the inward flame was burning more intensely—"cjère soeur si douce et si bonne."[175] Once he elaborated
on this fancy and asked "what's the good of a brother if you can't
tell him things?"[176] And even she came in time to relax her rigid
defenses enough to address him as "my dear Brother William."[177]
At the end of that letter she shows how much of her affection had
been transferred from her husband to Thackeray: "I say my prayers
for you every night and morning and feel very thankful for all your
affection. Bless you dear friend may God bless you and take care
of you always."[178]

A growing sense of how much Thackeray had supplanted him in
his wife's affections may have led Brookfield to insist on the separation in September, 1851. At that time he took his wife to Madeira,
on the ostensible plea of his ill health. Thackeray himself described

[169] The same, 86–7, 315, 352, 667.
[170] The same, p. 469.
[171] Professor Ray suggests (*Letters*, I, xcvii) that she confided to him how her husband
neglected her.
[172] The same, II, 478.
[173] The same, I, xcviii.
[174] The same, II, 477.
[175] The same, p. 503.
[176] The same, pp. 664f.
[177] The same, p. 738. Written in January, 1851.
[178] The same, p. 739.

the breaking-off to Mrs. Elliot and Kate Perry in a letter which is only partially reprinted:

The affair is at an end and the rupture complete. Monsieur [Brookfield] has spoken out like a man ... There is nothing more to be said or done ... There have been very high words between me and Monsieur in consequence of something I said to him that **was** quite unjustifiable ... But they'll probably leave London and the affair will end. I am going out of town and I don't know where. God bless you all.[179]

In the spiritual tempest that followed, Thackeray's moods veered like a weathercock. Yet one notices, blowing about in the gale, the stage trappings of the medieval drama which he had been enacting. One day Brookfield is a good fellow whom he has cruelly stabbed, while the writer himself and Mrs. Brookfield are both tortured souls in purgatory.[180] One recalls here a letter written in November, 1848, when he reminds his "dear sister" of how they had discussed death at the Clevedon interview:

I thought of myself as damned, and of you as an angel full of pity. Surely you will be able to make your way to me (wherever I may be) and give me one of your sweet smiles? I long for you to give me your blessing, my angel. When you look at me, when you think of me, I am in paradise.[181]

Or again he prostrates himself and begins kissing Mrs. Brookfield's feet in French:

... Je disais je l'aime je l'aime je l'aime ... Que je voudrais les baiser ces chere pieds de ma douce maitresse ... Je tremble d'amour quelquefois devant elle ... Bon dieu que ses yeux me poursuivent ...[182]

Then he turns against Brookfield and exposes him as a domestic tyrant, a breed which Thackeray—despite humorous avowals of his secret desire to be one—was always fair-minded enough to castigate.[183]

After this comes the greatest shock. Thackeray momentarily turns against the lady herself. Away goes his subservient pose, and his

[179] *Letters*, IV, 428. Written on September 23, 1851.
[180] The same, p. 429.
[181] *Letters*, II, 453.
[182] *Letters*, IV, 430.
[183] The same, p. 430.

manhood reasserts itself:

I wish that I had never loved her. I have been played with by a woman, and flung over at a beck from the lord and master . . . I treet [*sic*] her tenderly and like a gentleman: I will fetch, carry, write, stop, what she pleases—but I leave her . . . The thought that I have been made a fool of is the bitterest of all, perhaps.[184]

At the same time he surrenders the pose that his love was sacred and transcendent. Now he mentions practical reasons—apart from Mrs. Brookfield's timidity—why it was never consummated: "Any wrong was out of the question on our children's account."

A few weeks later Thackeray's faith in his "dear sister" is restored, and he reports her as "suffering more than I dare to think, God bless her."[185] The blame goes back to Brookfield, and facts come out to which Thackeray—the great exposer of shams—had hitherto more or less blinded himself:

He is full of queer ceremonies, punctilios unheard of amongst men of a franker sort. He clings to the fancy that nobody knows anything about his interior; and I shall of course hold my wagging tongue and speak of his affairs as little as possible . . . The poor fellow likes mysteries, and when his wife was you know in what a condition insisted that nobody knew or saw the circumstance.

In short the erstwhile "dear friend" was a bit of a sham.

As one watches the Brookfield affair recede into the limbo of Thackeray's past, certain inferences are plain. It marked, as I have said, a belated coming to maturity on his part since—for the first time in his life—he loved a mature woman passionately and selflessly. Yet because of the circumstances which made his love for Mrs. Brookfield a guilty passion by the standards of the time, Thackeray was forced to be, not an unmasker of sham, but a man deceiving himself with all sorts of poses and attitudes. When the affair was over, he spent some time utilizing its emotional aftermath in his writing. Then, feeling that the affair had left him a burnt-out shell, he spent the rest of his life living up to that pose.

184 The same, p. 431.
185 The same, p. 432f.

CHAPTER VI

Over the Crest

WHEN Thackeray had licked the wounds which his ego suffered from the quarrel with Brookfield, he spent nearly two years on what might fairly be called his last period of stimulating new experience. It began roughly during the winter of 1851–52, and ended in December of 1853 with that first attack of malaria in Rome which made him almost a chronic invalid for the rest of his life. Bad health thereafter overshadows all other factors in determining his moods, his conduct, and his literary achievement. Though that first bout of malaria seemed at the time a minor matter,[1] it became as important in its way as the flight from Taprell's, the loss of the patrimony, the marriage with Isabella, her insanity, the success of *Vanity Fair*, or the Brookfield affair. Thereafter melancholy was almost continuous and more pervasive than ever before in all phases of his life.

Thackeray's peace of mind was undoubtedly aided by the assurance that he could now blame his melancholy on an ulterior cause. Hitherto, when he had not performed his responsibilities to the top of his bent, he had been forced to blame himself, to lean on the self-portrait of himself as a weak, indulgent creature. Now that there was a valid excuse for not always performing admirably, he had less use for his unflattering self-portrait. Hence it became more an outward than an inward state of mind, more like the series of masks which he had already developed to aid him in his dealings with humanity.

Thackeray's goal in life during this whole time was the amassing of a capital sum whose interest would maintain his wife and daughters after his death. His mode of living was restless and peripatetic during the first part of the time. After he gave up lecturing in 1857 it was comparatively stable. His human relationships during these years were more satisfactory than at any time in his life except perhaps during the early years of his marriage. He had stabilized

---

[1] *Letters*, III, 328. Written on December 17, 1853.

the balance of authority as between himself and his mother. In America his affection for the Baxter family filled for a time part of the gap caused by the loss of Mrs. Brookfield. Then Anny and Minny came of age and themselves filled that role so that thereafter the mutual love of the trio satisfied the long starvation of the novelist's affection. Thackeray's professional achievement during this last dozen years of his life is marked by the decline from the brilliance of *Henry Esmond* and *The Newcomes* through the lesser radiance of *The Virginians* to the weaknesses of *Philip*. Concurrently with the latter came a sentimental success outside the field of narrative in *The Roundabout Papers*. The excellence of *Esmond* may be the more remarkable by virtue of its having been written partly between bouts of lecturing and partly during an actual lecture tour. *The Newcomes* similarly was written in the lull between *The English Humourists* tours and the barnstorming attendant on *The Four Georges*, and its composition was punctuated by repeated fits of illness.

Thackeray's failure as a debater in Cambridge[2] many years before had convinced him that he was too diffident to be a good public speaker. Hence he did not take to lecturing like a duck to water, even in the early days before its monotony began to pall. Yet the lecture platform offered huge compensatory rewards. In December, 1851, he confided to Lady Stanley: "the lectures though odious will be really a little fortune to me."[3] Ten months later he disclosed to the same confidante that "this peripatetic lecturing doesnt at all suit me . . . but it is more profitable than book-writing."[4] Part of the new elation that shows in his correspondence can be explained by the ease of this new way of earning money. Moreover it provided Thackeray with a fresh goal in life: the lectures were building the fund that would some day support Anny, Minny, and Isabella.

Vanity Fair had finally relieved Thackeray of the debts which had weighed on him ever since his breadwinning had been temporarily halted by Isabella's insanity. *Pendennis* and the *Punch* contributions brought in ample revenues for the next three years, but these revenues only kept pace with Thackeray's rather expensive scale of living. Lecturing, however, brought in money fast enough

[2] See above, p. 43.
[3] *Letters*, II, 816.
[4] The same, III, 100.

to permit some accumulation of capital. And for a time the building of that fund seemed very desirable since it kept Thackeray occupied—not too unhappily—and was in itself a worthy goal. His temperamental pendulum had swung in a new direction.

Yet after a year or so, one senses unhealth in the very vehemence of Thackeray's money-amassing and his almost miserly counting of his gains. The gambling craze of his young manhood, momentarily resurgent in his railway speculation in 1845,[5] was now resurrected in a new form. The stakes in lecturing were more certain than those of the gaming table, and the preparation and delivery of the lectures involved a little more work, but the prospect of rapid wealth was held out by both occupations. And Thackeray himself confessed that the loss of his patrimony was still rankling deep within him. He wrote: "if I can work for 3 years now, I shall have put back my patrimony and a little over—after 30 years of ups and downs."[6] The money-winning craze that the lecturing eventually developed in him was the obverse of the earlier gambling mania: one had destroyed his independent status; the other bid fair to restore it. And independent status was the hallmark of a gentleman.

Thackeray's own letters testify to his solicitude for his wife and daughters in case of his death. But worthy as was the feeling, it was not the only alternative to their starving in the streets. When he sailed for Boston on his first American tour in October, 1852, he asked Edward FitzGerald to be his literary executor. Between the lines of the letter is the implied hope that FitzGerald will guarantee a livelihood to Thackeray's family in case of the latter's death. To imply that the burden would not be great, the novelist pointed out:

my books would yield a something as copyright—and should anything occur I have commissioned friends in good place to get a pension for my poor little wife.[7]

Moreover, adds Thackeray: "I should have insured my life but for my complaint (a stricture) which I am told increases the annual payment so much that is not worth the premium." In other words, he was not uninsurable; life insurance for him would merely have been a poor investment. Yet that consideration would hardly have stopped his buying insurance had his family's future been really

[5] See above, p. 113.
[6] The same, IV, 155. Written on October 1, 1859.
[7] Letters, III, 99.

desperate. Probably the increased premium resulting from the stricture was no greater than his considerable annual wine and cigar bills. Significantly, Thackeray never complained about them.

So the fund for Isabella and the children, useful as it might be, was not a *sine qua non* to preserve them from real want in case of Thackeray's death. Yet he laid ever more stress on the need of building it as the novelty of lecturing wore off and its *ennui* grew. The thought of providing for his womenfolk spurred Thackeray to keep making platform appearances long after he had grown mortally weary of them.

Certainly during the winter of 1851–52 the lecturing was psychologically good for Thackeray because it kept his mind occupied. That preoccupation speeded his recovery from the separation from Mrs. Brookfield. Furthermore, since that blow had fallen in the midst of writing *Henry Esmond*, its author could transfer some of his misery to the ostensible narrator of that novel, its hero.

As early as November, 1850, when he finished *Pendennis*, Thackeray had a subject for his next novel, and by January of the following year, he reported that it was "biling up" in his "interior."[8] It was not to be satirical, as Thackeray was at pains to convey when he wrote: "in the next novel we are to have none but good characters. What is the use of examining folk who are quite otherwise."[9] Professor Ray places the beginning of *Esmond* in August, 1851,[10] only a month before the break with the Brookfields. Since Book I, which ends with Lord Mohun's slaying of Viscount Castelwood, was completed by February,[11] when Thackeray was convalescing from the worst pain of that business, the source of the basic relationships in that part of *Henry Esmond* is not hard to guess. The boy Henry is the novelist himself; Lord and Lady Castlewood are the Brookfields.

With these parallels in mind, it is easy to see that the main theme of this first book, the boy Henry's gradual winning of the Castlewood family's affection, corresponds to Thackeray's slow making of a place for himself in the Brookfield household. Henry's curiously

---

[8] The same, II, 708 and 736.
[9] The same, p. 744.
[10] The same, I, lx.
[11] The same, III, 15.

ambiguous status—somewhere between page, foster-son, cousin, or simply "kinsman"—reflects the novelist's efforts to win a defined place in the Brookfield family, even it it were that of "brother."[12] Henry's idolatry of Lady Castlewood is described in the same terms of courtly love which Thackeray habitually applied to Mrs. Brookfield. When Rachel first spoke to the boy, he,

who had never looked upon so much beauty before, felt as if the touch of a superior being or angel smote him down to the ground, and kissed the fair protecting hand as he knelt on one knee. To the very last hour of his life, Esmond remembered the lady as she then spoke and looked, the rings on her fair hands, the very scent of her robe, the beam of her eyes lighting up with surprise and kindness, her lips blooming in a smile, the sun making a golden halo round her hair.[13]

Even minor details lend credence to the parallelism. Rachel "was at this time scarce twenty years old," the age of Mrs. Brookfield when Thackeray first met her. Henry, like the novelist himself and like Barry Lyndon,[14] "had grown tall during his illness"[15]—in Esmond's case the smallpox that caused so much unhappiness in his patron's family.

Castlewood himself, of course, is no more like Brookfield than was his earlier literary parallel, George Osborne. Both men share with that reverend gentleman only their good looks, their vanity, and an inclination to take for granted the adoration of their wives. Lady Castlewood's devotion to her husband, on the other hand, is curiously and skillfully diverted to Esmond almost before the reader is conscious of the fact. In just such a way had Mrs. Brookfield's affections passed—at least in part—from her husband to Thackeray. The fatal duel which Castlewood fights with Lord Mohun— which has a historical counterpart too[16]—is the counterpart of Thackeray's break with Brookfield. The novelist's subconscious wish for the clergyman's death, expressed once in his killing off of George Osborne early in *Vanity Fair*,[17] results this time in the destruction of Castlewood at the end of the first book of *Henry Esmond*. Castle-

---

[12] See above, p. 170.
[13] Book I, chapter I. *Works*, XIII, 17f.
[14] See above, p. 108.
[15] Book I, chapter 9. *Works*, XIII, 91.
[16] See R. S. Forsythe, *A Noble Rake: The Life of Charles, Lord Mohun* (Cambridge, Mass., 1928).
[17] See above, p. 148.

wood's jealousy of Mohun leads to the duel just as Brookfield's jealousy of Thackeray had led to the break.

Of course Thackeray did not equate himself with a villain like Mohun: the novelist never could picture himself as a dashing swaggerer, successful in gallantry—much as he would subconsciously have liked to have been such a man. Even though Castlewood momentarily has jealous suspicions of Esmond, the guilt that Thackeray already felt in killing Castlewood would not let him commit the further enormity of making Esmond disloyal to his patron. Such an act would be tantamount to disloyalty on his own part to Brookfield, and such disloyalty would contaminate the "purity" of his feelings toward "his dear lady." So to prove the innocence of his own position in the affair, Thackeray has Esmond remain so loyal to his "dear lord" that he stands by him in the fatal duel and himself receives a near-fatal wound. This wound opens the way to the scene when Rachel visits Harry in prison and accuses him of being accessory to her husband's death. The injustice of her abuse is all the greater because she secretly loves Harry and not Castlewood.

Ample amends come to Esmond, however, on his return from the wars. Then Lady Castlewood tells him:

there is no sin in such a love as mine now; and my dear lord in heaven may see my heart; and knows the tears that have washed my sin away.

Furthermore it turns out that she loved him as early as the time when she watched by his bedside as he lay in smallpox. Made happy by that knowledge, Esmond observes that "the angels are not all in heaven."

And as a brother folds a sister to his heart; and as a mother cleaves to her son's breast—so for a few moments Esmond's beloved mistress came to him and blessed him.[18]

The confusion of usual heterosexual relationships in this passage is striking. It points not only to the pseudo-brother-and-sister bond between the author and Mrs. Brookfield, but also to the ending of the story, where Esmond marries Lady Castlewood after he has been passionately in love for many years with her daughter Beatrix. During this time Lady Castlewood has slipped into an almost maternal role in Henry's life; in fact, she has taken over the confidante's

18 Book 2, chapter 6. *Works*, XIII, 215.

part which Thackeray had hoped that his mother would assume as the repository of his feelings about Mrs. Brookfield. In that particular case, it would seem that Mrs. Carmichael-Smyth's jealousy had disqualified her,[19] and the honor of being confidante had gone to Mrs. Elliot and Kate Perry.

To many readers of *Henry Esmond* there has been something vaguely incestuous about the hero's marriage.[20] At the end of the story he espouses a woman who is not only the mother of his former love but who has also become his own foster-mother. Yet this solution seems entirely natural in the light of Thackeray's peculiar dealings with women. In the first place, he had perceived ahead of his age that there was something sexual about a mother's jealousy of her son's loves.[21] In fact, his life itself is living disproof of the notion that a man's love of his mother, his wife, his mistress, his sister, or his daughters are all different types of emotion. In certain instances, as in his feelings for Mrs. Brookfield, the novelist tried for obvious reasons to blind himself to the sexual character of his passion.

Thackeray's interest in a woman had little to do with the official nature of her relationship to him; his real concern lay in her capability of being adored by him or—better still—adoring him. At the center of his world stood the archetypal mother, basically Mrs. Carmichael-Smyth, who received and gave adoration in almost equal parts. In one direction her type coalesced into the mother-mistress, who is primarily a receptacle for male adoration. She is represented in Thackeray's eyes by Mrs. Brookfield, whose type in turn becomes a "mistress" like Beatrix Esmond, solely to be worshipped. On the other side, the archetypal mother merges into the mother-wife such as Rachel Castlewood, who is somewhat of a giver, but more of a receiver of adoration. She shades into the wife-daughter like Isabella Thackeray, Amelia Sedley, or the adult Anny and Minny Thackeray, all conditioned to yield adoration in torrents.

With such a scale of valuations, it is easy to see why Thackeray could blend portions of his mother, his wife, and his "dear lady" into the archetypal heroine of his novels, why he could address his "dear lady" as "sister," and why he could speak of his daughters

[19] See above, p. 166.

[20] Greig chronicles some hostile Victorian criticism of the Rachel-Henry Esmond relationship (*Thackeray: a Reconsideration*, pp. 163f).

[21] See above, p. 37.

as "my harem."[22] It also explains something of his tactlessness in appointing his mother and Mrs. Brookfield as twin angels to intercede for him in heaven,[23] and why he suffered from the jealousies between the different women in his life. Being linked together in his love, he felt egotistically that they should love one another. Yet at the same time he rejoiced in their jealousy because it was a proof of their love for him.

The mother aspect of Rachel Castlewood was by no means absent in the first book of *Esmond*. Even the reopening of Harry's wound in the prison by a wild gesture after his "dear lady" has berated him for her husband's death is a child's solution to the situation. After being scolded by his mother, the child hurts himself almost purposely so that he can be comforted by her.[24] Thereafter Rachel's maternal aspect becomes stronger as Beatrix draws toward herself those emotions in Harry which correspond to what Thackeray had felt for Mrs. Brookfield.

As always, the author loses emotional control over his subject when he becomes suffused with tenderness at thinking of his mother or Mrs. Brookfield. Hence it is hard to say which woman's image was dominant in his imagination as he wrote the dramatic passage where Rachel discloses to Henry that she knows his secret sacrifice of the family title to her son. After he has called her "dearest saint" and "purest soul" and explained what joy the sacrifice has given him, she flings herself on her knees and kisses his hands:

Don't raise me,' she said, in a wild way, to Esmond, who would have lifted her. 'Let me kneel—let me kneel, and—and—worship you.' [25]

Quite naturally, as his mother's own image became tarnished in Thackeray's eyes by the jealousy he found in her, he permitted Rachel Castlewood also to become increasingly jealous. She had first displayed this quality toward the boy Henry during his harmless friendship with Nancy Sievewright;[26] she had been intensely jealous

---

[22] See above, p. 115.

[23] See above, p. 163.

[24] Greig sees in Rachel's cruelty to Harry here a reflection of Mrs. Brookfield's feeling of guilt for her love of Thackeray: "Like Rachel, Jane wanted it both ways: she wanted to punish herself but to throw the blame on Thackeray" (*Thackeray: A Reconsideration*, p. 162).

[25] Book 3, chapter 2. *Works*, XIII, 332.

[26] Book 1, chapter 8. The same, p. 83.

of her husband's mistress;[27] and after her marriage to Esmond, that quality was the only flaw in her character.[28] So pronounced grew this trait in Rachel that one contemporary—and therefore pre-Freudian—reviewer could write: "Thackeray never really liked this woman himself, and successfully blends with every thrill of sympathy with her an undertone of profound aversion."[29]

With the character of Henry Esmond himself Thackeray had trouble. His letters had been full of the plaint that the book was gloomy and dismal, although to modern eyes it has no such faults. In fact, his novels and their autobiographic heroes were so intertwined in his imagination that he easily transferred qualities from one to the other. During most of the writing of *Esmond* Thackeray was, as we have seen, plunged in melancholy. Therefore he decided that the book was gloomy because he himself was too doleful to play his usual role of buffoon-satirist and punctuate its pages with quips and ridicule. Esmond, the autobiographical hero who was the author's mouthpiece, became "Don Dismallo," and his melancholy is so belabored by the author that the reader is hard put to find the traits in him that make all the other characters love him. Beatrix almost alone of the major individuals fails to give Esmond her untrammeled devotion. She atones for her coldness, however, in the sequel, *The Virginians*, by singing his praises with a feeling well nigh fervor.[30]

Yet if Esmond's devotion to Beatrix was based on what Thackeray had felt for Mrs. Brookfield, Beatrix was in one respect more like Thackeray himself than was Esmond. Although that hero could bring down "the most arrogant by a grave satiric way,"[31] his power to deflate egos only reflects the portion of Thackeray's satire which sprang from his bitterness and melancholy. The other part of it, that which welled up from an irrepressible gaiety, he gave to Beatrix. Like her predecessor, Becky, this most beautiful of Thackeray's heroines has a gift for satire. Perhaps that streak in her is partly an

[27] Book I, chapter 9. The same, p. 104.
[28] Preface. The same, p. 9.
[29] George Brimley, *The Spectator* (November 6, 1852). Reprinted in *Littell's Living Age* (February, 1864). XXIV, 327.
[30] Chapters 2 and 35. *Works*, pp. 20 and 368.
[31] Preface. *Works*, XIII, 10.

evasion of Mrs. Grundy. The author couldn't allege that Becky and Beatrix were sexually promiscuous, but since a satirical turn was a dubious asset in respectable Victorian womanhood,[32] he could subtly label the two women as outside the moral pale by making them satirists, especially of religious matters. Like Becky, Beatrix is such a scoffer:

"Oh, those parsons! I hate 'em all," says Mistress Beatrix ... "whether they wear cassocks and buckles, or beards and bare feet ... They try to domineer, and they frighten us with kingdom come; and they wear a sanctified air in public, and expect us to go down on our knees and ask their blessing; and they intrigue, and they grasp, and they backbite, and they slander."[33]

Beatrix like Thackeray saw clearly that some of her own waywardness was a reaction to her mother's saintliness. Once she poured out to Esmond her true opinion of Rachel: "Oh, what a saint she is! Her goodness frightens me. I'm not fit to live with her. I should be better, I think, if she were not so perfect."[34] Then she vents some sentiments reminiscent of Thackeray's annoyance with the Divine Aid that guided his mother's most minute concerns.[35]

She can't be frank with me quite; who is always thinking of the next world, and of her guardian angel ... Oh, Harry, I'm jealous of that guardian angel ... my mother's life is all for Heaven, and mine—all for earth. We can never be friends quite.

Thackeray's last dozen years of life was in truth a period of insight when many things were revealed to him. He had long cherished the notion that pampering mothers make dissipated sons, but only late in life did he see—as Beatrix saw—that over-pious mothers make wayward children. Naturally such a view would become dear to him insofar as it justified his own concept of himself as weak and worldly. So both Beatrix and her brother Frank are made out to be what they are because of their mother. In Frank's case the blame is laid on her piety, her parsimony, and her pampering ways; the boy was reared at Walcote "more like a poor parson's son than a young nobleman ... 'Twas this mistake in his early training ...

---

[32] As a prize example, consider Mrs. Arrowpoint's suspicions of Gwendolen Harleth in *Daniel Deronda*: "this girl is double and satirical. I shall be on my guard against her" (Chapter 5. *The Works of George Eliot*, "University Edition," VI, 67).

[33] Book 3, chapter 2. *Works*, XIII, 334f.

[34] Book 3, chapter 3. The same, p. 355.

[35] See above, pp. 154f.

that set him so eager upon pleasure when he had it in his power; nor is he the first lad that has been spoiled by the over-careful fondness of women.''[36]

In his next novel, *The Newcomes*, Thackeray's "rake" character is Lord Kew, whose waywardness is even more explicitly a reaction against pietistic education. His gentle mother—a widow of course—prays with "saintly love" and "pure supplications" for her boy's repentance. Then, as always in this stage of his life, Thackeray looks at the other side of the saint whom he is creating: Lady Kew's "mind was narrow." She failed to understand that "the tutors and directors she had set about" her son had driven "his high spirit into revolt." "When the young catechist yawns over his reverence's discourse, who knows but it is the doctor's vanity which is enraged, and not Heaven which is offended?''[37]

Thackeray loved his mother as much as ever during this last phase of his life. Furthermore she now recognized his authority in all matters pertaining to himself and his daughters except the girls' religious education. Yet he was more candid about the flaws in his love for her than ever before, in part no doubt because he was more detached and dispassionate about that love. For example, he could confess to Mary Holmes, a young music teacher who was a comparative stranger:

It gives the keenest tortures of jealousy and disappointed yearning to my dearest old mother ... that she can't be all in all to me, mother sister wife everything but it mayn't be.[38]

Then with the constant harping on the old string, he adds: "a jealousy after me tears and rends her."

The fact that Thackeray was willing, though not eager, to leave Anny and Minny with his mother during the two American tours bespeaks his confidence in the authority he had won during the governess feud.[39] Her attempt to use what authority she possessed to impose her religion on Anny and Minny was her last important defiance of her son. The stubborn resistance of Anny, at the age of fifteen, shows the early development of the character and intelli-

---

[36] Book 3, chapter 2. *Works*, XIII, 333.
[37] Chapter 27. *Works*, XIV, 485 f.
[38] *Letters*, III, 12f.
[39] See above, pp. 124f.

gence that was to make the child one of the foremost women of England. Her complaint to her father over her grandmother's domination shows a superb confidence in where her father's heart lay:

I am afraid Grannie is still miserable about me, but it bothers me when the clergymen say that everybody ought to think alike and follow the one true way, forgetting that it is they who want people to think alike, that is, as they do.[40]

To comfort Anny, her father sent her a letter marked "private." Despite this restriction the grandmother opened it and, having read it, sent her son a missive full of expostulations and tears. In rebuttal, he pointed out that, though loath to have secrets from her, he wished she would avoid subjects on which they couldn't agree.

And I know that in talking so there will be an occasion for fresh tears and pain . . . the question of reason becomes one of sentiment straightway: and you suffer pangs (and inflict them too) about what is a calculation, like the 3 angles of a triangle, of evidence probability and so forth. Parents have been made unhappy, children parted from them, people have killed persecuted . . . in all ages upon this question . . . Of course I am unhappy, and you knew I would not like it that my children should be sitting under a French Calvinist.[41]

Despite Thackeray's persuasiveness, his mother never did come round to his way of thinking. In fact this conflict became a case where the intolerance of the mother was visited upon the daughters. Ironically, during Anny's and Minny's sufferings after their father's death in 1864, Mrs. Carmichael-Smyth added fuel to their grief. As Anny explained it, they had "terrible religious discussions: Grannie's religious views were always very intense and she took our different habits of thought passionately to heart. It used to make us miserable to make her so unhappy. Minny would be made downright ill and I used to get half distracted."[42] Yet even iron will melt. By the end of that year Mrs. Carmichael-Smyth "said she had changed her mind . . . especially about religious things . . . she could now sympathize far more than she had once done with what my father used to think and say."[43]

Unfortunately Thackeray was not alive to witness that change of heart. It would have gladdened him had it occurred twelve years

---

[40] Letters, III, 141. Written on December 5, 1852.
[41] The same, p. 169.
[42] Thackeray and His Daughter, ed. Hester Thackeray Ritchie (New York, 1924), p. 133.
[43] The same, p. 136.

earlier when he was striving to make his wishes followed across three thousand miles of ocean. Only thus could he help Anny in her struggle over the religious ideas that he wished her to cherish.

At the time of this *contretemps* with Mrs. Carmichael-Smyth, Thackeray had other things on his mind, among the most important being Sally Baxter. The fact that the novelist did not have a known prototype for Beatrix when he wrote *Henry Esmond* highlights the curious fact that he discovered a living image of her when he got to New York, six months after finishing the book. There he met Sally Baxter. Soon he was writing to Mrs. Procter: "I have found Beatrix Esmond and lost my heart to her."[44]

Actually Sally's resemblance to Beatrix was probably superficial. She may have had as much beauty as the heroine of *Henry Esmond*. Quite certainly Sally possessed the accompanying knack of drawing circles of male admirers about her. No doubt there also were resemblances of appearance and speech between the two women which we have no way of knowing about. Yet Sally Baxter's claim to immortality will rest not so much on her resemblance to Beatrix Esmond as on being the prototype of Ethel Newcome. Thackeray wrote to his mother:

the end of my flirtation with Miss Sally Baxter here is that I have got a new character for a novel—though to be sure she is astoundingly like Beatrix.[45]

And on his return from the United States, he had only, as Professor Ray puts it, "to transfer his memories from New York to London,"[46] and Sally was ready for service as the heroine of *The Newcomes*.

Thackeray's brief attachment to Sally Baxter was in fact a rebound from the Brookfield affair. When Thackeray sailed from Liverpool in October, 1852, he had confided to Dr. John Brown that the change of scene should cure him of the last pain from losing his "dear lady." Then he added: "who knows when I come back I may tell you I'm in love with somebody else, and have begun Act I of another tragedy or farce."[47] Arriving in the New World in a state of mind so highly receptive to a new *amour*, the novelist succumbed almost instantly to Sally Baxter's beauty. But as proof of

[44] *Letters*, III, 154. Written on December 22, 1852.
[45] The same, p. 149.
[46] *Letters*, I, lxxxix.
[47] The same, III p. 91.

the psychological maturity that he had gained from the Brookfield affair, he recovered almost as speedily.

For one thing, Thackeray's affection for Sally was nearly indistinguishable from his affection for other members of her family. He had made himself an honorary member of the Baxter household as he earlier had of the Brookfields'. Then he had fitted the various females of the Baxter family into niches in his pantheon corresponding to those occupied by their counterparts back in England. Mrs. Baxter was Mrs. Carmichael-Smyth's deputy in the New World. As such the New York lady received letters from her counterpart thanking her for taking care of the novelist while he was out from under his mother's eye.[48] Sally's younger sister, Lucy, and her cousin Libby Strong corresponded to Anny and Minny, and they received letters from Thackeray[49] in just the tone of affectionate jocularity that he used in writing to his own daughters at this time. All four girls were daughter-wives who held places in his affections similar to that left vacant by Isabella. But Sally was twelve years younger than Mrs. Brookfield and the novelist was now twelve years older than he had been when he first met his "dear lady." Therefore his good sense recognized that Sally could not occupy the now-empty chief niche in his temple. Accordingly she became a sort of daughter-niece. His attitude toward her had more admiration and less affectionate familiarity than he felt toward the four younger girls.

Thackeray was still enough of a courtly lover to say half-jocosely to James. T. Fields: "I'm only a cipher in the young lady's estimation, and why shouldn't I sigh for her if I like."[50] Seemingly too the knowledge that their relationship could never lead anywhere roused in him a bitterness like that which he had felt at the loss of Mrs. Brookfield and for which he had found vent in *Henry Esmond*. Otherwise why should he, on the voyage back to England, have written letters to Sally "full of wit and jibes and scorn" which he tore up "because they were so bitter"?[51]

On Thackeray's second tour in the United States, he had not entirely recovered from Sally Baxter's charms. He failed to come down from Boston to attend her wedding to Frank Hampton in

[48] The same, pp. 271, 525.
[49] The same, pp. 163, 206, 215, 232, 259, 310, 368.
[50] The same, p. 244. Written on March 19, 1853.
[51] The same, p. 261. Written on May 3, 1853.

New York, excusing himself on the score of bad health and lecture engagements.[52] The excuse was certainly sincere and it did hurt Thackeray to be absent, but he later confessed to Mrs. Baxter some jealousy at seeing Sally given to another:

Some time—a good bit hence—I shall write to that lady you speak of—but now I can't; there's a something between us—I might sit with her for hours alone, and should not be able to open my mouth to Mrs. Frank Hampton . . . When my girls do that inevitable natural righteous thing—I know it will take me years to be reconciled to it.[53]

Apparently Sally at the time of her marriage was frightened at the thought of receiving legitimate admiration only from a husband. Perhaps too she was worried by the lack of intellectual stimulus in South Carolina. Since Thackeray was both her most illustrious conquest and her most cosmopolitan connection, she was anxious to maintain with him what he called a "sentimental friendship." Yet the Brookfield affair had taught him the danger of such bonds with married women, and through Mrs. Baxter he tried to make clear certain ideas to Sally:

it's quite best, when people of different sexes are married or unmarried, that those ultra sentimental friendship should be caught throttled and drowned in cold water.[54]

To his daughters Thackeray was more candid. Possibly as insurance against rousing their jealousy, he notified them whenever he saw the feet of clay under Sally's swirling crinoline: "Sally is not improved. She has been awfully flattered since I went away." And in regard to her marriage he didn't "envy the young man."[55] Further to placate Anny, he wrote her about Goethe's folly of falling in love at seventy-five with a schoolgirl, then—observing that Sally had just been married—he concluded:

I hope she will get over *her* passion for an old fogey who shall be nameless—It began to be a newsance at last to the old party, and very likely to the young one. My girls I suppose must undergo the common lot; but I hope they wont Sallify—Indulge in *amours de tête* I mean.[56]

[52] The same, p. 516. Written on December 11, 1855.
[53] The same, p. 542. Written on January 11, 1856.
[54] The same, p. 604.
[55] The same, p. 484. Written on October 30, 1855.
[56] The same, p. 523.

Sally served also as an object lesson to Anny and Minny on the forwardness and bad breeding of young American women:

From 16 to 22 is the age of women here and the girls have it all their own way. But I like the English way best and wouldn't have you two young fellows forward and commanding as the American girls are—as even Miss Sally Baxter is for which I have snubbed her a great deal though she is a noble young creature.[57]

Twentieth-century Americans, trained to look back on their mid-Victorian ancestresses as models of primness, may be surprised to read that Thackeray regarded these ladies in their youth as hoydens. Yet he went to some pains in *The Virginians* to express this idea graphically. Lydia van den Bosch, later Countess of Castlewood, is despite an eighteenth-century setting clearly modeled on young women to whom he had talked in America. After she has routed in verbal encounter her husband's aunt, Baroness Bernstein, before whom Castlewood and his family stand in awe, Lydia boasts:

'Guess I did it to tease old Madam Buzwig . . . She wants to treat me as a child, and do the grandmother over me. I don't want no grandmothers, I don't. I'm the head of this house, and I intend to let her know it. And I've brought her all the way from London in order to tell it her, too!'[58]

This contempt for the authority of her elders may have been as typical of Sally Baxter as it was of Lydia, but there is a coarseness of fibre about the fictional character which Thackeray can hardly have found in any member of the family which he adopted as his own in America. His opinion of the Baxters remained so high that he could write to Sally Hampton after his second American tour: "Though I don't love America I love Americans with all my heart—and I daresay you know what family taught me to love them."[59]

Sally Baxter as prototype for Ethel Newcome, Mrs. Shawe as the original of 'the Campaigner,'[60] and Major Carmichael-Smyth as the most important of various originals for Colonel Newcome,[61] all these

---

[57] The same, p. 224. Written on March 3, 1853.

[58] Chapter 73. *Works*, XV, 779f.

[59] *Letters*, III, 653.

[60] See above, p. 73.

[61] Thackeray himself repeatedly made the identification of his stepfather and Colonel Newcome (*Letters*, III, 464; IV, 57). That Colonel Carmichael (see above, p. 93) was also part of him was brought out in a letter from the novelist to Mrs. Gore: "Half of Colonel Newcome [Major Carmichael-Smyth] is down stairs now—the other half [Colonel Carmichael] is in London" (*Letters*, IV, 196). It is Professor Ray's belief (disclosed orally to the author) that Charles Carmichael's chief contribution to Colonel Newcome was his physical likeness as revealed in the illustrations.

are now well-accepted bits of Thackeray lore. It is also part of the basic body of truth that Clive Newcome is an autobiographical hero, that his boyhood uses more of his creator's boyhood than did that of Arthur Pendennis, and that Clive's marriage to Rosy Mackenzie was to imbed in fiction as much of Thackeray's married life as did the marriage of Philip Firmin in the later novel, *Philip*. Yet, paradoxically, *The Newcomes*, written between July, 1853, and June, 1855, draws less than any of the three preceding novels from the primary tensions of his life.

The mother-son-nexus—so important in *Pendennis* and *Henry Esmond*—is, as we have seen,[62] reduced in *The Newcomes* to a few peripheral relationships. Most notable are the shadowy foster-mother love of Mme. de Florac for the young Clive Newcome;[63] the briefly developed "smother-love" of Lady Walham for her son, Lord Kew;[64] and the tyranny of the Evangelical stepmother, Sophia Alethea Hobson Newcome, toward the young Thomas.[65]

Nor does much of the Brookfield affair survive in *The Newcomes* except in the pathos of Thomas Newcome's separation from Mme. de Florac and in Clive's pangs of unrequited love for Ethel. These he confides to Laura Pendennis,[66] as Philip Firmin was years later to pour out his requited passion for Charlotte Baynes.[67] The reader immediately recalls how Thackeray had made Mrs. Elliot and Kate Perry his confidantes when he was *épris* with Mrs. Brookfield and how Esmond had similarly vented his feelings about Beatrix to his "dear lady."[68]

The events of Thackeray's married life are, as we have seen,[69] reproduced after a fashion in the chronicle of Clive's marriage to Rosy, but the tale is rather like *Hamlet* with the role of the Prince of Denmark omitted. Isabella's best qualities were left out of Rosy and her weaknesses put into that luckless girl, with the result that Clive's pallid affection for his first spouse has little resemblance to Thackeray's deep and tender devotion for his "poor little wife."

[62] See above, p. 6.
[63] Chapter 47. *Works*, XIV, 637.
[64] Chapter 37. The same, p. 485. See above, p. 183.
[65] Chapter 2.
[66] Chapter 50. *Works*, XIV, 662.
[67] *The Adventures of Philip*, chapter 18. *Works*, XVI, 248.
[68] See above, pp. 178f.
[69] See above, p. 75.

The novelist's hatred of his mother-in-law, not his love of Isabella, supplies the driving power for the chapters describing Clive's marriage.

Thus the resemblance between Thackeray and Clive lies less in their inward make-up than in the outward circumstances of their lives—their Anglo-Indian parentage, their coming to England as half-orphaned boys to be cared for by devoted and undevoted relatives, their indifferent success as artists, and their marriages. But just as Thackeray chose to extract from Clive's career most of the counterparts to his own three greatest emotional experiences, so he chose to extract the autobiographical element from Clive's appearance, thoughts, acts, and emotions. Largely in consequence of this extraction, Clive is perhaps—as a character—the least satisfactory of the autobiographic heroes. As Saintsbury says:

> I not only do not take very much interest in him, but I have even no very clear idea of him. He seems to have been good-looking, amiable after a fashion, rather *gauche*, fairly clever with his hands, not much good with his head ... he is not ... quite made up. I see Pendennis perfectly; I see Philip pretty well. I don't quite see Clive.[70]

Thackeray tried, without too much success, to fill the lacunae in Clive's total personality with borrowings from artist friends, notably John Leech and John Everett Millais. The protective attitude of Arthur Pendennis, a "senior boy in a tailed coat," toward the engaging little Clive Newcome, a "newly breeched infant in the Petties,"[71] strongly suggests a passage in Lady Ritchie's *Memoirs*. She is echoing her father's oft-told reminiscences of Leech's first coming to Charterhouse:

> I am sure there was no one among all his friends whose society my father enjoyed more than he did that of John Leech, whom he first remembered, so he has often told us with a smile, a small boy at the Charterhouse, in a little blue buttoned-up suit, set up on a form and made to sing "Home, Sweet Home" to the others crowding round about.[72]

John Everett Millais first met Thackeray in March, 1852,[73] and the two men were soon friends. In fact, the novelist writes of having

[70] "Introduction to *The Newcomes*." *Works*, XIV, xxiv.

[71] Chapter 4. The same, p. 43.

[72] Hester Thackeray Ritchie, *Chapters from Some Unwritten Memoirs* (New York, 1895), p. 93.

[73] *Letters*, III, 231.

the famous pre-Raphaelite painter as his dinner guest in February, 1855,[74] when the writing of *The Newcomes* was going into the home stretch. Millais's career at the Academy schools[75] slightly resembles Clive's days as art student.[76] Both young men were conspicuously privileged among their fellow students by virtue of their affluence, good looks, and facility in their chosen profession. Doting parents gave the young Millais a background designed to make his budding career as comfortable and secure as possible. Similarly, Colonel Newcome was solicitous to provide for Clive's student days a home which would cater to his every foreseeable need.

But the case of Clive Newcome is only one example of a trend which began faintly in *The Newcomes* and showed itself more pronouncedly in *The Virginians*. Thackeray had exhausted the very best ore in his vein and was beginning to rely on slightly inferior stuff. The highly artistic management of this stuff made the circumstance hard to detect, for *The Newcomes* is probably, next to *Henry Esmond*, the most skilfully managed of the novels. The neat grouping of the huge *dramatis personae* around the central theme of worldly marriage, the dexterous introduction—with its farrago of beast fables on the subject of trickery and false pretensions, the graceful linkage of this fable with the various strains of allegory in the following narrative: these all attest to the high artistry of *The Newcomes*.

As to its sweeping panorama of characters, one feels that Thackeray was ransacking his ultimate resources to provide this display. Hitherto unexploited relatives like Great-aunt Becher were called on to provide persons like Miss Honeyman.[77] Certain of Brookfield's less pleasant traits were plastered on to the earlier Thackerayan lay figure of a Tractarian divine—sweet-scented, fragile, sycophantic, and hypocritical.[78] The result was the Reverend Charles Honeyman. Earlier lightly defined characters from minor works were brought forward and elaborated, as Mrs. Hobson Newcome

[74] The same, pp. 422f.

[75] See Francis Bickley, *The Pre-Raphaelite Comedy* (New York: Henry Holt, n.d.), chapters 3 and 4.

[76] *The Newcomes*, chapters 17 and 18.

[77] *Letters*, I, 4n.

[78] Earlier and briefer studies of the type are Lemuel Whey in *Mr. and Mrs. Frank Berry* (*Works*, IV, 333); Edmund Lavender in *Barry Lyndon* (chapter 18. *Works*, VI, 262f.); Young Oriel in *Our Street* (*Works*, X, 126ff.).

seems to have been sketched—partially at least—from the Lion-Huntress of Belgravia.[79] The barnyard allegory of the Pulleyn family seems to have helped Thackeray with his conception of Barnes Newcome's unhappy marriage to the Lady Clara Pulleyn.[80] The old Countess Kew seems at times less like the worldly, Thackerayan dowagers who preceded her[81] than like the witch who symbolizes her in two of Doyle's allegorical initial-letters at the heads of the chapters.[82]

Sally Baxter as Ethel Newcome represents the sole infusion of a vital new personal relationship into *The Newcomes*. Yet in Thackeray's life that relationship was a relatively minor one. Another more important bond was coming into being as Anny and Minny matured into womanhood, and use was to be made of it in *The Virginians*.[83]

[79] *Works*, VIII, 507–522.
[80] Chapter 28.
[81] See above, p. 65.
[82] See chapters 38 and 52. *Works*, XIV, 493 and 681.
[83] See below, p. 213.

CHAPTER VII

The Home Stretch

THE lowered opinion of the United States, which Thackeray expressed to Sally Hampton after the second American tour,[1] resulted largely from a closer experience during that tour with the vulgarities of the American scene. But the novelist also changed his mind about America because his psychological pendulum, having swung toward that country on the first tour, swung away from it on the second.

Two weeks after Thackeray's first landing in Boston on November 12, 1852, he had jubilantly written his daughters:

Going home, coming to New York! Law bless us—it's nothing. I hope I shall go home and come back again too—if they continue to like lectures by the Powers they shall have more and you young ladies will have a little fortune comfortable and assured when my jaws have ceased to wag. We are up 3 pairs of stairs in very snug rooms at a very good hotel. The people have not turned out with flags and drums to receive me like Dickens: but the welcome is a most pleasant one because there is no speechifying nor ceremony in it—Everybody has read Somebody's books.[2]

Of course there appeared that bane of the traveling celebrity—the hordes of people everywhere who must receive a handshake and some friendly words. But even they could not quell Thackeray's enthusiasm. Their constant calls at his hotel room provided an excuse not to write.[3]

While he was still enjoying this first enthusiasm over the New World, Thackeray's letters radiated a happiness that had been foreign to them since the social triumphs following the success of *Vanity Fair*. Before that it had rarely been visible since the exultation of discovering after his marriage that he could work and support a family. New environment alone could not work the change; Thackeray had never been exultantly happy on his Mediterranean Cruise, and his Irish tour had only brought him great joy when he was being lionized by Lever and his friends around the claret-laden

[1] See above, p. 188.
[2] *Letters*, III, 119.
[3] The same, p. 121.

board in Dublin. By 1852 the formula to bring Thackeray out of his melancholy consisted of new scenes plus stimulating associations, particularly if those associations had an atmosphere of triumph about them. And the cities of the United States seaboard were almost the only new spots in the world that could provide him with this kind of happiness. Once he had skimmed the cream from them—and it took him only a few weeks to do so—it was a conclusion that melancholy would again claim him for her own.

Yet Thackeray's spirits during the first tour remained generally good. The temporary spiritual refuge he had established with the Baxters helped keep him cheerful, as did his good health, for he wasn't sick a day during this tour. Moreover a protective coating was placed over the sordid realities of the American scene by the small groups of gentlemen who coalesced around him in the seaboard cities. In Boston, for example, there was "a very pleasant society of literary big-wigs with large old houses and good large libraries and good cellars with old wine, yea old claret of 44—but law! there's no time to drink it."[4] Providence was as jolly a place as Boston almost. There is always a knot of pleasant folks, fogeyfied, respectable, fond of literature with whom it is jolly to consort."[5]

Though these "fogeyfied" dignitaries enveloped Thackeray as eagerly on his second as on his first visit, the lure of greater lecture profits drew him south and west beyond the radiating good cheer of their well-warmed libraries and '44 claret. His fiercest grapple with the realities of American life came during his Mark Twainian voyage on a Mississippi River steamer from New Orleans to Cairo. Among his shipmates were a man with delirium tremens, a bearded lady, and a giantess. These worthies all ate with the blades of knives, and the practise amused Thackeray as always. Moreover he was then absorbed in a study of the American technique for circumventing handkerchiefs. "There's one elegant way of operating with one forefinger applied to one nostril which I'll show any company of ladies when I get home."[6] Yet he had to confess:

this country whiggifies me. The rabble supremacy turns my gorge. The gentlemen stand aloof from public affairs, and count no more than yonder Irish bog trotter . . . I couldn't bear to live in a country at this stage in its political existence.[7]

  [4] The same, p. 519.
  [5] The same, p. 530.
  [6] The same, p. 589.
  [7] The same, pp. 592f.

Thackeray was in fact about as offended with American vulgarity as was Dickens before him. But the author of *Vanity Fair*
showed more discretion in playing down his aversion than Dickens
had practised. It is not hard to determine the reasons for that
delicacy. First, there was the elder novelist's natural dislike of
giving offense; added to that was his gentlemanly feeling that the
Americans were his hosts; finally, there was his shrewd regard for
his American earnings. After telling James Russell Lowell about a
Boston reviewer who had accused him of planning a satire on the
United States, Thackeray denied that he could ever "compose a
book befouling the nest in which" he had "been made so comfortable.[8]"

Moreover, Thackeray had what might be called "a long view"
about America, an awareness that the vulgarities which had so
repelled Dickens were inevitable in a culture emerging from its
swaddling clothes. Traveling in Switzerland, for example, between
his two transatlantic tours, Thackeray found himself regarded by
fellow English tourists as the champion of American folkways.
Hence he was assaulted with complaints about the nasal voices,
the "knife-eating," the public cigar-smoking of the American tourists there. His defense was that the Yankees were "only what John
Bull was in 1815 ludicrous with his jargon, extravagance, and
follies."[9] Thackeray pointed out too that the barbarian British
tourist of 1815 had been compensated for by "our grands seigneurs
too, and gentlemen and ladies whom the world couldn't surpass
nor I doubt equal." Now, thinking of his well-bred American friends,
he wishes that some of them would come to Europe and advertise
their country's aristocracy as the "grands seigneurs" had advertised
that of England forty years previously. One is reminded of Thackeray's "doctrine of innate gentility" and his insistence that his
mother was the equal in breeding to any lady of title.[10]

As the great chronicler of snobbery, Thackeray of course noted
the failure of Americans by and large to square their democratic
pretensions with their notorious kowtowing to aristocracy. In *Martin
Chuzzlewit* Dickens had drawn the Morris family,[11] who are likable
at first because they are free of the vulgarity that marks nearly all

[8] The same, p. 167. Written in January, 1853.
[9] The same, p. 295. Written on July 21, 1853.
[10] See above, pp. 150f.
[11] Chapter 17.

the other American characters in the book. But the Morrises suddenly turn out to be ineffable snobs when they cold-shoulder Martin because he has come to America in the steerage. Thackeray in his fiction failed to redress the balance thus set askew by Dickens. In fact it would have been impossible for him to do so since he realized full well that the gentlemanly Americans, who were the only ones he liked, did not share the professed democratic sentiments of the vulgar majority among their countrymen. They were not hypocrites like the latter, professing egalitarian sentiments and failing to practise them; they simply did not profess such sentiments in the first place any more than did Thackeray himself.

He, however, avoided this question and other thorny issues by never really depicting an American gentleman of his own day in fiction. There are briefly mentioned background characters like the "United States dandies," Mr. Broadway Swells and Mr. Washington Walker of *The Kickleburys on the Rhine* (1850). These young men "drive the finest carriages, they keep the grandest houses, they frequent the grandest company." They have elegant curling beards, primrose gloves, cambric handkerchiefs and feet as small as men with "sixteen quarterings."[12] Clearly there is more ridicule than praise in Thackeray's feelings about them.

After he had seen America, Thackeray created the Warrington twins in *The Virginians*. But since their arrival in England took place a century before he wrote about them, the twins did little to help Victorian ladies and gentlemen appreciate the fine breeding of American aristocrats. On the other hand, Yankee vulgarians continued—as they had before 1852—to fit beautifully into the parades of snobs which Thackeray loved to paint in his books. His old enemy, Nathaniel Parker Willis, the brash young American correspondent, had served him many times as a model, most notably as John Paul Jefferson Jones in *Vanity Fair*.[13] Then there was Washingtod Jackson, the after-dinner speaker of *A Dinner in the City* (1847) who puts his English hearers to sleep even as he tries to curry their favor by hymning the glories of their cultural heritage.[14]

[12] *Works*, X, 283.

[13] Chapter 49, *Works*, XI, 615f. See Harold H. Scudder, "Thackeray and Nathaniel Parker Willis," *Publications of the Modern Language Association of America*, VII, no. 2 (June, 1942), pp. 589–592.

[14] *Works*, VIII, 206.

Englishmen of the day loved to ridicule Americans on account of their pathetic substitutes for the titles of aristocracy which they could never enjoy. Writing *The Roundabout Papers* near the end of his career, Thackeray was washing his score clear of old sneers and cynicisms. At that time he cried *peccavi* to this charge and stepped forward again as the champion of Americans, writing ironically:

How often have we laughed at the absurd mania of the Americans for dubbing their senators, members of Congress, and States' representatives, Honourable! We have a right to call *our* privy councillors Right Honourable, our lords' sons Honourable, and so forth: but for a nation as numerous, well educated, strong, rich, civilized, free as our own, to dare to give its distinguished citizens titles of honour—monstrous assumption of low-bred arrogance and *parvenu* vanity! Our titles are respectable, but theirs absurd. Mr. Jones, of London, a chancellor's son, and a tailor's grandson, is justly honourable, and entitled to be Lord Jones at his noble father's decease: but Mr. Brown, the senator from New York, is a silly upstart for tacking Honourable to his name, and our sturdy British good sense laughs at him. Who has not laughed (I have myself) at Honourable Nahum Dodge, Honourable Zeno Scudder, Honourable Hiram Boake, and the rest? A score of such queer names and titles I have smiled at in America.[15]

Akin to honorific titles were the military ranks to which the Americans were partial at this time. Mrs. Trollope in *Domestic Manners of the Americans* and Dickens in *Martin Chuzzelwit* had sprinkled the United States with generals and colonels. Now Thackeray had found some Americans of this stripe traveling on the continent. In *The Newcomes* there is General Zeno F. Pokey, who lives in Paris, where his wife's footmen disgrace him by smoking cigars in public.[16] Thackeray liked to have the names of such Americans suggest swine, and General Pokey's may have something to do with a pig in a poke, or it may be a corruption of "Porky." He finally returned to Cincinnati "to his original pigs"—as opposed to the footmen. "Had not Cincinnatus himself pigs on his farm, and was he not a general and member of Congress too?"[17] In this connection, one wonders whether Thackeray was recalling Mrs. Trollope's description of the pigs which were maintained as scavengers to keep sweet the highways and byways of Cincinnati.[18]

[15] "On Ribbons." *Works*, XVII, 378.
[16] Chapter 22. *Works*, XIV, 274.
[17] Chapter 46. The same, p. 603.
[18] Frances Trollope, *Domestic Manners of the Americans*, ed. Donald Smalley (New York: Knopf, 1949), pp. 39, 88f, 105.

At Baden the Newcomes met General Jeremiah J. Bung, whose name is hardly more complimentary than General Pokey's. The Bungs are not without graciousness, however; for Mrs. Bung allows that Ethel Newcome is the only English girl she has seen who is dressed smartly enough to hold her own at a party on Fifth Avenue.[19]

Thackeray's well-known strictures against the Irish, particularly Dean Swift, had earned him the enmity of James Gordon Bennett. This celebrated pro-Irish editor of *The New York Herald* had christened the novelist a "Cockney snob." In 1861 Thackeray took occasion in one stroke to pay back the *Herald*, to ridicule anew the "glamorous" foreign society reporting of his old enemy Willis, and to hurl a dart at American chauvinism and snobbery in general. In the novel *Philip* there is a parody of a "Letter from an Attaché"— namely Willis, to *The New York Emerald*—namely *The Herald*, describing a ball at the British Embassy in Paris. It is attended by one of Thackeray's porcine Americans, Colonel Z. B. Hoggins of Albany and "his lady." She and "the peerless bride of Elijah J. Dibbs" of New York

were the observed of all observers for splendour, for elegance, for refined native beauty. The Royal Dukes danced with nobody else; and at the attention of one of the Princes to the lovely Miss Dibbs, I observed his Royal Duchess looked as black as thunder. Supper handsome. Back Delmonico to beat it.[20]

During his first flush of enthusiasm over America Thackeray had professed to pooh-pooh even *The Herald's* hostile review with a "Who cares?"[21] By his second tour, however, he was—significantly— instructing his valet to read the reports of his lectures in advance of him. It was the man's duty to warn his employer away from any hostile comment,[22] although at the same time Thackeray was trying to maintain Anny's and Minny's spirits by trying to pretend that it "doesn't much matter."[23] Later he attributed a fit of melancholy to being "sore at the way in which the Press has treated your Papaw—very kindly in the main but with an ignorance and impertinence often that turns my stomach."[24] During the 1850's Irish

[19] Chapter 33. The same, p. 434.
[20] Chapter 25. *Works*, XVI, 377.
[21] *Letters*, III, 121
[22] The same, p. 505.
[23] The same, p. 489.
[24] The same, p. 512.

immigrants were whipping up anti-English sentiment in the United States to the extent that Thackeray could complain he was

invariably blackguarded by one paper in every town, perhaps two, with a curious brutal malignity and ignorance that makes me more sad than angry. They are always all Irish who do it. Bon Dieu, why will they lie so?[25]

He reports having been "whipped for a malignant attack upon Carlyle" by virtue of having included in his lecture on George III a gracious reference to the Eighteenth Century Lord Carlisle. After returning to London from this final American tour, Thackeray wrote to Sally Baxter—now Mrs. Frank Hampton:

Shall I ever come back to see you again? Not as a public performer. I won't go through the degrading ordeal of press abuse again. Those scoundrels managed last time to offend and insult the most friendly stranger that ever entered your country or quitted it—I like my dear old friends just as well as ever, mind you— but the public *non pas*.[26]

On his return from this second American tour, Thackeray was so saturated emotionally that he could tell Dr. John Brown there were no greater pleasures in life than beefsteak, potatoes and a bottle of claret:

What *is* a greater pleasure? Gratified ambition? accumulation of money? . . . Fruition of some sort of desire perhaps; when one is twenty, yes, but at 47 Venus may rise from the sea, and I for one should hardly put on my spectacles to have a look.[27]

As he wrote that passage he made a mistake common to victims of middle-aged apathy; he supposed that it was a fundamental change of character, when in fact it was more like a new mutation of the protective shell over his sensitivity. A man may have such delusions of apathy and still leap from his chair with a roar of pain if a sensitive nerve to his self-esteem is touched. So Thackeray roared like the bull of Bashan when Yates, a fellow-member of the Garrick Club, lampooned him[28] or when Anny's first literary effort was attacked.[29]

Thackeray's sensibility during this last phase of his life expressed

[25] The same, p. 585.
[26] The same, p. 612. Written on July 12, 1856.
[27] The same, IV, 115.
[28] See above, p. 12.
[29] *Letters*, IV, 410 n.

itself in an ever-increasing nostalgia, the form of sentimentality most natural to the aged. Sentimentality is a form of wish-fulfillment, a way of weaving fantasies in which one's thwarted sensual appetites for tender experiences are gratified. Since Thackeray had erected a shell of premature and artificial old age around himself to protect him from emotional upheaval, he was forced to exclude from his fantasies any future sentimental wish-fulfillment. Because he lived in expectation of imminent death, he could never experience those wishes. Hence his wish-fulfillment was retroactive, a feeling that the past should have been different and better. But to wish such thoughts rationally would be to exclude his imperfect self from sharing in that better past, so he recreated the actual past, not as it was, but as he would like it to have been. Obviously the emotion that makes boyhood unhappiest is fear, so that must be excluded from nostalgic revery. Thackeray's master Carlyle, who had deeper insight than his pupil, on revisiting the beautiful landscapes of his boyhood wondered: "Why is the past so beautiful? The element of *fear* is withdrawn from it for one thing. That is all safe, while the present and future are all so dangerous."[30]

Carlyle's statement implies that pain of some kind must play a part in the original experience before valid nostalgia can be evoked. The correctness of his insight is borne out by Thackeray's wide and varied nostalgic reveries. One remembers how he wept as a man in his thirties when he recalled the coach that used to take him back to school.[31] And the pain of an old love—probably what he had felt for Isabella—started a nostalgic reminiscence as early as 1844 during the writing of *Barry Lyndon*.[32] A similar emotion was transferred from the author's mind to that of Arthur Pendennis when that hero started reading an old novel he had begun during the agonies of the Fotheringay affair:

And what meant those blots on the page? As you come in the desert to a ground where camel's hoofs are marked in the clay, and traces of withered herbiage are yet visible, you know that water was there once; so the place in Pen's mind was no longer green and the *fons lacrymarum* was dried up.[33]

[30] Quoted by James Anthony Froude, *Thomas Carlyle: A History of His Life in London* (New York, 1884), I, 17.
[31] See above, p. 18.
[32] See above, p. 109.
[33] Chapter 41. *Works*, XII, 518.

Whatever the state of Arthur's *fons lacrymarum*, the various wells of nostalgia in his maker's heart had a way of flowing at the most unexpected times, even when he visited Cambridge with Brookfield in 1849 and whiffed the odor of stale food in the dining room of his old college:

the thing to me most striking was . . . the smell of the dinner exactly like what I remember aforetime—Savoury odors of youth borne across I dont know what storms and deserts struggles passions poverties hopes hopeless loves and useless loves of twenty years!—There is a sentiment suddenly worked out of a number of veal and mutton-joints and surprizes me just as much as it astonishes you.[34]

Thackeray's nostalgia came then in part from perceiving that the *vanitas vanitatum* philosophy had removed all goals from the future and forced him to turn his eyes back to the past. And like the "vanity of vanities" philosophy itself, this awareness came in time to be not only an attitude but a pose—in fact, part of Thackeray's self-portrait.

What then had become of that other old pose, that of the buffoon? In earlier days it had provided Thackeray with a long row of literary egos under whose assumed names he could perform and amuse and satirize: Major Gahagan, James Yellowplush, Jeames de la Pluche, George FitzBoodle, and—most long-lived and popular—Michael Angelo Titmarsh. During the first half of the fifties, Thackeray's new occupation—lecturing—gave him a new variation of the buffoon's mask—that of the traveling quack.

Even prior to his very first series of lectures, before a distinguished London audience in May, 1851, Thackeray wrote to the Carlyles a note which he signed "Equilibrist and Tightrope dancer in ordinary to the nobility and the Literati." Appended was a comic drawing of himself as a tightrope walker.[35] In arranging his *English Humourists* tour through the English provinces in April, 1852, he requested a friend in Birmingham to "consider whether now is a good or bad season for mountebanks to perform" in his city.[36]

The money was of course Thackeray's motive:

It's not a proud position certainly to lecture from town to town—but the money—but the children? If by a little posture making I can put money in their little purses shouldn't I.

[34] *Letters*, II, 510.
[35] The same, p. 775.
[36] The same, III, 42.

The novelist had grown accustomed to performing antics in his books before the huge, invisible reading public. However, his innate aristocratic prejudice made him wince at troubling himself that he might please a visible public to whom he felt superior. Telling Dr. John Brown how he was kowtowing to the merchants of Glasgow, he referred to "the great and illustrious Titmarsh cap in hand to a fat cotton or rum spinner."[37] Considering the scholarly character of the lectures and Thackeray's dignified presentation, this sensitivity seems uncalled for. Yet in view of his complex psychology, it was inevitable, and the motley garb of the mountebank was a cover for this wounded pride. Moreover that garb protected the lecturer's self-esteem if his efforts failed, for by assuming a quack's role he gave notice that he—Thackeray himself—was not involved emotionally in the success or failure of the lecture.

As the years went on, however, and the irritation and boredom of lecturing increased, Thackeray got the strength to carry on only from the psychic release that came with laughing at his comic self-portrait of the mountebank. Telling Mrs. Baxter of his plan to carry the *Four Georges* as far west as the Mississippi, he observed: "I shall go on my way like an old Mountebank (I get more ashamed of my nostrums daily) and send round the hat through the republic."[38] And weary unto death with the constant visitors, the supper parties, and the lionization of his role, he wrote to Anny and Minny from Boston: "You see my letters are not those of a human being but of a travelling lecturing quack."[39]

It was naturally a relief to see England again after such trying experiences as those of the second American tour. Thackeray's psychic pendulum swung back so strongly toward his homeland that he even enjoyed barnstorming the length and breadth of Great Britain to deliver the *Four Georges* lectures during the winter and spring of 1856–1857. This euphoria of mind had many causes beyond the mere joy of being home. One was the discovery of how his reputation had so ballooned that lecturing was as profitable in pleasant British surroundings as in unpleasant American locales. Another reason for this happiness was the fact that reading the

[37] The same, p. 32.
[38] The same, p. 166.
[39] The same, p. 514.

Georges had become too automatic even to disgust the lecturer any more.[40] Then there was the greater responsiveness of the British audiences, a trait that came from their deeper knowledge of the lecturer's subject matter. Even more important was the sheer joy of reaping the "golden harvest" of the lecture platform and being able to write home:

So you need none of you spare yourselves anything—not carriages horses fires comforts of any sort—when for 2 hours talking we can have 50£—mind this my dear old GP. and that if you will draw on Lubbocks for 50£ I have written to them to cash the bill.[41]

With affairs in such a happy state, life's vicissitudes seemed minor: blue devils, "spasms," the troublesome stricture, the malaria—much improved since a quinine treatment in New York—all smote Thackeray periodically and frequently, but only one or two lectures had to be cancelled on account of illness. There is no doubt too that he enjoyed illness. A stoic about the pain that came with the onset of his various attacks, he was a valetudinarian in convalescence, enjoying the luxury of bed-rest, free for the moment of responsibility, and hovered over solicitously by Anny and Minny.

The *Four Georges* drew only two unpleasant reactions from British groups. Thackeray was amused by Scottish objections[42] to the inclusion of Mary Stuart among the great adulteresses of history.[43] He was relieved at being boycotted by "the great world" of London because of his highly derogatory lecture on the Queen's uncle, George IV. If Thackeray's erstwhile aristocratic friends had troubled to read his published works, they would have learned how any thought of that royal gentleman made him froth at the mouth. His changed attitude since *Vanity Fair* days toward the "great world" is the measure of his increased moral stature. At that time he had virtually gone on his knees to pray that social triumph would not turn his head.[44] Now the severance of that connection affected

---

[40] The same, IV, 22.
[41] The same, III, 634.
[42] The same, pp., 629, 630.
[43] "George the First." *Works*, XIII, 714 f.
[44] See above, p. 152.

him about as deeply as the loss of an old tooth. On hearing that Minny's *debut* could not take place, he lapsed into irony:

I hear that I am in disgrace with the fashionable world for speaking disrespectfully of the Georgyporgies—and am not to be invited myself, much more to be allowed to take others into polight Society. I writhe at the exclusion.[45]

When Thackeray was *in extremis* a year-and-a-half later, in miserable health, and plagued with a thousand gadfly vexations while he staggered along under the gigantic succubus of *The Virginians*, these little crosses might have seriously troubled him. And had his fellow Garrick Club member, Edward Yates, chosen the early months of 1857 instead of the summer of 1858 to lampoon him in the press, Thackeray might have laughed the matter off. As it was he treated Yates like one of the hidden human serpents of whom he had such a morbid fear,[46] and rode him unmercifully out of the club.

The Carmichael-Smyths were, as usual, difficult to deal with during the British lecture tour of 1856–1857. Here too Thackeray had so grown in stature since the 1840's that the querulousness of his aged parents was now merely a problem of ways and means to him. No longer did it present searing emotional crises. Major Carmichael-Smyth was sinking fast and demanded constant nursing from his wife. She bore up heroically in the presence of her husband, but—as compensation—started making demands on her son and granddaughters. To her usual weapon of pathos, she added a nervous illness of her own, as well as the seriousness of her husband's condition, to make periodic calls that would bring to her side Anny, Minny, and their father. Thackeray wanted to provide lodgings and attendants for the old couple near his current residence in Onslow Square, Brompton,[47] but his stepfather—who hated London—refused to leave Paris. Anny and Minny kept the situation patched up by making long visits to Paris, generously forsaking the pleasant London life now attainable by virtue of their father's wealth. Thackeray waited, secretly looking forward no doubt to his step-father's death as a solution of the problem. He had outgrown the old fears of divided authority that used to come when he

---

[45] *Letters*, IV, 17. Written, on February 8, 1857.
[46] See above, p. 12.
[47] *Letters*, III, 638.

had had to send Anny and Minny to their grandmother, or when she had come to live with him.

Some of Thackeray's ebullience in the winter of 1856–1857 came from a feeling that he had almost found the pot of gold at the rainbow's end. He was about to become a *rentier* who could devote his life to anything he wanted. The two choices that appealed most to him were a return to the artist's life or a career in parliament. For years he had surveyed the former through the same rose-colored spectacles which he had long used in seeking the elusive sinecure that had never materialized.[48] While he had been writing *The Newcomes*, Thackeray had found himself imaginatively reentering the old world of his twenties in describing Clive's visit to Rome. Then came into play both nostalgia and Thackeray's fondness for finding farther hills greener, especially after he had visited Rome in the winter of 1853–1854.

The simplicity of the student's life there, the greatness and friendly splendour of the scenes surrounding him, the delightful nature of the occupation in which he is engaged, the pleasant company of comrades, inspired by a like pleasure over a similar calling, the labour, the meditation, the holiday and the kindly feast afterwards, should make the Art-students the happiest of youth, did they but know their good fortune. Their work is for the most part delightfully easy. It does not exercise the brain too much, but gently occupies it, and with a subject most agreeable to the scholar.[49]

As the embodiment of the ideal calling, the character of J. J. Ridley the artist is almost canonized. His studio light throws an aureole about his head as he works at "his glorious but harmless war":

With these he achieves conquests, wherein none are wounded save the envious: with that he shelters him against how much idleness, ambition, temptation! . . . Art is truth: and truth is religion: and its study and practice a daily work of pious duty.[50]

[48] In September, 1848, Thackeray applied unsuccessfully for the position of Assistant-Secretary at the General Post Office (*Letters*, II, 427, 431, 432, 433n; IV, 391). In 1851 he was hoping for some sinecure in the gift of the Lord Chancellor (*Letters*, II, 791). In 1854 he put out feelers for a post vacated by John Lockhart's death, the Auditorship of the Duchy of Lancashire (the same, III, 404). In February, 1855, he was advised to apply for a police magistracy, but failed to do so (the same, p. 417). In the same month he learned that he might have had a position in the Board of Trade (the same, p. 425).

[49] Chapter 39. *Works*, XIV, 507.

[50] Chapter 65. The same, p. 851.

The presence in *The Newcomes* of the two worldly, snobbish artists, Smee and Gandish, does not detract from Thackeray's conviction that the true artist's life is a priestly calling. Writing *Philip* near the end of his life in 1861, he still held the same convictions. Ridley appears in that book, again under a halo of studio light, again blessedly happy at his calling. Again the author explains at length his view that art is challenging enough to absorb, but not taxing enough to exasperate its practitioner.[51]

In seriously considering a return to an art career in 1857, Thackeray was thinking inconsistently. He would not need any income from his painting, and he had long since proved to himself that he lacked the talent to excel in the profession. In fact as early as 1852 he had reported to his mother from Vienna, after a bout of tramping through galleries, that looking at pictures always made him "want to give up everything . . . and turn painter." Even then he had known that the best way to cure the feeling "would be to set to work for a month—to see that I can't do it, and give it up in disgust."[52] With this awareness in 1857, when he considered going back to painting, Thackeray should have regarded his new occupation as nothing more than a hobby. Yet, just at that time, the sight of some paintings in Glasgow by the now forgotten Mrs. Hugh Blackburne made him dismiss the thought:

> I was so confounded by Mrs. Blackburne's prodigious genius and saw that she had a talent so infinitely superior to my little one—that I thought I had best blow that poor little farthing candle out, and think of it no more.[53]

Why should an amateur give up an occupation that brings him happiness merely because a professional far excels him? The answer is that Thackeray was still visualizing his life in terms of glory and fame. A week later, however, he saw his potential art career more clearly as a mere gentlemanly avocation. He was telling Mrs. Carmichael-Smyth of his dilemma in choosing between painting, parliament, or the writing of history during the Golden Age that had seemingly dawned for him. Ease, and "perhaps Conscience" urged

[51] Chapter 6. *Works*, XVI, 74f.
[52] *Letters*, III, 60.
[53] The same, IV, 4.

him to "retire and paint pooty little pictures."[54] Clearly he now saw his paintings-to-be in their true light.

His abortive parliamentary career is one of the *curiosa* of Thackeray's life. Clearly he would not have been happy in the treadmill of parliamentary duties. But there was at play here the same atavistic instinct which made him regard his whole professional life as an atonement for the prodigality—such as it was—of his youth. During his money-amassing period of the 1850's, he more than once compared his new fund of capital with that which he had once frittered away. One gains the impression that he felt the replacement of that exact sum would restore him to a once-cherished status. While still in America in 1855, he had estimated his earnings, current and prospective, and exclaimed: "why then, at 50, I shall be as I was at 21."[55] In October of 1859, shortly after the completion of *The Virginians* and during the planning of *The Cornhill Magazine*, he was to write: "If I can work for 3 years now, I shall have put back my patrimony and a little over."[56] Ironically fate was to grant him just those three years plus a little more—fourteen months in fact—of life. During that time he was able to recoup his patrimony augmented by a small overplus.

The status which Thackeray felt had been forfeited by the loss of his patrimony was that of the hereditary aristocrat. One of the symbols of such a man was a seat in parliament. Hence it is clear that this particular prestige symbol—a "vanity" by definition—still had value in Thackeray's eyes during the happy months of 1857. But it took more than the allurements of prestige to make him face the hazards of a parliamentary election. The paucity of political reference in his novels has blinded readers to the fact that he was keenly interested in politics. Anyone taking the trouble to read the *Punch* contributions, particularly the chapters of *The Book of Snobs* that did not find their way into the collected edition,[57] will be struck by Thackeray's astuteness as a political commentator. But the feud in 1851 with the *Punch* staff over the lampooning of Napoleon III had virtually brought to an end his contributions to

[54] The same, p. 7.
[55] The same, III, 528.
[56] The same, IV, 155
[57] Chapter 17–23. *Works*, IX, 328–358

that magazine. The manuscript of an undelivered speech which he had written for a meeting of the Administrative Reform Association on July 11, 1855, shows the same astuteness.

Clearly there lay in Thackeray's make-up a vein of political acumen, even though he professed to dislike politics when he first mentioned his new ambitions in a letter to Sally Baxter Hampton: "when I am independent what shall we do? Hush—perhaps have a try at politics for which I dont care now—but one must do something and when you begin to play you get interested in the game."[58] Three weeks later Thackeray was refusing a borough offered by the Whig Whipper on the ground that he preferred to stand as an independent.[59] Five days later he was saying "there's a great career before me if I will but run it," and three days afterward he reinforced this statement, observing that the remark was "not swagger but a fair look at Chances in the face:

Just when the novel-writing faculty is pretty well used up here is independence a place in Parliament and who knows what afterwards? Upon my word I dont seem much to care, and fate carries me along in a stream somehow—Shall I float with it or jump on shore? I shant be happy in politics . . . but with the game there, it seems faint-hearted not to play it.[60]

As he approached the actual task of standing for parliament, Thackeray's innate reluctance showed itself. In March he refused a Scottish seat because he knew it was impossible to conform to his constituents' anti-Catholic and Sabbatarian views.[61] By July, 1857, he had decided to stand for Oxford.

The election turned out just as one would expect. Thackeray and his opponent, Edward Cardwell, conducted their mutual exchanges on the highest level of gentlemanly courtesy, while Thackeray's henchmen—without his knowledge—carried out their activities on the practical level of politics. After he had lost the election by the small margin of sixty-seven votes and had learned that his supporters had been bribing voters, he declared he would have had to surrender his seat had he won.

The Sabbatarian issue was raised again during the campaign and

[58] *Letters*, III, 653. Written on December 10, 1856.
[59] The same, IV, 3f.
[60] The same, p. 7.
[61] The same, p. 31.

Thackeray refused to temporize, despite certain constituents' strong aversion to the opening of places of amusement on Sundays. Here the novelist's refusal was an extension into the outside world of the unresolved quarrel between his mother's Evangelicalism and his theological liberalism. Although he spoke well on the hustings and went through all the distasteful duties of canvassing, one suspects that he was not too anxious to win. After the election Thackeray regarded the whole thing as a hoax. Writing to Dr. John Brown on January 2, 1858, he reported:

the Oxford election cost £850. It was a cowardly robbery of a poor, innocent, rightly-served man. And if I had won—that is the beauty of it—I should have been turned out, my agents, in spite of express promises to me, having done acts which would have ousted me. May the present be a luckier year to me, and a happy one![62]

Never did a wish receive less fulfillment; 1858 was a dark year for Thackeray. The last months of 1857 had been marred by the financial panic in the United States, and that in turn had spread to Great Britain. Although Thackeray's original fear for his American dividends had proved unfounded, his well-known generosity turned him into a virtual one-man alms bureau for British friends and acquaintances who suddenly found themselves penniless. His benefactions, plus the gradual upward curve of his living expenses, discovered him at the end of 1857 no richer than at the beginning. And he was still confronted with the task of writing another novel, for on his return from America, Bradbury and Evans had lured Thackeray with the colossal bribe of £6,000 to sell himself once more into Egypt. At the time he had expected that huge sum to insure completely a life of leisure. Now his hope proved vain; even with the £6,000 he would only maintain his present way of life and approach a little nearer to the final goal. Thus Thackeray felt much as Alice was to feel in her famous race with the Red Queen. He had to run ever faster just to stay where he was.

This feeling of futility must have had something to do with the weakness of *The Virginians* as compared with the earlier novels. Yet there were other reasons for the decline of Thackeray's narrative power. Professor Ray has attributed it, in part at least, to

[62] The same, p. 64.

the basic change which had come over him with the collapse of the Brookfield affair.[63] He cites as autobiographical a passage in *The Virginians* which describes Henry Esmond after his withdrawal to Virginia:

A something had occurred in his life, which had cost a tinge of melancholy over all his existence. He was not unhappy—to those about him most kind—most affectionate . . . but there had been some bankruptcy of his heart, which his spirit never recovered. He submitted to life rather than enjoyed it.[64]

Then Professor Ray goes on to say:

Thackeray's withdrawal from the give-and-take of intense personal relationships changed the character of his fiction, for his capacity for emotional realization in his novels depended to a marked degree upon the pressure of his current emotional experience. The quieter pages of his later books reflect his experience remotely and with subsiding force and spontaneity.[65]

Thackeray's renunciation of "the give-and-take of intensely personal relationships" was unquestionably a major factor in his waning creative ability. But the sad ending of the Brookfield affair—however important it may have been as an emotional landmark—does not seem to me to have been the principal cause of that renunciation. It was one of his poses to attribute his latter-day melancholy to a broken heart. That pose was widespread in his time; its origins lie far back in the middle ages; Byron had given it fresh impetus, and the Victorians—especially the Victorian women—loved it. But Thackeray's years, his position as a family man, and the need of protecting Mrs. Brookfield—all prevented him from striking the attitude too publicly. Before anyone but Mrs. Elliot, Kate Perry, and a few other intimates, he had to drape the attitude—not over himself but over one of his thinly disguised autobiographical heroes.

Even if Thackeray had never loved and lost Mrs. Brookfield, he would have striven to eliminate from his life all personal relationships in which there was an element of conflict. Such a policy was inevitable in his nature with its sensitive abhorrence of pain. His life had been a gradual drawing into his hands of all reins of authority so that others could not set themselves to oppose him. To use one

---

[63] "The 'Unwritten Part' of *Pendennis* and *Esmond*," *The Listener* (August 4, 1949), p. 198.
[64] Chapter 3. *Works*, XV, 28.
[65] "The 'Unwritten Part' of *Pendennis* and *Esmond*," p. 198.

of his favorite metaphors, he wanted to be the Turk in his harem. There was still the unresolved religious struggle with his mother, but both had adjusted themselves to that; Mrs. Carmichael-Smyth knew enough not to bring up the subject of religion and, if she had, it was hardly the stuff from which a writer like Thackeray could weave fiction. He was too cautious of his public.

Thackeray's conflicts during his last decade of life were with large groups: his lecturing public, the electors of Oxford, the contributors to the *Cornhill Magazine*, and his readers. While these groups were, in different degrees, psychological extensions of his personal circle, there was this difference: he could assume authority from the start with his intimates like Isabella, Anny, or Minny, or he could gradually assume it, as he had done with his mother and was doing with Mrs. Brookfield when her husband moved her away from him. But this control could not be exercised over large groups outside his circle. When he could not dominate, his tendency was to retreat.

Thackeray retreated from the lecture audiences of the small towns in the United States by never going back to them with more lectures. He could no longer endure the criticisms that ignorance had levied on him. In the difference with the Scottish and Oxford electors over the Sabbatarian issue, he had effectually retreated by refusing to compromise. The quarrel with his contributors to the *Cornhill* was that which every editor has to face and win—the right to reject unsatisfactory contributions finally and without recourse. Thackeray first tried to mollify unsuccessful contributors who offered tales of personal hard luck with their manuscripts. The mollification consisted of paying off these unfortunate men and women with gifts out of his own pocket. In the end he retreated by surrendering the editorship. Furthermore, it should not be forgotten that his whole literary career since *Vanity Fair* was a retreat from his satirical position under pressure of the Victorian mistrust of satire.

But whether Thackeray's withdrawal from intense personal relationships was caused by the Brookfield affair or by psychological factors far older, it was, nevertheless, largely to blame for that waning narrative ability that becomes marked with *The Virginians*. Some external causes also bore their part in the change. Though he had often been forced to rise from a sickbed to meet the monthly deadlines of *The Newcomes*, the experience had then been sufficiently new to be a challenge. Moreover ill health then was at that time an excuse to decline the constant dinner invitations which were an even greater hazard to literary production. Now Thackeray no longer had the heart to pass up these invitations unless sickness actually had him in its grasp. And the writing of monthly numbers in bed or in a convalescent's chair had become too familiar to be any longer a challenge. It requires the iron will of a Parkman to carry forward creative writing year after year in the face of invalidism. Though Thackeray was not the weakling he thought himself, his will was certainly not of iron. So continual illness had its share in his waning powers.

Another external cause for Thackeray's waning power lay in the mere fact of his being a celebrity. None of the demands on his time that celebrity entails had passed him by. Yet he was without the technique that most important persons have since developed of shielding themselves from the public. His time and energy were at the mercy of a gigantic correspondence, the pressure from alms-seekers, and the demands of past acquaintances, current friends, and would-be acquaintances. Such pressures are not the sort from which novels are born. Yet by isolating himself from them, a writer isolates himself from the springs of life which must nourish his creation.

Then there was the decision to graft his new novel, *The Virginians* upon a stem provided by the Preface to *Henry Esmond*, penned four years previously. Here Rachel Esmond Warrington, purportedly writing in 1778, chronicles the settlement of her family in Virginia and the highlights of its early existence there. Thackeray's decision to start *The Virginians* from that point inevitably dictated an American locale for a considerable part of his new novel. It is significant that he moved the action as quickly as he dared to England and kept it there as long as possible before moving it back to Virginia. For his research into Colonial America had an academic flavor; it didn't bring to life the period as the research into George III's England had vivified its period when he had prepared *The Four Georges*. For that reason the English portions of *The Virginians* escape much of the contrived, lifeless quality of the average historical novel, where the local color is acquired by research, not by experience. But in writing *Esmond* Thackeray had not only been saturated in the Queen Anne period; he had poured into his manuscript the pain of losing Mrs. Brookfield. In *The Virginians* he had no such recently experienced passion to distil into fiction. He started by digging from mothballs his old theme of a widow's tyranny over her son. Then he applied to it a modification which he had worked out three years before with Sophia Alethea Hobson Newcome: Mrs. Esmond Warrington was given twin sons.[66] Unfortunately, their attitude to one another is mawkish and totally unreal. Because Thackeray had never had a brother, he could not conceive even the minor irritations which grind away like sand between the most affectionate of brothers and which alone can make a relationship interesting.

Thackeray also resurrected his relationship with his grandmother,[67] to serve as model for the Bernstein business. It will be recalled how that dowager, who is in reality Beatrix Esmond grown old, had formed Harry Warrington in the mold of an eighteenth-century gentleman. Another relationship in *The Virginians*, that of General Lambert and his two daughters, bears out Professor Ray's statement that Thackeray could only "recover something of his earlier vigor" in the act of "describing a situation approximating one in which he was still involved."[68] For Anny and Minny served, by their father's own admission, as the models for Theo and Hetty Lambert.[69] The General himself was modeled on Thackeray as he was in the 1850's, even down to such details as the worthy soldier's fondness for Montaigne,[70] or the way both had of using a tooth-extraction as a symbol for painful experience.[71]

Only one tiny rift marred Thackeray's perfect relationship at this time with his daughters; he was gnawed by a jealous fear that they might marry and leave him. During the second American tour he had discouraged Anny's romantic interest in one Creyke, a penniless, tubercular young clergyman with expensive tastes.[72] In the fictional situation depicted in *The Virginians*, when Hetty Lam-

---

[66] See above, p. 5.

[67] See above, p. 65.

[68] "The 'Unwritten Part' of *Pendennis* and *Esmond*," p. 198.

[69] "I am afraid the 2 Lambert girls in the Virginians are very like them" (*Letters*, IV, 81).

[70] *The Virginians*, chapter 57. *Works*, XV, 592. Cf. *Letters*, II, 245f.

[71] *The Virginians*, chapter 33; *Works*, XV, 339. Cf. *Letters*, II, 19, 235; IV, 226; *Mr. Brown's Letters to His Nephew* (*Works*, VIII, 312); *Mr. Thackeray in the United States* (*Works*, X, 609); *Henry Esmond*, book 3, chapter 4 (*Works*, XIII, 361).

[72] *Letters*, III, 524.

bert evinces such an interest in Harry Warrington, Lambert covers up his jealousy with just such a jest as Thackeray might have used:

> On Tuesday morning I am king of my house and family. On Tuesday evening Prince Whippersnapper makes his appearance, and my reign is over. A whole life is forgotten and forsworn for a pair of blue eyes, a pair of lean shanks, and a head of yellow hair.[73]

A few months before this passage was drafted, the novelist had been writing his daughters in the same vein about non-existent suitors:

> already Anny is deploring the departure of her youth. Her gentle sighs breathed on the artless paper made me wonder whether TOMKINS had not made his appearance;—I shall be very glad to see him—Dont give him the Liverpool Port if you ask him to dinner . . . the young beggar does not know about wine yet.[74]

Despite his jealousy there is little doubt but that Thackeray wanted to see his daughters happily married. That feeling is implicit in a description to his mother of their sadness at the marriage of a younger friend. Quoting the story of Jephthah's daughter, Thackeray wrote: "They are both of them beginning to bewail their Virginity in the mountains."[75]

Yet the plot of *The Virginians* had to develop suspense by creating a struggle between General Lambert and his daughter Theo over her right to marry George Warrington. There is nothing in the General's character to suggest that his once flippantly expressed jealousy would make him seriously oppose the happiness of a child whom he loved dearly. Nor does Thackeray make jealousy his basis for the General's opposition; it is motivated entirely by a stubborn sense of honor. Lambert will not sanction a match which lacks the approval of the young man's mother, Mme. Esmond Warrington, who—for her part—will not accept a daughter-in-law with only a penny for her portion.

Thus the conflict between the young lovers and the heroine's father is inadequately motivated. But another aspect of the situation must be considered too. In describing their separation, Thackeray was in a sense reliving the separation from Isabella that had taken

[73] Chapter 33. *Works*, XV, 338f.
[74] *Letters*, IV, 33. Written in March, 1857.
[75] The same, p. 272. Written on July 5, 1862.

place during his own betrothal.[76] Hence the enforced separation of Theo and George is moving, and its depths give depth to the characters themselves.

Also it is quite probable that Thackeray's feelings about a son-in-law were ambivalent. Jealous as he might have been toward the man who would probably claim one of his daughters, that man could also take the place of the son he had always wanted. And men commonly want sons who possess what they themselves feel to be their own lacks. In Thackeray's case these lacks would best be supplied by a youth of the "head boy" type such as he had idolized in his schooldays,[77] a "frank, manly young" hero, good-looking, pleasure-loving, and without much depth of intellect. Young Frank Castlewood had been such a character; so was Harry Warrington as he laid siege to the heart of Hetty Lambert. In this sense, the author's failure to marry Harry and Hetty to one another marks a rueful acceptance of the fact that his own ideal son was not the ideal mate for his darling Minny.[78]

On turning from the Warrington and Lambert families to some of the other characters in *The Virginians*, one sees where Thackeray's powers are failing. Bernstein is one of his great creations because she is a logical extension into old age of Beatrix Esmond and because she is partly a recreation of Mrs. Butler.[79] But the Miles Warringtons are a pallid reproduction of the Evangelical, hypocritical, snob families that the novelist had portrayed more vividly in the Hobson Newcomes and elsewhere. And other characters are variations of familiar types that have interesting beginnings but end nowhere. Sampson starts to go beyond the renegade parson but falls below the stature of Charles Honeyman in interest. The Earl of Castlewood has traits that differentiate him from Thackeray's stock "wicked lord" of the eighteenth-century, but not enough of them. Castlewood's sister Maria combines not very successfully the "adventuress" traits of Becky Sharp or Beatrix Esmond with the doting softness of Amelia Sedley. Great things might have been done with her had Thackeray still possessed his old cunning.

[76] See above, p. 71.

[77] See above, pp. 20f.

[78] Late in *The Virginians* Thackeray endows himself as George Warrington with just such a son, whom he calls Captain Scapegrace (Chapter 92. *Works*, XV, 979).

[79] See above, p. 65.

So in *Philip* remarkable possibilities inhere in Dr. Firmin, the hero's father, who is the first full-length man of medicine in the Thackerayan canon. Firmin is a curious combination of pathos and villainy, but he gets packed off to America before the story has gone far and never comes back. His sin lay in being too much like a cuckoo; he was growing so lustily in the nest of the author's imagination that he was thrown out lest he endanger those more tender chicks, his own son and Charlotte Baynes. With such fledglings of his own brood Thackeray was more at ease. Philip was a mixture of "the artist as a young man"[80] and of one George Morland Crawford.[81] Charlotte Baynes was a more accurate portrait of Isabella than Rosy Mackenzie had been,[82] and Mrs. Baynes is a less vicious lampoon of Mrs. Shawe than Thackeray had perpetrated in 'The Campaigner.' General Baynes seems to have had much of Colonel Carmichael in him, and some of Mary Carmichael found its way into Mrs. Baynes. Hence, as Professor Ray observed, Thackeray recovered "something of his earlier vigour" because he was "drawing on memories too bitter ever to lose their sting"—in this case the feud he had conducted with Mrs. Shawe over the right to marry Isabella, which figures in the book as "the duel fought over Charlotte Baynes by Philip and Mrs. General Baynes."[83]

Because Thackeray's emotion was strong as he relived those poignant days of his courtship, Mrs. Baynes is not another Campaigner, nor is General Baynes a repetition of Colonel Newcome, nor is Charlotte just another Rosy. But the background characters do not fare as well. The Talbot Twysdens as a family are of the same stripe as the Miles Warringtons; Talbot himself is a faded Pitt Crawley Jr. or Barnes Newcome; and his wife and daughters are only réchauffée versions of a hundred earlier Thackerayan mothers and daughters in the world of London snobdom.

Here again, as in the case of the digressions, it was easier for Thackeray to apologize than to mend his ways. Even as he finished *Philip* in August of 1862, he wrote "De Finibus," the *Roundabout Paper* for that month, in which he pictured his imaginary critics as

[80] See above, p. 54.
[81] *Letters*, II, 721n.
[82] See above, p. 75.
[83] "The 'Unwritten Part' of *Pendennis* and *Esmond*," p. 198.

saying: "what a poverty of friends the man has! He is always asking us to meet those Pendennises, Newcomes, and so forth. Why does he not introduce us to some new characters?"[84] Thackeray excuses himself by saying, "the dish which one man devours, another dislikes." But that apology is compounding his error. To admit that one only likes the old and familiar is an admission that one is incapable of new growth.

Paradoxically, the exculpatory digressions of Thackeray's later years are full of both affirmation and repudiation. When he wanted to use an old literary device, whether in the field of plot construction, character-building, or ideology, he affirmed his fondness for it. When he was tired of such a habit, or saw that a favorite idea was no longer tenable, he repudiated it in one way or another.

Our novelist's dislike of managing a plot, for example, can partly be blamed on his aversion to effort, but it derives also from a distaste for certain artificial conventions of the day regarding suspense, surprise, and coincidence. He had always seen the element of sham implicit in these conventions, but had conformed to them in some slight degree. Even his last three full-length novels, *The Newcomes*, *The Virginians*, and *Philip*, are finally resolved by the discovery of a lost document establishing the hero's right to certain property. Here the repudiation consists in making the discovery so coincidental and out-of-keeping with the rest of the book that it is obviously an artificial device.

Furthermore in *Philip* Thackeray goes a step further; he apologizes to his readers in advance for following the plot convention of artificially prolonging the hero's courtship:

All I can promise about this gloomy part is, that it shall not be a long story. You will acknowledge we made very short work with the love-making, which I give you my word I consider to be the very easiest part of the novel-writer's business. As those rapturous scenes between the captain and the heroine are going on, a writer who knows his business may be thinking about anything else—about the ensuing chapter, or about what he is going to have for dinner, or what you will; therefore, as we passed over the raptures and joys of the courting so very curtly, you must please to gratify me by taking the grief in a very short measure. If our young people are going to suffer, let the pain be soon over.[85]

[84] *Works*, XVII, 590.
[85] Chapter 23. The same, XVI, 333.

Nine months later, when he wrote *The Roundabout Paper*, "On a Peal of Bells," Thackeray was even more candid:

There is a great deal of carpenter's and joiner's work in novels which surely a smart professional hand might supply. A smart professional hand? I give you my word, there seem to me parts of novels—let us say the love-making, the 'business', the villain in the cupboard, and so forth, which I should like to order John Footman to take in hand, as I desire him to bring the coals and polish the boots.[86]

Thackeray had two excuses for digressing from his story when he felt like expounding pet ideas. One excuse was implicit in his role of lay preacher, which gave him the right to repeat ideas *ad libitum*. He could argue that a congregation will never be rid of its sins, and therefore its minister is justified in reiterating his sermons forever. Thackeray reasons in that vein when he wishes to extenuate his repetitions of the *vanitas vanitatum* theme in both *The Virginians* and *Philip*:

I know it is an old story, and especially that this preacher has yelled *vanitas vanitatum* five hundred times before. I can't help always falling upon it.[87]
O me! O my beloved congregation! I have preached this stale sermon to you for ever so many years. O my jolly companions, I have drunk many a bout with you and always found *vanitas vanitatum* written on the bottom of the pot![88]

Another convenient way to excuse moralizing digressions was to pretend that the appreciation of them was the test of a discriminating reader. Conversely, the lack of such discrimination branded the reader as a mere sensation-seeker. Thackeray used that method of chastising his public in *The Roundabout Paper*, "De Finibus":

perhaps of all the novel-spinners now extant, the present speaker is the most addicted to preaching. Does he not stop perpetually in his story and begin to preach to you? When he ought to be engaged with business, is he not for ever taking the Muse by the sleeve, and plaguing her with some of his cynical sermons? I cry *peccavi* loudly and heartily. I tell you I would like to be able to write a story which should show no egotism whatever—in which there should be no reflections, no cynicism, no vulgarity (and so forth), but an incident in every other page, a villain, a battle, a mystery in every chapter. I should like to be able to feed a reader so spicily as to leave him hungering and thirsting for more at the end of every monthly meal.[89]

[86] *Works*, XVII, 607.
[87] *The Virginians*, chapter 26. *Works*, XV, 276.
[88] *Philip*, chapter 2. *Works*, XVI, 18.
[89] *Works*, XVII, 596.

Thackeray may have defended to the very end his right to digress and to be cynical in his digressions. But certain of his favorite cynical ideas were, nevertheless, repudiated in the mellow mood of his later years. *The Virginians*, for example, contains a supreme repudiation, that of the universal evil of hypocrisy:

Oh, let us be thankful, not only for faces, but for masks! not only for honest welcome, but for hypocrisy, which hides unwelcome things from us! Whilst I am talking, for instance, in this easy chatty way, what right have you, my good sir, to know what is really passing in my mind?[90]

The sequel to this passage shows what chiefly prompted Thackeray's willingness to extenuate hypocrisy. In the following sentence, one should substitute "spasms" for "gout," the "importunities of needy people" for "the eldest son's college bills," and a "large London magazine" for "the Stoke Pogis *Sentinel*." Then one will have a picture of the cheerful visage with which the unhappy novelist often confronted his public during the 1860's:

It may be that I am racked with gout, or that my eldest son has just sent me in a thousand pounds' worth of college bills, or that I am writhing under an attack of the Stoke Pogis *Sentinel* . . . I say that humbug which I am performing is beautiful self-denial—that hypocrisy is true virtue. Oh, if every man spoke his mind, what an intolerable society ours would be to live in![91]

The characteristic sicknesses, financial demands, and press attacks of Thackeray's later years forced him more than ever to adopt this stoical mask over his inward trouble. It covered not only his social intercourse, but his letters, and even his published works. As Michael Sadleir has described those later years:

He was constantly ailing, subject to fits of acute depression, over-worked, harried, and haunted by the fear of leaving the two daughters he so dearly loved inadequately provided for. Rather than betray his physical sufferings, his nervous dejections, his financial worries, he evolved a social manner and a sentimental, jocular, self-mocking style of letter-writing.[92]

In other words, since circumstances had forced on Thackeray the need of wearing a mask, he was now willing to grant that other men too had a right to wear one. The tolerance was extended, in *The*

[90] Chapter 56. *Works*, XV, 577.
[91] The same.
[92] "Thackeray's Letters Reviewed," *The Twentieth Century and After* (August, 1947), CXLII, 82.

Virginians, to children and servants because "where there is not equality there must be hypocrisy."[93] This last concession really stemmed from an earlier abrogation of Thackeray's general rule against hypocrisy. The sufferings of certain women of his acquaintance under the tyranny of their husbands had led him in the late '40's to enunciate the "doctrine of justifiable female hypocrisy."

A certain Mrs. Edward Marlborough FitzGerald had been persistently abused by a husband (no relation to FitzGerald the poet) who had climaxed his enormities by bringing his mistress into his house and introducing her to his daughter. After the separation Thackeray had tried to help the wife, but she had refused to disclose to him her full misery. His comment was: "You were a hypocrite too—for which indeed I love and honor you."[94] In *Mr. Brown's Letters to his Nephew* (1849) Thackeray glorified the wifely arts of the clinging Amelia Sedleys of the world: "Say they are not clever? Their hypocrisy is a perpetual marvel to me, and a constant exercise of cleverness."[95] And after the parting from Mrs. Brookfield, Thackeray disclosed that the sufferings of that lady had helped him to evolve his doctrine. "The misfortune of poor Wms. mood is that it makes perforce hypocrites of you and all who approach him—these 'lies'—are called virtues in women—they are part of the duty which my dear has set herself, and in which I say God speed her."[96] Thereafter disquisitions on women as the licensed flatterers and hypocrites of the fireside become a set theme in Thackeray's letters and novels.[97]

The gradual relaxation of Thackeray's hold on all activity which called for effort and conflict, his increasing desire to be left in peace, the nearly incessant melancholy of his later years—all these were marked by one break. At the end of 1859 he became the first editor of *The Cornhill Magazine*. The princely bribe of a £1,000 annual salary offered by the publisher George Smith was more than he could resist, especially when "the immense success of the first number" caused the sum to be doubled.[98] To top it all, Smith promised Thackeray "£350 a month for the exclusive rights to serialize his

[93] Chapter 30. *Works*, XV, 310.
[94] *Letters*, II, 340. Written on January 18, 1848.
[95] "On Love, Marriage, Men, and Women." *Works*, VIII, 325.
[96] *Letters*, IV, 430. Written in September, 1851.
[97] See *Letters*, IV, 56; *The Newcomes*, chapters 40 and 64 (*Works*, XIV, 530 and 830); *The Virginians*, chapter 90 (*Works*, XV, 969); *Philip*, chapter 23 (*Works*, XVI, 337).
[98] *Letters*, IV, 148n.

future novels in [the new periodical], to issue them thereafter in
volume form, and to resell them for American editions and foreign
translations."[99]

Even at that late date in his career, the stimulus of new responsibilities and new associations swung Thackeray's temperamental pendulum back toward happiness. This happiness grew ecstatic with
the phenomenal success of the first issue of *The Cornhill*. As Professor
Stevenson remarks, his "hysterical jubilation revealed much more
than merely his satisfaction with an enlarged income. It marked the
release from a deep inward shame that had gnawed him for twenty
years. At last he had made a resounding success, and in the very
same sphere in which he had lost the bulk of his patrimony."[100]

The brief duration of Thackeray's editorship was, of course, foreseeable from the start. Despite the princely salary, and in spite of
the subordinates who took over most of the administrative routine,
the novelist had by March, 1862, had enough. He surrendered the
post. In his famous farewell letter to *The Cornhill's* contributors and
correspondents, Thackeray placed the bulk of his worries on "the
daily Tasks of reading, accepting, refusing, losing and finding the
works of other peoples."[101] These same vexations were the "Thorns
in the Cushion" of which he had complained in a famous *Roundabout
Paper*.[102] Yet even if all such responsibilities had been taken over
by others, he would still have found some excuse for resigning.

The most permanent fruit of Thackeray's connection with *The
Cornhill* were "The Roundabout Papers," which he contributed to
it with decreasing regularity from the inception of the magazine
until his own death in December, 1863. Here was the logical end-
product of the growing discursiveness of the novels. No longer need
he bother with the technique of plotting, which in *The Virginians*
and *Philip* had been a shriveled, atavistic incumbrance to the flow
of his thought. The narrative lines of those novels had not been,
like the plots of *Vanity Fair* and *Esmond*, vital parts of a narrative
organism. And it is those *Roundabout Papers* that represent the free
play of Thackeray's humourous ego which are probably the most
immortal of his essays. "On a Lazy, Idle Boy," "Tunbridge Toys,"

[99] Stevenson, *The Showman of Vanity Fair*, p. 357.
[100] The same, p. 364.
[101] *Letters*, IV, 260.
[102] *Works*, XVII, 397ff. Published in July, 1860.

"De Juventute," "Round About the Christmas Tree," "De Finibus," "On a Peal of Bells," "On a Pear-Tree," "Dessein's," and others have in common a limpid stylistic grace; a tendency to nostalgia; and a sentimental moralizing that epitomize the later Thackerayan manner.

Quite naturally the substance of these essays is the substance of most of Thackeray's novels—himself and his past experience. But another group of *Roundabout Papers* shows an avowed determination on his part to be objective. For one thing, they deal with the England of the 1860's, not that of the 1820's and 30's. "On Ribbons" urges the establishment of an Order of Britannia for heroic mariners; "On Some Late Great Victories" deals with contemporary pugilism; and "The Notch on the Axe" concerns itself with the craze for spiritualism. "On Two Roundabout Papers Which I Intended to Write" satirizes Du Chaillu's recent explorations in Africa, and "A Mississippi Bubble" jests about conditions of travel in the United States. "On Half a Loaf" attacks that country for its policy on foreign investments during the Civil War. "On Alexandrines" is a tribute to the new Princess of Wales.

It is as if Thackeray was feebly but manfully struggling, at the very end of his career, to climb out of his old groove. His last piece of fiction too, the *Denis Duval* which was left unfinished at his death, gives more evidence of the same wish. It breaks new ground in its choice of unfamiliar material and depicts the lives of the Huguenot émigrés in the Cinque Ports during the later Eighteenth Century. There are no pictures of fashionable society; Thackeray's beloved military types are scrapped in favor of naval men; the old recurring symbols and images are few and far between, and digressions are almost eliminated. Action is so plentiful that the reader gains the impression of a story with much of *Henry Esmond* in it, quite a bit of Thackeray's beloved Dumas père, and something of Wilkie Collins.

It is foolish to speculate on how far Thackeray could have broken out of his ways had not death taken him. Certain it is that the end which he had long sought came suddenly in the form of apoplexy on Christmas Eve, 1863. He was in his bed in the great house at Palace Green, Kensington, which a kinsman had jestingly called "Vanity Fair."[103] It was built with the fruits of Thackeray's desperate money-

103 *Letters*, IV, 213.

gathering during his last years, and its architecture was that of the Queen Anne period. Its style was chosen because the house was supposed to witness a new task. That was to be a labor which promised to be utterly congenial, if any task could be lastingly congenial to a man who had tired of everything in which he had long persevered. He was to write the history of Queen Anne's reign— if ever he should find himself sufficiently in control of his unearned income to stop writing novels.

In his house at the time of Thackeray's death were three of the five women who had controlled his life. Anny and Minney Thackeray were there, still unwedded. So was Mrs. Carmichael-Smyth. The daughters who had been so happy under his domination were sorely stricken by his death. The mother—bereft of her husband for two years—had long been restless and melancholy. She was tormented by fears for her son's soul. Mrs. Brookfield was freed by the novelist's death from the restrictions imposed by her husband against communication with his family. She stood by and gave them consolation. Long since past consolation or domination, Isabella Thackeray was to live on for thirty years.

Index

NORTHWESTERN UNIVERSITY
The Graduate School
1950

From time to time, The Graduate School of Northwestern University authorizes through the Editorial Board of *Northwestern University Studies* the publication of monographs in various fields of learning. A list of these publications appears below. Orders and inquiries are to be addressed to The Graduate School, Northwestern University, Evanston, Illinois.

Northwestern University Studies in the Humanities

No. 1. *Tales from the French Folk Lore of Missouri*, by Joseph Médard Carrière $4.00

No. 2. *Kant's Pre-Critical Ethics*, by Paul Arthur Schilpp $2.50

No. 3. *Luise Hensel als Dichterin*, by Frank Spiecker $1.50

No. 4. *The Labors of the Months in Antique and Mediaeval Art*, by James Carson Webster (Out of print)

No. 5. *Forgotten Danteiana*, by J. G. Fucilla (Out of print)

No. 6. *Speech Development of a Bilingual Child, Volume I*, by Werner F. Leopold (Out of print)

No. 7. *L'Histoire de Gille de Chyn*, edited by Edwin B. Place $2.50

No. 8. *The Aesthetic Process*, by Bertram Morris $2.25

No. 9. *The Classical Republicans*, by Zera S. Fink $4.00

No. 10. *An Historical and Analytical Bibliography of the Literature of Cryptology*, by Joseph S. Galland $5.00

No. 11. *Speech Development of a Bilingual Child, Volume II*, by Werner F. Leopold $5.50

No. 12. *Writings of John Stuart Mill*, by Ney MacMinn and others $2.50

No. 13. *Political Forgiveness in Old Athens*, by Alfred P. Dorjahn $2.50

No. 14. *Education for Journalism in the United States from Its Beginning to 1940*, by Albert Alton Sutton $2.00

No. 15. *Analytical Syllogistics*, by Delton Thomas Howard $4.00

No. 16. *Fair Rosamond*, by Virgil B. Heltzel $3.00

No. 17. *The Nonsense of Common Sense* (Lady Mary Wortley Montagu), edited by Robert Halsband $3.00

No. 18. *Speech Development of a Bilingual Child, Volume III*, by Werner F. Leopold $5.00

No. 19. *Speech Development of a Bilingual Child, Volume IV*, by Werner F. Leopold $5.00

No. 20. *Critical Prefaces of the French Renaissance*, by Bernard Weinberg $5.00

No. 21. *A Critical Bibliography of the Published Writings of Romain Rolland*, by William Thomas Starr $3.50

No. 22. *Le Panorama Littéraire de l'Europe* (1833–1834), by Thomas R. Palfrey $3.00

No. 23. *Juan de Segura: Processo de Cartas de Amores*, edited with introduction, translation, and commentary by Edwin B. Place $3.00

No. 24. *The Poems of Aimeric de Peguilhan*, edited and translated with introduction and commentary by William P. Shepard and Frank M. Chambers $4.50

No. 25. *Thackeray: The Sentimental Cynic*, by Lambert Ennis $5.00

No. 26. *William Warner's Syrinx, or A Sevenfold History*, edited with introduction and notes by Wallace A. Bacon $5.00

No. 27. *Matthew Arnold: The Ethnologist*, by Frederic E. Faverty (In press)

Northwestern University Studies in the Social Sciences

No. 1. *Predicting Criminality*, by Feris F. Laune $1.50

No. 2. *Shamanism in Western North America*, by Willard Z. Park (Out of print)

No. 3. *Seventy Years of Real Estate Subdividing in the Region of Chicago*, by Helen Corbin Monchow (Out of print)

No. 4. *The First Scientific Exploration of Russian America and the Purchase of Alaska*, by James Alton James $2.00

No. 5. *Compulsory Health Insurance in the United States*, by Herbert D. Simpson (Out of print)

No. 6. *The Neapolitan Revolution: 1820–1821*, by George T. Romani $4.00

Northwestern University Studies in Mathematics and the Physical Sciences

No. 1. *Mathematical Monographs*, by D. R. Curtiss, H. T. Davis, H. L. Garabedian, H. S. Wall, E. D. Hellinger $2.25

No. 2. *A Catalog of Illinois Algae*, by Max E. Britton $3.00

Northwestern University Studies in the Biological Sciences and Medicine

No. 1. *A Study in Neotropical Pselaphidæ*, by Orlando Park $7.50

Not in series

Galileo, Two New Sciences, translated by Henry Crew and Alfonso de Salvio $3.50

Remittances should be made payable to Northwestern University, and should be sent with orders to The Graduate School, Northwestern University, Evanston, Illinois

Prices include postage